The Design of
Biographia Literaria

The Design of
Biographia Literaria

CATHERINE MILES WALLACE

Department of English, Northwestern University

London
GEORGE ALLEN & UNWIN
Boston   Sydney

**George Allen & Unwin (Publishers) Ltd,
40 Museum Street, London WC1A 1LU, UK**

George Allen & Unwin (Publishers) Ltd,
Park Lane, Hemel Hempstead, Herts HP2 4TE, UK

Allen & Unwin, Inc.,
9 Winchester Terrace, Winchester, Mass. 01890, USA

George Allen & Unwin Australia Pty Ltd,
8 Napier Street, North Sydney, NSW 2060, Australia

First published in 1983

British Library Cataloguing in Publication Data

Wallace, Catherine Miles
    The design of Biographia Literaria.
1. Coleridge, Samuel Taylor. *Biographia literaria*
I. Title
808.1   PR4476
ISBN 0-04-800016-7

Library of Congress Cataloging in Publication Data

Wallace, Catherine Miles.
    The design of Biographia Literaria.
Includes bibliographical references and index.
1. Coleridge, Samuel Taylor, 1772-1834. Biographia
literaria. I. Title.
PR4476.W34 1983   821'.7 [B]   82-20791
ISBN 0-04-800016-7

Set in 10 on 11 point Plantin by Typesetters (Birmingham) Limited
and printed in Great Britain
by Mackays of Chatham

Contents

Preface

Arthur Symons said it best: '*Biographia Literaria* is the greatest book of criticism in English, and one of the most annoying in any language.' Many have agreed that Coleridge's brilliance comes shrouded in an obscure, infuriating intricacy. In order to analyze that intricacy, and yet not to write a book as labyrinthine as the *Biographia* itself, I have 'at all times endeavoured to look steadily at my subject': the order and relation of parts that I call 'design'. I occasionally discuss Coleridge's plagiarisms and his misquotations, but only when they create or solve interesting rhetorical problems. I discuss Coleridge's personal history only when such details reveal particularly well how he creates a 'literary life'. I discuss Wordsworth in somewhat greater detail, but I am not centrally concerned with illuminating that friendship and its theoretical disputes. Wordsworth appears in *Biographia Literaria* partly as an individual, but more centrally as the ideal philosophic poet – and in all instances as Coleridge's idea of him. I step outside that conception only when recourse to Wordsworth's criticism proves requisite to the full understanding of how Coleridge designs his counter-argument. None the less, the Wordsworth portrayed in my pages remains the *Biographia*'s image of him. Major work needs to be done on each of these issues.

In evaluating *Biographia Literaria* as a discourse, I do not commonly engage philosophic 'first questions' in my own right: I am not a philosopher. I do point out how Coleridge's conclusions depend upon assumptions usually drawn from Christianity. I also describe how the coherence of his theory depends not only on the validity of these assumptions, but also upon the ways in which they modify and restrict each other. But in my own analyses I ordinarily grant the validity of these starting-points.

And it should be admitted from the start that I have thoroughly enjoyed the puzzles Coleridge's discourse presents. One day a colleague commented ruefully to me that one must be a true 'Coleridgean' to love the *Biographia*. Perhaps so. But it is also true that one who becomes fond of bitter tastes never calls them sweet. I regularly distinguish between the intricacy that derives from the sophistication of Coleridge's thinking, and the obscurity that derives from the manner of his composing. Yet both his errors and his intricacies reflect consistent habits: comprehending the design as the work of both a genius and an exhausted, troubled man can render more easily accessible what is permanently valuable in *Biographia Literaria*.

This book is intended for three general kinds of readers. First, of course, sworn 'Coleridgeans'. For them, the crucial issue will be my argument about how Coleridge composed – an argument tested against the *Biographia* because it is so central among his works. Secondly, those interested in the *Biographia* only in parts. *Biographia Literaria* is, alas, usually read only in parts except by the most determined; and so I allowed a certain pragmatism to prevail in my own design. This book is written so that one can discover how the 'interesting' parts fit into the whole structurally, conceptually, and rhetorically. Biographers, philosophers, Wordsworthians, literary theorists or historians, and students of poetry can each select the chapters that pertain to the parts of the *Biographia* that matter to them. My third set are those whom Coleridge himself addressed – not literary professionals of any ilk, but that wider group of people who care about literature, who value its contributions to human culture, who seek reasonable principles of critical judgment. Accommodating the needs of these readers has at times required that I verge upon an old but useful format, the so-called 'commentary'. Coleridgeans will recognize, I trust, a certain familiar irony in this: just a few comments, if the right comments, can illuminate much.

After my manuscript had been sent to Allen & Unwin, Cambridge University Press published Kathleen Wheeler's *Sources, Processes and Methods in Coleridge's 'Biographia Literaria'*. In a few places I have noted major points of disagreement, but these comments are necessarily limited in scope. Our agreements, however, are many. We both argue, in her words, that 'The reader of the *Biographia* must at all times be aware that his intellectual activity is a primary subject of the text' (p. 107). The complementarity of our works may be more than coincidental: at slightly different times, and unknown to each other, we both studied with John Wright at the University of Michigan in Ann Arbor. Mr Wright directed my dissertation, which underlies the present study; I am delighted to acknowledge how much I owe to the rigor and detail of his criticisms at that stage. More recently, this study or parts of it were evaluated by Don H. Bialostosky, Charles O. Hartman, J. R. de J. Jackson, Lawrence Lipking, and Philip C. Rule, SJ. To each I am grateful for good advice. Errors and infelicities that remain are my responsibility. Both early and late, my work with Coleridge has been shared by Warren H. Wallace, MD, to whom my debts and my gratitude are deepest of all.

Abbreviations

Acknowledgments

I would like to thank Marilyn Gaull, editor of *The Wordsworth Circle*, for permission to reprint 'The function of autobiography in Coleridge's *Biographia Literaria*', an essay that appears here as chapter one; and William Kupersmith for permission to reprint portions of an essay first published in *Philological Quarterly* as 'Coleridge's theory of language'.

1 The Chamois Hunter

> The musician may tune his instrument in private, ere his audience have yet assembled: the architect conceals the foundation of his building beneath the superstructure. But an author's harp must be tuned in the hearing of those, who are to understand its after harmonies; the foundation stones of his edifice must lie open to common view, or his friends will hesitate to trust themselves beneath the roof.
>
> *The Friend*, I, 14

> A man's principles . . . are the life of his life.
>
> *The Friend*, I, 97

In this half of the century, the familiar portrait has been redrawn: we no longer see Samuel Taylor Coleridge as a genius helplessly mired in addictions, neuroses and morbid Christianity. Growing numbers of scholars have demonstrated the depth and subtlety of Coleridge's thought. His originality has been re-evaluated; his reputation has grown. *Biographia Literaria* deserves a new look as well. Like Coleridge himself, it is not a rambling, foggy, inconsistent traveler toward isolated, cryptic insights. It is a formal and rhetorical whole designed to engage the reader not simply as a philosopher-critic, but as a person, as a union of intellectual, emotional and moral powers. Its design reveals a coherent and genuinely imaginative vision of the necessary character of modern discourse.

Yet it is a difficult book. At first glance, there is ample evidence that *Biographia Literaria* is a fragmented disaster whose difficulties can neither be resolved nor understood: the 'missing' transcendental construction in chapter XIII; the incorporations from Schelling; its origin as a preface to *Sibylline Leaves*. Such evidence appears to justify Carlyle's malefic description:

> . . . instead of answering [a question], or decidedly setting out towards an answer of it, he would accumulate formidable apparatus, logical swim-bladders, transcendental life-preservers and other precautionary and vehiculatory gear, for setting out; perhaps did at last get under way, – but was swiftly solicited, and turned aside by the glance of some radiant

new game on this hand or that, into new courses; and ever into new; and before long into all the Universe.[1]

'Solicited' is the central word here: seduced, enticed, led astray. The Victorians said Coleridge lacked 'will power'; the moderns that he was hopelessly 'neurotic'.[2] Yet the principle remains the same: the formal disorder of the works reflects the personal disorder of the man.

But the evidence for *Biographia Literaria*'s formal disorder shrivels abruptly if examined in strong light. The infamous chapter XIII, for example, culminates an extensive pattern of reference to the intellectual powers of Englishmen; it is an elaborately planned appeal to the philosophic reader. Philosophic readers have been appropriately disappointed: the strategy succeeds at least in part. But such readers err in judging this chapter a neurotic break, or a failure of nerve, or a change in plan literally unexpected by its author. There is substantial evidence to the contrary.[3] In a parallel way, the *Biographia*'s origin as a preface reflects no reprehensible spontaneity on Coleridge's part: one finds plans for the *Biographia* in letters and notebook entries dating back at least to the autumn of 1803.[4] The plagiarisms from Schelling have been evaluated in general by Thomas McFarland, and in painstaking detail by Elinor Stoneman Shaffer, both of whom conclude that the literal appearance of plagiarism is misleading.[5] In the light of recent scholarship, this traditionally *prima facie* evidence loses its impressive appearance.

But the reputation of *Biographia Literaria* has also rested on the experience of many attentive and informed readers. For a text so often described as unreadable, it has been read more often and valued more highly than quite makes sense. The paradox is revealing: there is no frustration quite the equal of intuiting a coherence that refuses to emerge into the full daylight of objectifying comprehension. There are, in fact, many brief descriptions of the *Biographia*'s general thematic unity. Shawcross is exemplary. He attributes 'the miscellaneous character of the book' to the poor state of Coleridge's 'health and spirits', but goes on to say:

> It is with this end in view ['the desire . . . to state clearly, and defend adequately, his own poetic creed'] that, in the autobiographical portion of the book, he describes the growth of his own literary convictions; that, in the philosophical, he seeks to refer them to first principles; and that, in the criticism of Wordsworth's poetry and poetic theory, he emphasizes the differences which, as he imagines, exist between Wordsworth and himself. (*BL*, I, xcii)

Coleridge's complaint seems to the point:

> Now surely a [work] the contents and purposes of which are capable of being faithfully and compleatly ennumerated in a sentence of 7 or 8 lines, and where all the points treated of tend to a common result, cannot

justly be regarded as a motley Patch-work, or a Farrago of heterogenous Effusions! (*LS*, 114 n)[6]

This general thematic unity is seldom denied.[7] Yet it is one thing for an attentive reader to perceive the relations among the topics Coleridge discusses; it is something altogether different to perceive that Coleridge so manages his discourse as to define exactly how 'all points treated of tend to a common result'. A sympathetic reader can link the parts to a postulated common result, but this does not prove that *Biographia Literaria*, as a discourse, generally succeeds in establishing these relations through various formal and rhetorical strategies. Such strategies comprise what I call 'design': the blueprint of the whole, regarded both as a governing structure, and as the intent or governing idea implicit in and enacted by this structure.

The generations of scholars and critics succeeding Shawcross have explicated Coleridge's 'literary convictions' and his 'first principles' to reveal a thinker known to very few in 1907: a Coleridge who is erudite, philosophically acute, and humanly profound. As we have more and more fully seen how his intricacy of mind engages complex human questions, it becomes less possible to believe that so great a thinker could have been so fundamentally incompetent a writer. Common sense questions whether such extraordinary powers of concentration and synthesis could have been so entirely suspended when he sat down to compose. He himself often insisted that genius and command of language vary together. His books are not perfectly written – whose are? – but their difficulty resides primarily in the complexity of his ideas, and in the complexity of design these ideas require for their intelligible presentation. Coleridge knew he would be charged with obscurity; he often tried both to defend himself, and to preclude the charge through elaborate explanations of his principles in writing. Understanding these principles alleviates much of the confusion and frustration that so many readers experience.

Coleridge's desire to make his readers think, to make them engage genuine ideas, underlies the design of *Biographia Literaria*. It also accounts in part for the book's reputation as excessively difficult reading. In what he regarded as 'the finest passage in the *Friend*', Coleridge acknowledges the problems he creates for his readers.

Alas! legitimate reasoning is impossible without severe thinking, and thinking is neither an easy nor an amusing employment. The reader, who would follow a close reasoner to the summit and absolute principle of any one important subject, has chosen a Chamois-hunter for his guide. Our guide [Coleridge himself, as The Friend] will, indeed, take us the shortest way, will save us many a wearisome and perilous wandering, and warn us of many a mock road that had formerly led himself to the brink of chasms and precipices, or at best in an idle circle to the spot from whence he started. But he cannot carry us on his shoulders: we must strain our own sinews, as he has strained his; and make firm footing on the smooth rock for ourselves, by the blood of toil from our own feet. (*F*, I, 55, and n. 2)

Feet that are sticky with blood – it is a lurid image, but all too often it has struck me as entirely apt. Owen Barfield grants that the relation between subject and object is no doubt the *pons asinorum* of Coleridge's philosophic endeavor, but then argues that 'the concept, and perhaps the *experience*, of thinking as an *act*, or as an "act and energy," are the toll-gate in the middle of the bridge, the barrier that has to be opened before we can get across'.[8] Barfield demonstrates how thoroughly this central concept influences all of Coleridge's thought; my major concern is the way in which it shapes his composition.

Coleridge's compositions are designed to make the reader engage a particular problem or issue in ways that will lead him to the conclusions that Coleridge has already reached. He wants to make us think things through for ourselves, under his tutelage. To the extent that his particular interests are all versions of a predominant interest in thinking itself, one can say that he writes in ways designed to help us think about thinking. That is no small ambition. Further challenges to the reader emerge from the fact that Coleridge seldom accommodates to lesser energies or lesser talents than his own. He may lead us away from precipices, but he does not hesitate to lead us up rough and steep paths if these take us where he wants to go.

Some of the reader's troubles derive from Coleridge's lack of skill in the fine art of enticing tired minds to further and further effort. But often the reader stumbles because the way is genuinely and irreducibly difficult. As Sara Coleridge notes, the original thinker cannot rely on 'known ways and smooth well-beaten tracks': he forces his readers into unaccustomed mental exercise.[9] Both contemporary and modern readers have echoed this image of a difficult path to describe the effort Coleridge's discourse requires.[10] The image is particularly apt: as Coleridge often observed, the Greek word we translate as 'method' translates literally as 'way' or 'path' or 'mode of transit'. The 'Essays on Method' in *The Friend* claim that valid method demands powerful imagination. So does reading the *Biographia*. As Bishop C. Hunt, Jr, observes, 'what we might call the "dramatic" element in philosophy, the process of search and its written reenactment, assumes a larger significance. Much of Coleridge's best writing can be read as a kind of dramatic monologue in prose, a mimetic representation of the mind in the act of thinking something through.'[11] Thinking along with Coleridge as he thinks something through demands more than energy or learning. It requires that we read his prose with the same use of the same skills we engage when we read his poetry.

When Coleridge asserts that he wants his readers to *think*, he means that we must develop and exercise the ability to observe our own minds. We must acquire the self-consciousness that is secondary imagination's most basic act. His clearest statement of this requirement is the distinction between *thinking* and *attending* in *Aids to Reflection*:

> It is a matter of great difficulty, and requires no ordinary skill and address, to fix the attention of men on the world within them, to induce them to study the processes and superintend the works which they are themselves carrying on in their own minds; in short, to awaken in them both the faculty of thought* and the inclination to exercise it. For alas! the largest part of mankind are nowhere greater strangers than at home.

He who would explicate creativity itself requires a thinking audience no less than he who would explicate 'moral or religious truth'. Whether the critic's 'inward experiences' be those of reading or of writing, his reader needs the imaginative power of self-consciousness as a prior condition to understanding imagination itself in rigorous theoretical terms. 'The primary facts essential to the intelligibility of my principles I can prove to others only as far as I can prevail on them to retire *into themselves* and make their own minds the objects of their stedfast attention' (*F*, I, 21).

Alone and unbalanced, this requirement provides nothing less than a license for solipcism. But, despite what has been asserted in his name, Coleridge was no advocate of an 'autonomous' imagination.[12] His many explanations of the relation between ideas (the content or object of thinking) and experience reveal how his method excludes the irresponsible and the eccentric. Ideas and laws are correlative terms, strictly defined.[13] An idea is a subjectively originating set of relations exactly echoed by relations observable in experience. An idea whose counterpart is a law of the natural world can be 'objectively' or physically demonstrated. One who understands will be compelled to assent. An idea whose counterpart is a law of the mind cannot be physically demonstrated, because it has a psychic not physical referent. Furthermore, assent cannot be logically compelled because the spirit itself is essentially free: it cannot be coerced into generating the confirming mental experience. None the less, 'At the annunciation of *principles*, of *ideas*, the soul of man awakes, and starts up, as an exile in a far distant land at the unexpected sounds of his native language, when after long years of absence, and almost of oblivion, he is

---

*Distinction between thought and attention. – By thought is here meant the voluntary reproduction in our minds of those states of consciousness, or . . . of those inward experiences, to which, as to his best and most authentic documents, the teacher of moral or religious truth refers us. In attention we keep the mind passive: in thought, we rouse it into activity. In the former, we submit to an impression – we keep the mind steady, in order to receive the stamp. In the latter, we seek to imitate the artist, while we ourselves make a copy or duplicate of his work. We may learn arithmetic, or the elements of geometry, by continued attention alone; but self-knowledge, or an insight into the laws and constitution of the human mind and the grounds of religion and true morality, in addition to the effort of attention requires the energy of thought. (*AR*, 69 and n)

suddenly addressed in his own mother-tongue' (*LS*, 24). The imaginative person intuitively and immediately grasps the truth of a valid idea. Experience confirms – although it cannot demonstrate – the validity of ideas about non-physical realities. For instance, experience illustrates but does not prove the existence of God:

> Assume the existence of God, – and then the harmony and fitness of the physical creation may be shown to correspond with and support such an assumption; – but to set about *proving* the existence of a God by such means is a mere circle, a delusion. It can be no proof to a good reasoner. . . . (*TT*, 22 February 1834)

Historians face the same situation as theologians:

> If you ask me how I can know that this idea – my own invention – is the truth, by which the phenomena of history are to be explained, I answer, in the same way exactly that you know that your eyes were made to see with; and that is, because you *do* see with them . . . this idea, not only like a kaleidoscope, shall reduce all the miscellaneous fragments into order, but shall also minister strength, and knowledge, and light. . . . (*TT*, 14 April 1833)

As *Biographia Literaria* explains in detail, the same is true of literary critics. They must illustrate their ideas by particular reference to texts, while yet remembering that criticism is not an empirical science.[14]

Coleridge's intent to make his readers think, to make them engage ideas, accounts for the oft-lamented 'digressive' texture of his works, especially the *Biographia*. In *The Friend*, he cites Plato approvingly: '"It is difficult, excellent friend! to make any comprehensive truth compleatly intelligible, unless we avail ourselves of an example. Otherwise we may as in a dream, seem to know all, and then as it were, awakening find that we know nothing"' (*F*, I, 148). His 'examples' seem digressive in part because they are lengthy, and in part because he obviously enjoys them for their own sake; but primarily they seem so because they form no part of an induction. They relate not to each other, but to the ideas they illustrate. They are not particulars from which he generalizes and concludes according to the logical principles governing the use of evidence. The rational and imaginative reader who tries (consciously or unconsciously) to synthesize the anecdotes into a proper induction will be driven to distraction.[15]

This lack of 'system' creates hazards for the unwary, but it is easy enough to discern Coleridge's motives. According to Coleridge, strictly objective observation, abstraction and generalization are a waste of time, because the number of potentially relevant particulars is nearly infinite. Without a prior idea or, as Jackson so aptly paraphrases, a good *hunch*, 'the life of an ante-diluvian patriarch would be expended . . . in merely polling the votes, and long before he could [have] commence[d] the process of simplification, or have arrived in sight of the law' (*F*, I, 485).[16] Hence, for one who possesses an idea, the role of particulars in a discourse can be largely rhetorical. And yet for Coleridge this role is not rhetorical in the degraded sense. Because empirical confirmation stands prominently among the tests for a valid idea, Coleridge's particulars are 'illuminations' somewhat as Blake uses that word. They comprise one of the major strategies whereby he tries to prevail upon and help his readers to 'retire into themselves'. As a consequence, one who reads the *Biographia* ignoring its 'digressions' wastes his time no less surely than the empirical patriarch: these illuminations are crucial to the full intelligibility of Coleridge's principles.

To the problems inherent in the strategy one must add the fact that, as Coleridge himself admitted, he tended to offer too many of these illuminations. '[M]y illustrations swallow up my thesis – I feel too intensely the omnipresence of all in each, platonically speaking . . .' (*CN*, II, 2372). As De Quincey so shrewdly observed, that excess can confuse Coleridge's audience, and obscure the idea he is trying to illuminate:

> Coleridge, to many people, and often I have heard the complaint, seemed to wander; and he seemed then to wander the most, when, in fact, his resistance to the wandering instinct was greatest – viz., when the compass and huge circuit by which his illustrations moved travelled farthest into remote regions before they began to revolve. Long before this coming round had commenced most people had lost him, and naturally enough supposed that he had lost himself. . . . However, I can assert, upon my long and intimate knowledge of Coleridge's mind, that logic the most severe was as inalienable from his modes of thinking as grammar from his language.[17]

In the most practical of ways, then, the 'digressive' texture coherently reflects Coleridge's desire to help his readers think about ideas. Even for the most astute reader, the strategy probably fails at times, partly because it so easily breaks down into the excessive indirectness characteristic of Coleridge, and partly because any reader habituated to sustained abstract argument may be annoyed or unduly distracted by the change of pace. But it will fail less often for a reader who understands in advance what Coleridge is doing, and why.

An example of my own will illustrate the character of Coleridge's illuminations. Shawcross dismisses most of chapter II: 'the irritability of men of genius' is 'a quite irrelevant topic' (*BL*, I, 212). Irrelevant to what? To poetic diction? To autobiography? One who accepts Shawcross's judgment ignores Coleridge's first major account of the psychological consequences of imagination. The 'irritability' issue forges the major link between the controversy over *Lyrical Ballads* and the theory of imagination. Without a firm grasp of this link – and the principal metaphors that subsequently call it into play – one is apt to miss nearly half of what the *Biographia* says about imagination. Shawcross's error is provoked by the conclusion of chapter I: a profusion of anecdotes superficially concerned with Coleridge's delight in literary parody. Yet, on a closer look, the 'Higgenbottom' sonnets illustrate that the simple style he advocates can easily descend into the trivial. This story, and the related stories centered around 'The Ancient Mariner', reveal Coleridge as a man blessed with a good-humored, common-sense balance both in his theories and in his personality. Chapter II focusses sharply on this question of balance in personality and in literary style as evident in great poets and anonymous critics; it smoothly and coherently develops the argument about diction introduced in the preceding chapter by tracing qualities of diction to an origin in qualities of mind. The discontinuity that misled Shawcross resides only in the illustrations Coleridge uses: the first chapter draws primarily on memories of his youth and early manhood; the second on his knowledge of literary history and his encounters with contemporary criticism.[18]

Coleridge's desire to make his readers think explains more than the book's superficially digressive texture. It explains the principal feature of the design: its fusion of personal history and philosophic argument. To understand this design, one must first recognize that the *Biographia*'s autobiography is art – not chronicle. One must distinguish between Coleridge the author and 'Coleridge' the created narrator, the hero of a story that has a coherent development and formal unity that only art can impose upon a real life. Coleridge the author adapts his own history to perfect it as the vehicle for a philosophic inquiry into the distinction between fancy and imagination. The diversity of his own experience supplies the illustrations that progressively reveal the idea of imagination: the stages of the reader's intuition of this idea correspond to the stages of 'Coleridge's' intellectual life. As George Watson observes, *Biographia Literaria* follows 'a plan neither narrative nor logical but a disconcerting combination of the two'.[19]

Sara and H. N. Coleridge, and J. Shawcross, have pointed out the differences between this created self and the real man; but the necessarily delicate analysis of these differences should be done only by a psychologically astute biographer. For present purposes what matters most is that Coleridge turns the primary autobiographical act of self-creation into a vehicle for philosophic and literary discourse. This central feature of the *Biographia*'s design in part reflects his commitment to the ideal unity of poetry and philosophy.[20] But in part it also solves major practical problems. The philosophic analysis is not complete, yet it presents itself as capable of formal closure. The strictly literary unity of the autobiography seeks to bridge this gap by eliciting the reader's confidence that closure can be attained. The autobiographical narrative, in turn, is often and severely interrupted by abstract logical arguments. But the created self is a metaphysician from boyhood; he incorporates these arguments – not without strain, at times – as accounts of his scholarly endeavors.

The synthesis of autobiography and philosophy serves another, more crucial purpose as well. It helps Coleridge convince his readers of something he cannot prove logically: that the theory of imagination does not lead to pantheism. The created self is deeply religious and repeatedly concerned with the moral consequences of materialist philosophies. We may judge that his theory is wrong, or formulated badly; but we cannot doubt that it is orthodox in intent. For this person, the pursuit of philosophic questions and the discovery of identity have been a single process. For us, the development of a philosophic inquiry and the growth of the critic's mind are a single story. Although for practical reasons it is sometimes convenient to distinguish the text as autobiography from the text as philosophic discourse, ultimately these two aspects are inseparable. They are polar opposites informing the *Biographia*'s design; their unifying or originating power is Coleridge's idea of imagination.

Early in chapter IX, one dense footnote focusses many scattered hints that the design of *Biographia Literaria* is a conscious innovation on the received form of philosophic writing:

> . . . [the word] *discourse* [as used in *Paradise Lost*] . . . does not mean what we *now* call discoursing; but the *discursion* of the *mind*, the processes of generalization and subsumption, of deduction and conclusion. Thus, Philosophy has *hitherto* been DISCURSIVE; while Geometry is *always* and *essentially* INTUITIVE. (*BL*, I, 109 n)

Coleridge saw himself as devising a philosophic work that would be intuitive at least in part, because it is impossible to define 'imagination' by discursive methods alone. Geometry is always intuitive, in Coleridge's terms, because the geometer seeks to communicate an idea that finds perfect echo in nature's laws (*PhL*, 107–8). That is, both the idea of a triangle and a triangle drawn in sand will have angles whose sum is one hundred eighty degrees. The triangle in sand is not the law, but the symbol of the idea (whose corresponding law is mathematical). Geometry is unique among fields of inquiry because mathematical statements fully describe both the idea in the mind and the law in nature. In other fields, the discursively formulated law is not so perfect. 'An IDEA, in the *highest* sense of that word, cannot be conveyed but by a *symbol*; and, except in geometry, all symbols of necessity involve an apparent contradiction' (*BL*, I, 100). Except in geometry, symbols can be explicated discursively only as contradictions in terms: the idea can be conveyed symbolically (through some equivalent of the triangle in sand), but the symbol itself is paradoxical.[21] That is why 'a great idea can be taught gradually, that is by considering it as a germ which cannot appear at any one moment in all of its force' (*PhL*, 173). In most fields, the 'great idea' *must* be taught gradually if it is to emerge from a discursive text.

Except in geometry, then, symbols communicate ideas more adequately than discursive logical formulations, because a symbol holds together the contradictions that logic can only break apart. A symbol, Coleridge explains, 'is characterized by a translucence of the Eternal through and in the Temporal. It always partakes of the Reality which it renders intelligible; and while it annunciates the whole, abides itself as a living part in that Unity, of which it is the representative' (*LS*, 30). The symbolic relation between Eternal and Temporal, or between God and Man, cannot be defined through logic; and every symbol participates in this relation.

McFarland's work suggests that the systematic understanding, once fully engaged by extended, close, logical analysis, will always object to a discourse that tries to present a symbolic resolution to logically defined problems. Yet, as he also shows, no closed logical system could accommodate Coleridge's complex view of human reality. I suggest that Coleridge himself knew this full well: the understanding cannot fully grasp the symbolic reality known through reason. A closed logical system excludes the divine:

> The inevitable result of all consequent Reasoning, in which the intellect refuses to acknowledge a higher or deeper ground than it can itself supply, and weens to possess within itself the center of its own System, is – and from Zeno the Eleatic to Spinoza and from Spinoza to the Schellings, Okens, and their adherents, of the present day, ever has been – Pantheism under one or other of its modes, the least repulsive of which differs from the rest, not in its *consequences*, which are one and the same in all, and in all alike are practically atheistic, but only as it may express the striving of the philosopher himself to hide these consequences from his own mind. (*F*, I, 523 n)

When he claimed that he would one day render his system acceptable to the understanding, he probably intended to fuse a Kantean demonstration of understanding's inadequacies with an essentially imaginative and symbolic portrait of the realities known directly only by reason. Such a discourse would not be a closed logical system, but a work of art – some variation, perhaps, on 'the first genuine philosophic poem' that he wanted Wordsworth to write. It would not have persuaded the understanding *per se* but, rather, it would have kept the understanding within its proper limits. Assent would not have been a conclusion by the powers of analytical intellect alone, but a moral and imaginative act of all our powers in concert.

In *Biographia Literaria*, 'imagination' is the title of an idea whose symbolic forms include poetry (see also *LS*, 29). If we are to grasp this idea, so as to assent or to refuse assent, then the *Biographia* cannot limit itself to 'deduction and conclusion'. These cannot render its idea fully accessible to the inquiring reader. These cannot bring the reader to what J. Robert Barth, SJ, calls a symbolic 'encounter' with the idea of imagination – not the theory, but the idea that the theory can only describe paradoxically.[22] And thus the created self who is not a pantheist, whose history is not quite Coleridge's own, cannot be regarded as merely a device. Like all good metaphors, the created self is neither a lie nor an ornament. It is Coleridge's response to Hume's demonstration that closed logical systems cannot adequately describe the character of the mind, or the nature of reality. Any orderly explanation – any human act creating order – is grounded in an act of faith. This is not directly nor necessarily a faith in God but, rather, a faith in the possibility of order and knowledge that for many individuals has culminated in religious experience. The modern philosopher, by whatever particular title he or she is known, must offer more than just the logical proofs we have come to distrust as partial at best. The philosopher must also evoke our faith in the order he has discovered. He or she must appeal not only to logic, but also to imagination, to our intuitive (rather than sensory) relation to the world around and within us. If something in our souls does not 'awake and start up', we distrust the theory even before we have detected its error.

Coleridge responds to Hume's challenge by creating 'Coleridge' as a gradually emerging symbol of the fusion of actual human experience and rigorous philosophic inquiry: questioner and question are subjective and objective poles of the unity that is the examined life. As Barth explains, 'the making or perceiving of a symbol is for Coleridge a kind of act of faith. It is meant to evoke a response of the whole person, in faith, hope, and love. It is a commitment of self to someone other than one's self.'[23] 'Coleridge's' history is designed to elicit our faith in the idea 'imagination' even before rigorous proof has been established. We are first to trust the man, and then his theory. The coherence of the man's life and the validity of the theory are two forms or manifestations of a single integrity. As Richard Mallette argues, 'the narrator's personality . . . steps forth at every junction to shape and mould our experience. . . . The total effect . . . lends to the *Biographia* an imaginative unity that would otherwise be lost in a work that attempts to survey the horizonless landscapes of literary theory, practical criticism, philosophical disquisition, and personal autobiography.'[24]

But put questions of consent aside for now: the theory remains inaccessible until one understands this character 'Coleridge'. The *Biographia*'s speaker is in part an ironic self-parody by a man who knew himself all too well. The speaker is garrulous, he is eclectic and distractable, he is learned in the 'obscure' and the 'useless'. His manner of telling reflects these qualities: his story turns freely, abruptly, from one thing to another. Only after several readings does one perceive the inexorable, orderly momentum of the whole: the impromptu is rarely random. The speaker's freely associational leaps are exquisitely calculated to insist, over and over again, that the thinker finds unity within apparent diversity. Minor issues reflect major questions because all significant problems are ultimately interrelated. Gradually one discovers the central concerns that unite and direct these associational shifts.

With that recognition comes another: Coleridge is an exceptionally witty, playful writer. As he develops the contrast between his speaker and anonymous critics, he transvalues the elements of his self-parody: the speaker is eclectic and antiquated only to those enamored of a facile, inconsistent, popularized Lockeanism. His diffident double negatives point emphasis to issues too profound for this degraded group to recognize. His unexpected leaps land him always in the heart of the matter. One who reflects carefully on the abrupt shifts will always find his way to basic questions about fancy and imagination. The strategy is at once arrogant and entertaining: it is an intriguing style occasionally carried too far. Even the best reader may be occasionally confused, not by the subtlety of the relations *per se*, but by the unpredictability that the strategy generates. As Jackson explains, 'the reader is not permitted to know where he is being taken, or why he is being taken there; by obscuring the end in view, the intricacies of the way are allowed to become confusing and even irritating'.[25] I suspect that Coleridge's judgment may have been overwhelmed at times by the potent combination of his anger at anonymous criticism, and his delight with parody. And perhaps, as in any autobiography, fiction merges with fact: both the author and the speaker are 'responsible' for the reader's periodic bewilderment.

Although this 'speaker' clearly lacks the full artifice of Browning's speakers, he is far more deliberately a construct than the speakers of most autobiographies. Coleridge's created image may quite aptly resemble himself, but 'he' also serves such definite ends so well that analysis requires some means of distinguishing creator from creation. Coleridge's celebrated introspective powers should lead us to expect such delicate complexity in his intellectual autobiography. Richard Haven suggests that Coleridge was 'a born psychologist trying to write as a metaphysician', that 'Coleridge's philosophy should be seen not as an unsuccessful attempt at a logical analytical system, but, like his poetry, as a projection, an "elaborated transformed symbol", of his own psychological experience'.[26] Much recent scholarship has stressed Coleridge's extraordinary fidelity to his own moral and intellectual experience, fidelity sustained despite the enormous difficulty of reconciling the diverse elements into an intelligible whole. Autobiography is the natural vehicle for such a mind, because it allows him to present experiences that illuminate major speculative insights, but it does not require formal logical unity. The autobiography of a richly imagined 'self' can make arguments Coleridge wants to make, and yet bear up under the strain of the gaps that emerge when these arguments are separated from their autobiographical enactment.

Although Coleridge's later works are generally clearer, and more skillfully persuasive, *Biographia Literaria* remains the central text for the study of Coleridge's prose. As James Olney explains in *Metaphors of Self: The Meaning of Autobiography*:

... a man's lifework is his fullest autobiography [.] ... When, moreover, a man writes, in addition to his other works, something that is confessedly autobiographical ... then we may expect to be able to trace therein that creative impulse that was uniquely his: it will be unavoidably there in manner and style and, since autobiography is precisely an attempt to describe a lifework, in matter and content as well. A man's autobiography is thus like a magnifying lens, focusing and intensifying that same peculiar creative vitality that informs all the volumes of his collected works; it is the symptomatic key to all else that he did and, naturally, to all that he was.[27]

Coleridge achieves what Olney describes even more fully than conventional autobiographers: his intellectual autobiography portrays not the *man*, but the man *thinking*. In *Biographia Literaria* one meets face to face the thinker whose methods inform all the other works: he who believes his intuitions and then seeks confirmations; he who attributes to others his own ideas, and uses others' texts without attribution; he whose penetrating syntheses revise the habitual patterns of understanding. Both Coleridge's vitality and his peculiarity are most evident in *Biographia Literaria*: one who grasps the design of this most rewarding, most frustrating text will more easily follow Coleridge's track anywhere else.

Coleridge's desire to make his readers think about genuine ideas underlies the *Biographia*'s digressive texture; his fusion of autobiography and philosophy creates the necessary supply of anecdotal illuminations. These features of the design are a coherent, intelligible response to problems arising from the unity of ideas and laws. But this does not explain – nor explain away – all the difficulties impeding the *Biographia*'s readers. The design is also characterized by peculiar or inadequate transitions for which there is often no defense. Prudent authors of difficult arguments take particular care with transitions. Their transitions integrate parts, subordinate parts to whole, and repeatedly orient the reader within sequences of patterns large and small. Such transitions separate form from content by commenting on the form as such; this helps the reader to monitor his comprehension of major structures. Coleridge's argument is exceedingly difficult, but his transitions are hardly prudent. Often they are cryptic, just a sentence or two catapulting us into strange new terrain. More often, they seem to establish only a whimsical, undisciplined, associational flow. The speaker seems to ramble unbearably, just as Carlyle described.

In part, I grant, Coleridge's transitions are terrible. They suggest an incredible insensitivity to audience. Perhaps he so quickly penetrated to fundamental issues in his own reading that he failed to perceive the needs of blunter minds. A person as well read and as astute as Coleridge himself might have little trouble recognizing the unifying issues, but the rest of us are too apt to discover the central points only by wandering in circles. In other works, Coleridge seems to realize the useful (albeit mechanical) function of the conventional transition: major divisions commonly begin by commenting on the form as such. These transitions are often clumsy and intrusive because the underlying duality of form precludes tidy logical summary.[28] But they help, if only in assuring the reader that the author is executing a deliberate plan. This is no small matter: without confidence in the ultimate coherence of the whole, one would not expend the effort Coleridge's prose requires.

Yet the famous Coleridgean carelessness does not explain everything. It is also clear that the autobiographical fiction of *Biographia Literaria* makes it difficult for Coleridge to write transitions that maintain our sense of order, unity, and progression. Had Coleridge continually specified the relations between philosophic and autobiographical movements, and between the parts of these and the definition of imagination, then the autobiographical fiction would have become palpably fake. No real life is so direct, so fortuitously ordered. Coleridge's solution is to orient the reader primarily to the life and times of 'Coleridge' rather than to the evolving definition of imagination: as he explains, 'I have used the narration chiefly for the purpose of giving a continuity to the work' (*BL*, I, 1). But this solution has its awkward moments: in the opening lines of chapters IX and XIV, for instance, the abrupt return to autobiography may disorient even the most careful reader.

His fusion of narration and philosophy also creates problems. The definition of imagination does not unfold in a direct, clear, logical fashion, so the reader's progress and his locale within this definition cannot be sketched briefly. Furthermore, Coleridge cannot easily separate form and content by commenting on the form as such: his dual design *enacts* its principal idea to a far greater extent than one commonly finds. The form is to make us think; the content is to tell us what thinking is – which is to say, to render us conscious of what we are doing as we ponder the issues *Biographia Literaria* raises. Kathleen Wheeler explores this self-reflexivity by analyzing passages that refer both to the theory of imagination and to the experience of reading the text itself. She argues that German Romanticism provides both a motive and a rationale for such writing. So does the tradition of spiritual autobiography.[29] For these passages to function as they must, the work as a whole must systematically lead the reader to reflect on them both objectively, for what they say, and subjectively, for why or how they emerge at particular places. The work does so, I contend, by engaging our sympathies with both the madcap adventures and the scholarly endeavors of its most colorful speaker. Transitions cannot locate the reader within this process, because there is little reason to assume that all readers of the same chapter are at the same 'point' in understanding the idea of imagination. Like the youthful speaker himself, the new reader may not fully appreciate the implications of certain experiences or discoveries. When Coleridge's transitions fail, it is often because he presumes that more is understood at a given point than an actual reader is likely to understand, even after several attentive readings. And many subtle but quite adequate transitions will fail, of course, for the reader who assumes that there can be no unity within the diversity of *Biographia Literaria*.

Although Coleridge's design impedes conventional transitions, it encourages – and perhaps requires – the unity that metaphors can provide. The cinque-spotted water-insect for instance, belongs to an elaborate pattern of imagistic reference to imaginative synthesis. Light and water recurrently signal the rhetorical power of imaginative works. These metaphors, and others, both signal and generate the complex unity of *Biographia Literaria*'s many discrete issues. They establish its character as an essentially imaginative – not logical – discourse because they simultaneously develop the speaker and elucidate his ideas. Some have condemned Coleridge's densely imagistic passages as pious or poetic excrescences in what ought to be sober philosophy. But to ignore these lines is to mutilate the text, and its ideas.

How does one read a text of such complexity? What methods are adequate? Arthur Symons makes the basic point: 'one who is ceaselessly attentive will be ceaselessly rewarded'.[30] But even reasonably ceaseless attention reaches a point of diminishing return: by creating a form nearly as difficult as his ideas, Coleridge risks losing our interest in either. But recognizing the *Biographia*'s duality, recognizing its mediation between philosophy and narrative, enormously simplifies the reader's task. From the character of the design it follows that each chapter *must* be read both as a stage in the speaker's intellectual development, and as a stage in the effort 'to effect . . . a settlement of the long continued controversy concerning the true nature of poetic diction; and . . . to define . . . the real *poetic* character of the poet, by whose writings this controversy was first kindled' by demonstrating that fancy and imagination are 'two distinct and widely different faculties' (*BL*, I, 1–2, 60). Only if each part is read in both ways will all the relations among parts become evident. Without such bifocal vision, the whole remains fragmentary and, at times, rudely incoherent. In the chapters that follow, I will often distinguish between the two aspects both to demonstrate this method, and to reveal how the two strands of development are sustained and interwoven. But distinction is not separation: philosophic and autobiographical aspects provide objective and subjective accounts of a single idea that cannot be fully defined from either perspective alone.

Yes, *Biographia Literaria* is difficult – but it is not impossible. Its real flaws do not amount to so much when one considers the clarity, the acuity, and the grace that are generally evident. The reader's greatest burden is imposed not by these flaws, but by the complexity of Coleridge's thought. Coleridge wants his readers to think, and so he writes in ways designed to encourage and to require that effort.

2 Starting-Points

> As to the Persecution of Bigots, I have all my life been
> exposed to them – and in for a penny, in for a pound.
> Nay, the latter is the better policy; for it is the Nature
> of these Cattle to hate in an inverse ratio to the
> magnitude of the Difference.
> Letter to Hyman Hurwitz, 10 March 1820, *Collected
> Letters*, V, 21

The first four chapters most clearly reveal how Coleridge weaves auto-biography and inquiry into a single fabric. The speaker describes his youthful encounters with both genius and its anti-type, the fanatic. From his position in the autobiographer's 'present', he offers some apparently extraneous speculation about the psychological differences between geniuses and fanatics. Take these speculations seriously, examine them closely, and you find a major account of the psychological consequences of imaginative power. The speaker attributes his youthful ability to distinguish genius from fanatic not to any precocious insight into such matters, but to the rigor of his education. He repeats his teacher's principles of writing, and derives from them the literary principles that shaped his youthful taste in poetry. His explanation of these principles allows Coleridge to define complex connections between imagination and language. He further develops the relations among personality, imagination, and language by characterizing the speaker as a genius who responds in imaginative ways to the imaginative deficiencies of anonymous critics. Coleridge also maps out the *Biographia*'s future development when he presents the youthful speaker as seeking to substantiate these relationships. And note that Coleridge does all this without extensively committing himself to any single explanation of the complex he is sketching. This enables him to discuss parts *as parts* later on – a flexibility that proves crucial as he maneuvers past pantheism.

Philosophy and autobiography are so closely woven in these first four chapters that in most of what follows I shall be separating them: this is the least confusing way of revealing their complementarity. But, before getting into that, let us look for a moment at the *Biographia*'s opening paragraph. It is an extensive and entirely accurate account of what is to come; it directs the reader along rational and fruitful paths through the complexity of these opening chapters. But it is paradoxically unlikely to operate in this way for the new reader, who undoubtedly needs such assistance most keenly. This first paragraph proclaims the book's intent to resolve the controversy about poetic diction, and to define 'the real *poetic* character' of Wordsworth. To resolve the controversy about diction requires two things. First, it demands a proper theory of diction itself. Secondly, it demands an explanation of the controversy as such: an analysis of the anonymous critic's response to Wordsworth's genius. To define Wordsworth's 'real *poetic* character' is to define his particular character: he is the first genuine philosophic poet; he is the first to combine Shakespeare's objectivity with Milton's subjectivity so as to write about both subject and object simultaneously – so as to write about perception itself. But to define Wordsworth's particularity requires first that one define the type of which he is an instance: what is 'real *poetic* character'? For Coleridge, poetic diction and the psychology of genius are aspects of the more encompassing question, 'what is imagination?' This introductory statement of purpose orients the reader both to major issues and to principal relations among major issues, if one reads very closely. He relies on this statement – no doubt unduly – to project patterns of emphasis into the first four chapters.

The statement functions so poorly in directing such emphasis, however, because it competes so awkwardly with what appears to be the major statement of purpose.

> It will be found, that the least of what I have written concerns myself personally. I have used the narration chiefly for the purpose of giving a continuity to the work, in part for the sake of the miscellaneous reflections suggested to me by particular events, but still more as introductory to the statement of my principles in Politics, Religion, and Philosophy, and an application of the rules, deduced from philosophical principles, to poetry and criticism. (I, 1)[1]

This sounds like an immethodical miscellany. Coleridge seems to set out three domains of inquiry – politics, religion and philosophy – and to note that from the philosophy will be deduced the means of settling the Wordsworth controversy. But Wordsworth is no mere *exemplum*, no simple application of one of three inquiries: he and the controversy swirling about him are Coleridge's central illuminations of his theory of imagination. The 'statement of my principles' anticipated here can only be one high unified set – a theory of the mind's activity – that will have implications in all directions.

His 'not the least important' intentions concerning Wordsworth are an accurate but off-handed prediction that the implications most centrally explored will be those having to do with genius and poetry. To make sense of what follows, one must simply remain alert for the enunciation of principles. A substantial number of these appear promptly in chapter II, which presents itself as an exploration of the speaker's puzzling experiences as recounted in chapter I. This mode of development also gives a particular content to the first paragraph's sketch of the relation between autobiographical narration and principles.

Regarded as autobiography, these four chapters define the sequence of influences from the days at Christ's Hospital until approximately 1796. (This record of influences will continue to the end of chapter IX.) These influences introduce four of Coleridge's principal working assumptions, although without as yet offering much justification for them. First, the accounts of Boyer and Bowles provide an initial statement of the criteria for good poetry. From the Reverend Bowyer (more properly, *Boyer*) of Christ's Hospital he learned that all good writing is precise, that poetry is the most precise form of writing, and that the logic that a poem follows is difficult because subtle, complex, and dependent upon 'fugitive causes' (I, 4–5). His attribution to a teacher forms part of a pattern of statements about the importance of education, a pattern evident everywhere in Coleridge's work (I, 7–8; I, 27 n; II, 116–17).[2] The suggestion that a Boyer-like 'index expurgatorius' should be hung in courts of law uses humor to enforce a serious suggestion: imprecise thinking and writing threaten public welfare. This public dimension will later grow: the necessary features of precise language generate the truth-claims advanced on behalf of poetry, philosophic criticism, and philosophically grounded inquiry in all fields.

Bowles's sonnets encourage Coleridge to seek a detailed and philo-sophically grounded understanding of Boyer's 'more fugitive causes' of the logic and language of poems. Such philosophic grounding is necessary to refute the judgments of those whose taste has been formed by 'Mr. Pope and his followers' (I, 11–14). The speaker's first attempt to organize his ideas about poetry results in two aphorisms. The first reformulates Boyer's teachings: 'whatever lines can be translated into other words of the same language, without diminution of their significance, either in sense, or association, or in any worthy feeling, are so far vicious in their diction' (I, 14). The speaker consistently describes bad poetry as either translatable, or as a translation (I, 13). The broad definition of 'significance' gradually develops into a theory of language that defines the kind of precision poetry achieves. Only as that theory is delineated (in chapters XIV to XXII) do we see the necessary connection between precision and the second aphorism, 'the poem . . . to which we *return*, with the greatest pleasure, possesses the genuine power, and claims the name of *essential poetry*' (I, 14). Coleridge later argues that such precise control over the whole domain of significance initiates in the reader an imaginative activity closely akin to the poet's own. Such activity generates a delight – the aesthetic response – that sustains repeated reading (II, 10–11).

Secondly, Bowles's influence leads the speaker to develop a criterion for philosophy: the philosopher must maintain a proper balance between 'metaphysic depths' and 'history, and particular *facts*'. Neither can philosophy exclude 'the love of nature, and the sense of beauty' (I, 10). The 'preposterous pursuit' to which the speaker refers is not metaphysics itself, but metaphysical inquiry that excludes both the particular and the promptings of the heart.[3] The lines from *Paradise Lost* that the speaker cites to describe his youthful excursion into lifeless philosophy are Milton's description of a pastime in Hell. As Satan fights his way up through Chaos, the angels remaining in Hell amuse themselves with what Milton calls 'Vain wisdom all, and false Philosophy'. Philosophy without faith, Coleridge obliquely suggests, is not just preposterous – it is demonic. The speaker later asserts that those who deny our immediate knowledge of a common physical world are but schoolmen who 'live and move in a crowd of phrases and notions from which human nature has long ago vanished' (I, 179). The faint echo of St Paul suggests that such systems are not just foolish but immoral; the sharp accusation that such a philosophy is built on the abuse of words is an equally serious charge. Bowles's sonnets (and the 'amiable family' of Mary Evans) draw the speaker back from the abyss of false philosophy.[4] He turns to literature, and seeks a philosophically rigorous understanding of literary merit. His first attempt results in the two aphorisms we have already examined.

Coleridge uses this broadly inclusive definition of philosophy to distinguish between his system and pantheism. This crucial distinction rests in large measure on his claim that epistemology must begin by assuming immediate knowledge of both an independent world and a personal God; it must begin here because in his heart he finds it impossible to doubt that he possesses such knowledge. Without these two principles, or within a more conventional definition of philosophy, what Coleridge proposes in *Biographia Literaria* is clearly pantheist.[5]

The lines from Milton imbedded in the account of youthful philosophizing do more than support an inclusive definition of philosophy; they also define theology as one of the speaker's longstanding interests:

> Of providence, fore-knowledge, will, and fate,
> Fixd fate, free will, fore-knowledge absolute,
> And found no end in wandering mazes lost.
> (*Paradise Lost*, II, 559–61)

The speaker's inquiry into these matters proves extensive. The character of will occupies most of chapters V to IX. Foreordination is not an explicit issue, but human freedom and moral responsibility certainly are. The relation between human will and divine knowledge occupies chapter IX, parts of chapter X, and all of chapters XII and XIII. Yet this inquiry is neither demonic nor sterile, because it is animated and in part motivated by the speaker's faith not only in God, but also in a particular world immediately known.

Yet note that there is very little in chapter I to alert us to the density and precision of these few apparently casual statements about the speaker's youthful interest in 'metaphysic depths'. Any good reader will remember what has been said about precision, or permanent literary value, or the anger of fanatics, because these receive the conventional emphasis of repetition. But these few statements about philosophy, although theoretically part of the 'influences' pattern that ought to convey adequate emphasis, are quite apt to be forgotten. Only the experienced 'Coleridgean' will realize that Coleridge's introspective habits and his knowledge of *The Prelude* would have made him an extraordinarily self-conscious autobiographer. Without such confidence, a self-disciplined reader is unlikely to examine these remarks as closely as they require. This instance is further complicated by the extent to which many of Coleridge's contemporaries would regard any excursion into 'metaphysic depths' as a 'preposterous pursuit'. The speaker's ironically self-critical remarks eventually accumulate into a distinction between the good or philosophic reader, and the Lockean blockhead. But at this very early stage the fine distinctions underlying the word 'preposterous' are all too apt to be missed.

The third influential figure is Southey. The praise of Southey is abundant, yet qualified. His poems are full of pathos and just reflections, but they are never described with terms signaling imagination (I, 40; cf. I, 57–60; II, 13–20). He merits attention as a moral influence on the imprudent and impulsive speaker, and as a member of the so-called Lake School. Coleridge denies that he, Southey and Wordsworth form any school but 'that of good sense confirmed by the long-established models of the best times of Greece, Rome, Italy, and England' (I, 36 n). Reviews of Southey's work demonstrate the principles of anonymous criticism (which is thus implicitly opposed to 'good sense' and the whole Western tradition). The defense of Southey proceeds side by side with a listing of these failures: mistaking poetic genre or intent; exaggerated attention to isolated flaws; the lack of principles of judgment; and vicious personal attack (I, 43–4; I, 47). In short, both their concrete particulars and their abstract theories are deficient: by the criteria for philosophy just proposed, such criticism is entirely fraudulent. This account of the defamation of Southey is designed to reinforce the reader's faith in the public need for such principles as the speaker learned through Boyer and Bowles. The speaker asserts that critics must 'support their decisions by reference to fixed canons of criticism, previously established *and deduced from the nature of man*' (I, 44, my italics). Chapters V to XVI seek to fix such canons in exactly this way. The need for this kind of foundation, here asserted, will only later be justified by the relation between imaginative power and particular features of good poems.

Wordsworth himself is the final influence celebrated in these chapters. Through Wordsworth and criticism of *Lyrical Ballads*, the speaker recognizes the differences in kind between the synthetic imagination and the associative fancy. As a result, his quest for a firm foundation in 'the nature of man' takes a specific direction: to define these two terms as an aid both to the poet and to the 'philosophical critic' (I, 62). The form of this inquiry is described as complementary to Wordsworth's inquiry – a fiction later discarded because it would obviate the need for any practical discussion of poetry.[6]

> But it was Mr. Wordsworth's purpose to consider the influences of fancy and imagination as they are manifested in poetry, and from the different effects to conclude their diversity in kind; while it is my object to investigate the seminal principle, and then from the kind to deduce the degree. (I, 64)

The paradoxical form of Coleridge's intent is easily resolved. Coleridge often insisted that when the mind acts, the whole mind acts, not some single faculty. One may distinguish among the mind's characteristic activities, although one may never regard these acts as entirely independent of each other, as if they were distinct computing programs that could be separately engaged. Coleridge's distinguishing among characteristic activities *per se* yields difference in kind, and his 'seminal principle' is an idea about the character of all mental activity. Wordsworth's distinguishing among *products* of mental acts, however, can go no farther than differences in degree. And the clearest understanding of these differences in degree requires a prior understanding of the difference in kind, because differences in degree are relative and contingent. Coleridge sharply disagrees with Wordsworth whenever it appears that Wordsworth's relative distinctions are contingent upon a seminal principle derived from Lockean materialism.

Judgments of degree dominate these early chapters, as part of the motive to the inquiry into kind. They also dominate most of the second volume, as Coleridge puts the abstract inquiry to practical use. The speaker's judgments often assert relative degrees of imaginative power. The later Wordsworth is more imaginative than the early Wordsworth; the same is true of Southey (I, 58; I, 40). Pope's translation of the *Iliad* is pseudo-poetry, but his original compositions are the work of genius (I, 26 n). The 'faulty elder poets' are better than the 'moderns', but they are still primarily fanciful (I, 15). Only anonymous critics seem entirely to lack imaginative power. In them we see what Barfield calls degraded fancy.[7] But this is only an appearance: they lie to make money (I, 28–9; II, 129).

In the fourth chapter, Coleridge defines 'true poetic genius' by describing Wordsworth (I, 56–60). The influences traced in these chapters, and the chronology-breaking speculations to which memory gives rise (e.g. chapter II) have inexorably led to the recognition that the imaginative qualities of genius are responsible for both the precision and the truth of genial production. The influence and the poetic genius of Wordsworth culminate and summarize the first four chapters, so as to provide a major autobiographical link between the philosophic inquiry and the practical criticism. I will deal with the figure of Wordsworth in chapter IV more fully below.

The first four chapters also define the personality of the speaker in ways designed both to establish the validity of Coleridge's ideas, and to prepare for their orderly exposition within an autobiographical context. The crediting of influences, for instance, achieves more than an initial statement of working assumptions. In its continuity through the first nine chapters, this pattern also defines the speaker as a humble man, as one quick to give others their due because 'the obligations of intellect [are] among the most sacred of the claims of gratitude' (I, 9). The very controversial acknowledgment to Schelling (I, 102–5) forms part of this extensive movement. Yet this humility is no simple thing.[8] By crediting others with ideas basic to his argument, Coleridge can offer unequivocal assertions of the truth and importance of the ideas at issue without making the speaker unbearably arrogant. Ideas credited to others are often presented as if *a priori* truths. Yet, since egotism is always inversely proportional to genius, the speaker's grateful attributions indirectly suggest that he is a genius himself. This pattern of attributions may also be a distant echo of what Geoffrey Yarlott calls Coleridge's need for 'sheet anchor' relationships to help him sustain a modicum of genuine self-confidence and its attendant productivity.[9]

Whatever its psychological resonance, the pattern also reflects Coleridge's profoundly conservative character: the genius does not proclaim revolutionary new truths, but instead rediscovers and revitalizes the wisdom of the ages (I, 60; I, 66). Such conservatism underlies Coleridge's view of history as well, a view evident in the *Biographia* and elsewhere.[10] By contrast, those lacking imagination are 'ingenious' and endlessly seek novelty (I, 11; I, 27–8; I, 27–8 n). The speaker's character and personality are most substantially and colorfully defined by this comparison to anonymous critics. The ongoing contrast begins with the account of the education of an anonymous critic that immediately follows the description of the speaker's education. The speaker's humility and deference are highlighted by the 'self-conceit, shallowness, arrogance, and infidelity' taught to future anonymous critics. The portrait of such reviewers and the comparison between them and the speaker often reflect eighteenth-century satires and satirical methods; Hazlitt responds brilliantly in kind. The 'anonymous critic' figure plays an important role in the exposition of the theory of imagination, but it is also a lively and utterly polemical response to the abuse Wordsworth and his circle had suffered.[11]

The speaker's generous good humor (which also sharply distinguishes him from anonymous critics) enforces the need for philosophically grounded critical principles. At the end of the first chapter, two anecdotes (one in the text, one in a footnote) recount the speaker's parodies of his own poetic diction and his epigram critical of 'The Ancient Mariner'.[12] In each instance, someone expects that he will be outraged by the anonymous verse. The first paragraph of chapter II extends the comedy into serious issues: why should we credit the ideas he (or any other critic) advocates? Why do we suppose that a poet seriously defending himself against a critic only proves himself 'irritable'? The current situation of both criticism and the arts reveals that many poets and most critics are engaged in no more than a frivolous game of politics and personalities, a game that threatens all genuine writers (see I, 27 n; I, 25–9; II, 87). Lacking principles 'derived from the nature of man', poets and critics alike lack the absolute standards necessary to give intellectual substance to their arguments.

In chapter X such advocacy of principles and principled argument will be cited as evidence of philosophic genius (I, 125; II, 39). This strikingly complements the speaker's serenity, objectivity, humor and lack of egotism. Coleridge portrays the speaker as a genius so as to establish both a theoretical and a rhetorical ground for the speaker's authority. The speaker himself never advances the claim: he seems 'unconscious' of the implications of what he reveals about himself. Yet the distinction between 'speaker' and Coleridge himself is very delicate at this point. I believe that Coleridge was essentially conscious of the pattern, because its extra-ordinary consistency is managed with great care to avoid direct claims, and because it serves an important rhetorical aim: we must be convinced that the speaker is capable of solving the enormous philosophic problem postponed in chapter XIII.

At the end of chapter II the speaker explains that poets have a reputation for irritability simply because their expression, on any topic, will be more lively than that of the less gifted writer (I, 30). Such an explanation indirectly justifies his most lively condemnations of anonymous critics, seeking to resolve the apparent contradiction between the genially diminished sense of self and such eruptions. As I will show in more detail later, these descriptions provide a set of images whereby Coleridge can briefly characterize a man or his work as inadequately imaginative. The speaker's occasional tempestuous excess supplies the imagery so characteristic of Coleridge's dense prose; it solves a major problem of first-person narration.

In the light of several indications that the speaker is a genius, many of his self-critical remarks cannot be taken literally. The most frequently misunderstood of these concludes chapter IV. Because it is so often quoted in misleading fragments, I will quote the entire paragraph:

Yet even in this attempt ['to investigate the seminal principle' of the difference between fancy and imagination] I am aware, that I shall be obliged to draw more largely on the reader's attention, than so immethodical a miscellany can authorize; when in such a work (the

Ecclesiastical Polity) of such a mind as Hooker's, the judicious author, though no less admirable for the perspicuity than for the port and dignity of his language; and though he wrote for men of learning in a learned age; saw nevertheless occasion to anticipate and guard against 'complaints of obscurity,' as often as he was about to trace his subject 'to the highest well-spring and fountain.' Which, (continues he) 'because men are not accustomed to, the pains we take are more needful a great deal, than acceptable; and the matters we handle, seem by reason of newness (till the mind grow better acquainted with them) dark and intricate.' I would gladly therefore spare both myself and others this labor, if I knew how without it to present an intelligible statement of my poetic creed; not as my *opinions*, which weigh for nothing, but as deductions from established premises conveyed in such a form, as is calculated either to effect a fundamental conviction, or to receive a fundamental confutation. If I may dare once more adopt the words of Hooker, 'they, unto whom we shall seem tedious, are in no wise injured by us, because it is in their own hands to spare that labor, which they are not willing to endure.' Those at least, let me be permitted to add, who have taken so much pains to render me ridiculous for a perversion of taste, and have supported the charge by attributing strange notions to me on no other authority than their own conjectures, owe it to themselves as well as to me not to refuse their attention to my own statement of the theory, which I *do* acknowledge; or shrink from the trouble of examining the grounds on which I rest it, or the arguments which I offer in its justification. (I, 64–5)

No literally 'immethodical miscellany' provides 'deductions from established premises' or a grounded theory with supporting arguments. For Coleridge, 'immethodical' would be a term of deepest condemnation; and yet the headnote printed opposite page 1 distinctly echoes *The Friend*: 'He wishes to spare the young those circuitous paths, on which he himself had lost his way' (I, civ; compare *F*, II, 48–9 and *F*, I, 55 and n). The geographical metaphor is repeated exactly in the extract from Hooker;[13] and, in Coleridge's terms, no genuine reasoner will be immethodical. Furthermore, the balance between particular and general or theoretical, characteristic of the young Coleridge's philosophical work, also characterizes correct method (*F*, I, 448–524). The delicately allusive play leading to substantial ideas, so common in Coleridge's prose, entirely undercuts the self-description 'immethodical miscellany'.

So why the irony? It acknowledges how the work will appear to the unimaginative, while encouraging the sympathetic reader to question his own – not Coleridge's – abilities (cf. I, 160–1). Hooker addressed 'learned men in a learned age'; the speaker, however, must address 'the public' (I, 41–2). Yet this public reads carelessly and inattentively (I, 26–7 and n). Beginning here, the speaker explains and laments that the necessary difficulty of his topic will limit his audience (I, 73–4; I, 105–7; I, 149); all of chapter XII, from the perspective of autobiography, is an elaborate explanation of why this public will be confused, and what they will fail to understand. As the pattern develops from this point to chapter XII, responsibility gradually shifts from the speaker to the reader.

The irony, then, is directed not against himself, but against the dim and inattentive reader for whom he will seem obscure every time he deals with first principles. The unequivocal undermining of 'immethodical miscellany' as a description of the *Biographia* presumes at least a rudimentary knowledge of method; that is, that method involves such things as deductions, fundamental proofs and confutations, grounds, arguments, and established premises. This maneuver constitutes a second appeal to the reader whom the speaker assumes will share his own response to the excesses of anonymous criticism (cf. I, 50).[14] As responsibility for following the argument progressively shifts on to this reader, he is more and more clearly portrayed as sharing the speaker's judgment of 'the public' and its anonymous magazine-writers. When the speaker ceases transcribing chapter XIII, we are to see that as a helpless surrender to the practical power of the deficient multitude. The lines of judgment are so strictly drawn that an actual reader is to perceive every obscurity in the text as evidence of his own imaginative poverty – as long, of course, as he remains within the conceptual and rhetorical universe of *Biographia Literaria.*[15]

The reputation of the book, then and now, suggests that this dubious strategy failed. To the informed and sympathetic reader who finds the *Biographia* obscure, the pattern may constitute a high-handed shirking of authorial responsibility. The problem, I suspect, is not primarily that Coleridge is this arrogant; but that he is rather inept at the 'interpersonal' skills involved in an author's relation to his readers. He does not often enough and clearly enough distinguish between the genuine troubles of an attentive reader, and the perversely deliberate noncomprehension of magazine-reading blockheads. His sardonic remarks about those who cannot follow his arguments may provoke a defensive anger that subverts his rhetorical intentions. Later I will point out other instances of Coleridge's clumsiness in identifying and relating to a consistently imagined audience.

The gap in chapter XIII concludes another aspect of self-portraiture that first appears in these introductory chapters. The speaker describes himself as impractical, and constitutionally oblivious to the public consequences of his acts (I, 31–2). He is, as a result, quick to depend on the influence of such practical, foresightful, and dutiful men as Southey (I, 49 n). Yet in reading *Lyrical Ballads*, friends admired principally for judgment prove themselves deficient (I, 53–4).[16] Since the judgment concerns literary not practical matters, the speaker is not deceived. But when one of these 'judicious' friends advises against publication, the speaker immediately stops transcribing. This is clearly worse imprudence. Coleridge seems here to be operating ironically within the eighteenth-century opposition between judgment and genius. The portrait of the speaker as an imprudent genius subject both to his own frailties and to the miscomprehension of Englishmen serves primarily to validate the claim that Coleridge could prove that his theory of imagination is compatible with Christianity. It is intended to imply that the sympathetic reader might come to Highgate to read the withheld manuscript, or at least anticipate its rapid publication. Needless to say, these implications were false.

To summarize the autobiographical aspect: the chronological sequence and self-portraiture in these first chapters provide the starting-points of Coleridge's argument, and the conceptual and rhetorical foundations on which it will be built. Regarded as philosophy, these chapters begin to build that argument, to define imagination by contrasting fanatics (or pseudo-poets) with geniuses. The structure of this definition reveals what R. H. Fogle calls the classically Coleridgean method. A prior unity is dissolved into subjectively oriented and objectively oriented aspects, and then reconstituted as a whole.[17] Here, Coleridge defines imagination through describing both the psychology and the works of the two contrasting types of mind. The fourth chapter ends approximately where the first began – with the desire to resolve the controversy by explaining fancy and imagination. As one always finds with Coleridge's circular progression, the second formulation substantiates or illuminates the first by drawing all that has intervened into coherent relation.

The psychology of the fanatic differs from that of the genius because the fanatic, who suffers 'a debility and dimness of the imaginative power', must consequently rely on the 'immediate impressions of the senses'. The genius, on the other hand, 'is affected by thoughts, rather than by things; and only then feels the requisite interest even for the most important events and accidents, when by means of meditation they have passed into *thoughts*' (I, 20). This same domination of the physical generates the pseudo-poetic diction of modern poetry, which sacrifices both passion and intellect to an elaborate, incoherent imagery (I, 15, I, 26 n). (The pseudo-poet, of course, may be a temporally prior form of the anonymous critic, who is the *Biographia*'s foremost example of the fanatic (I, 25–9).)

The same 'dimness of the imaginative power' accounts for temperamental differences between fanatics and geniuses. Most of chapter II describes the notable serenity of Chaucer, Spenser, Shakespeare and Milton, contrasting it with the virulent hostility of anonymous critics (I, 19–20). The explanation for this state of affairs presents a major idea: 'The passion being in an inverse proportion to the insight, *that* the more vivid, as *this* the less distinct; anger is the inevitable consequence' (I, 19). The controversy concerning *Lyrical Ballads* demonstrates this clearly. Although two-thirds of the poems in this collection were quite good, anonymous critics focussed their attention on the few flawed pieces. These flawed pieces 'provoked direct hostility when announced as intentional, as the result of choice after full deliberation' – as if the flawed poems rather than the good ones reflected the intent of the Preface (I, 51–4). The inconsistency of such critical judgment is self-evident, and the anonymous critics dimly sense this contradiction:

> In all perplexity there is a portion of fear, which predisposes the mind to anger. Not able to deny that the author possessed both genius and a powerful intellect, they felt *very positive*, but were not *quite certain*, that he might not be in the right, . . . [and sought] alleviation by quarrelling . . . and by wondering at the perverseness of the man, who had written a long and argumentative essay to persuade them . . . that they had been all their lives admiring without judgment, and were now about to censure without reason. (I, 52)

The controversy that the speaker wants to resolve arises, *as a controversy*, from the characteristic response of the deficient mind to the powerful genius of Wordsworth. Such genial power, in context with the flaws in the Preface and in a few poems, inevitably ignited these volatile fanatics.

Throughout the *Biographia*, excessive passion of any sort, but especially exorbitant anger, signals the lack of imaginative and intellectual power – often through images of swarming bees, swirling storms, or other naturally violent events (e.g. I, 19, 32; II, 7). 'Genial', by contrast, means both 'characteristic of genius' and 'cordial or kindly'. References to hostility or serenity, and to stupidity or insight, help sustain the development of the theory of imagination in and through an autobiographical narrative principally recounting the speaker's encounters with other people or their writings.

The works of fanatics are distinguished from the works of geniuses through several metaphors. At issue is the fact that, despite their reliance on the senses, fanatics observe poorly and thus write incoherently. In Pope's translation of the *Iliad*, cited as the source for decadent modern imagery, it is difficult at times to tell whether 'the sense or the diction be the more absurd' (I, 27 n). Moderns sacrifice both intellect and passion to 'the glare and glitter of a perpetual, yet broken and heterogeneous imagery, or rather to an amphibious something, made up, half of image, and half of abstract meaning' (I, 15). In such poetry, we see nothing clearly, nor are we brought to understand anything distinctly. The false light of 'glare and glitter' contrasts sharply with the '"frequent bursts of overpowering light"' characteristic of Wordsworth's *Descriptive Sketches*, a volume which announced 'the emergence of an original poetic genius above the literary horizon' (I, 56–7). The traditional association of light and enlightenment makes distinctions among qualities or sources of light a natural image for the imagination; this image is largely responsible for the first link between the terms 'imagination' and 'self-consciousness' (I, 165–7).

As one would expect, the works of frauds are also fraudulent: 'The difference indeed between these and the works of genius is not less than between an egg and an egg-shell; yet at a distance they both look alike' (I,

26). The fanatic's anger reveals his intellectual emptiness, 'even as the flowery sod, which covers a hollow, may be often detected by its shaking and trembling' (I, 25). In contrast to such indictments, Coleridge advances major truth-claims on behalf of genuinely imaginative works, works which arise from 'the union of deep feeling with profound thought; the fine balance of truth in observing, with the imaginative faculty in modifying the objects observed' (I, 59). The subjective synthesis of passion, observation and thought results in a poem that synthesizes power, beauty and truth. Coleridge particularly stresses the union of truth with the power to elicit response that characterizes the great poem:

> In poems, equally as in philosophic disquisitions, genius produces the strongest impressions of novelty, while it rescues the most admitted truths from the impotence caused by the very circumstance of their universal admission. Truths of all others the most awful and mysterious, yet being at the same time of universal interest, are too often considered as *so* true, that they lose all the life and efficiency of truth, and lie bed-ridden in the dormitory of the soul, side by side with the most despised and exploded errors. (I, 60)

These ideas reappear in different form as the 'plan' for *Lyrical Ballads* (II, 5–6). This blend of truth and power is consistently represented by images of health, dew and refreshing rain (I, 59; II, 121). By contrast, the fraudulent anonymous critic has 'intellectual claims to the guardianship of the muses [which] seem, for the greater part, analogous to the physical qualifications which adapt their oriental brethren for the superintendence of the Harem' (I, 42): the image deftly combines debility and perversion.

The contrast of fanatics and geniuses serves generally to enforce this link between truth and aesthetic power. The philosophic inquiry in chapters V to XIII substantiates the truth-claim by defining the cognitive function of imagination; the further discussion of poetic diction in chapters XIV to XX substantiates the link between truth and aesthetic power by defining the imaginative origins of language itself – origins briefly signaled here by the link between verbal precision and poetic genius. These two definitions are at once the most central and the most vulnerable of Coleridge's arguments: they are philosophically, although not rhetorically, dependent on the metaphysics that chapter XIII does not provide.

I want to clarify one possible misunderstanding concerning the contrast between the genius and the fanatic. The fanatic does not suffer an excess of fancy. He suffers an excessive reliance on the senses, or a deformed, exaggerated sensibility. Poets 'from Donne to Cowley' are witty or fanciful. They do not achieve the balance and unity of true poetic genius, but true poetic genius is extremely rare. Even those who are more imaginative than these 'elder poets' (Bowles, for instance, or Cowper) are never described as geniuses. They are far less imaginative than Wordsworth.

A footnote at the end of chapter II clarifies this issue. The true poet is not 'irritable' because his 'profound sensibility' is counter-balanced by the associative power (fancy) and the modifying power (imagination) (I, 30 n). The fanatic's anger reveals the deficiency of this balance. 'GENIUS itself consists' in imagination; but fancy is 'a component equally essential', as the criticism of Wordsworth's poetry will later show (I, 30 n; II, 104–5). These intellectual powers are the polar opposites of the physical powers of sense and passion; like centripetal and centrifugal forces, they remain necessarily in balance. Fanatics and pseudo-poets can neither observe well, nor control their passions, because their fancy and imagination are feeble.

The image from physics deserves close attention. Centrifugal and centripetal forces are two manifestations of a single power (attraction) exhibited in or by the relations of bodies having mass. The outward-directed centrifugal force (sensibility) is not truly a force at all, but a way of naming a particular perspective on or experience of the inward-directed centripetal force. In the familiar physics-class example, the man sitting on the ball being twirled on a string only *feels as if* he and the ball are being flung outward. Actually, his movement is possible only through the inward pull exerted along the string. This is, I submit, a quite precise image for what Barfield calls Coleridge's theory of '"separative projection"'. We inexorably *feel as if* there is a real, independent, physical world. Any science (of things or minds) that is concerned with knowledge must accept as axiomatic that we can know an external physical world that actually does exist. But metaphysics in its strict sense – as ontology – must recognize the *logical* priority of (inward-directed) imaginative power: that is, the priority of self-consciousness.[18] The image reappears later to illumine the polarity of being and knowing (I, 188).

The image in this passage implicitly links Coleridge with Newton, just as Kant had compared himself to Copernicus.[19] In chapter IX the speaker describes such a 'completion' of the master's work as the task he shares with Schelling (I, 103–4). A later footnote explaining the meanings and relationship of words 'I' and 'me' further identifies Coleridge's position for the philosophically experienced reader (I, 52–3 n).

I will have much more to say about imagination and self-consciousness later on. For now, one need only note that genius requires both fancy and imagination for its effective manifestation. The opposite of genial imagination is not fancy, but a literally mindless empiricism. The passage also reveals a most fundamental trait of Coleridge's prose: his metaphors are highly cognitive. They often (perhaps always) define relationships and ideas that will be explained 'literally' only later.

One final issue deserves attention: in what ways do these philosophical and autobiographical aspects interrelate? Coleridge says that he uses the chronological narrative 'chiefly for the purpose of giving a continuity to the work' (I, 1). Any substantial continuity has its roots in the structure of ideas and arguments presented; the sequence of influences reveals such origins. Like the landscape of Wordsworth's boyhood, the figures of Boyer and Bowles loom high because they foster the speaker's intellectual and moral character. They impress upon him and elicit from him the values and habits of mind that subsequent influences (Southey, Wordsworth, the anonymous critics) refine or draw farther into distinct consciousness. These values and habits prepare him to recognize both genius and fanaticism for what they are: the operations of imagination account for both, and for their productions as well. The speaker's forthcoming inquiry reflects his native philosophic bent, and arises – as do all genial productions – from the balanced power of his ideas (about language), his observations (of writers), and his passion (for true understanding and fair judgment).

3 The Associative Fancy

24th March, 1808. In how kind and quiet a manner the *Conscience* talks to us, in general, & at first – how *long-suffering* it is, how delicate, & full of pity – and with what pains when the Dictates of Reason made impulsive by its own Whispers have been obstinately pushed aside, does it utter the sad, judicial, tremendous Sentence after which nothing is left to the Soul but supernatural aid. O what an aweful Being is Conscience! and how infra-bestial the Locks [sic], Priestleys, Humes, Condilliacs [sic] and the dehumanizing race of fashionable Metaphysicians. *Metapothecaries*, said one *sportively*, but I *seriously*, should say *Cata*physicians (i.e. *Contra*naturalists) when I spoke of them as *Agents*; but when I regard them merely in *themselves* & *passive*, I should call them *Hypo*physicians, i.e. *below Nature. Zoophytes?* – Nay, there is no contradiction in anything but degraded man. (*CN*, III, 3281)

The first four chapters demonstrate well the so-called 'circularity' of Coleridge's discourse. He presents a series of interrelated terms ('precision', 'beauty', 'truth', 'serenity', 'anger', 'insight', 'intellectual dimness'), each of which he links to 'fanatic' or to 'genius'. These terms appear in each chapter; progressive development unfolds the *relations* of the terms, not just their meanings in the usual sense. One idea controls all these relations: the center of the circle is *will*. Chapter V begins an extended inquiry into will, and particularly into the relation between will and imagination.

Chapter V begins this inquiry by distinguishing three levels of will, and by asserting that the nature of will is epistemology's central problem:

There have been men in all ages, who have been impelled as by an instinct to propose their own nature as a problem, and who devote their attempts to its solution. The first step was to construct a table of distinctions, which they seem to have formed on the principle of the absence or presence of the WILL. Our various sensations, perceptions, and movements were classed as active or passive, or as media partaking of both. . . . [C]onjectures, however, concerning the mode in which our perceptions originated, could not alter the natural difference of *things* and *thoughts*. . . . Our inward experiences were thus arranged in three separate classes, the passive sense, or what the school-men call the merely receptive quality of the mind; the voluntary; and the spontaneous, which holds the middle place between both. (I, 65–6)

Coleridge's attempt to base his criticism on principles 'established and deduced from the nature of man' (I, 44) formally begins with this account of the 'traditional' analysis of human nature. Later we learn that secondary imagination operates at the spontaneous level of will. It is 'an intermediate faculty, which is at once both active and passive' (I, 86). As chapter V proceeds, Coleridge asks whether associationism can account for the spontaneous activity of mind; and he concludes that it cannot. The laws of association describe the operations and the materials of fancy, but imagination itself operates in other ways. Imagination does not associate; it synthesizes. What *that* distinction entails will be stated in chapters XII and XIII, and explained coherently in the chapters on Wordsworth.

This table of distinctions provides the epistemological and structural foundation of the *Biographia*'s inquiry into imagination. It functions here as a substitute, in some ways, for Coleridge's more usual foundation: the distinction between reason and understanding. As the reader winds his way through chapters V to XIII the table slowly grows. The completed table looks like this:

	I	II	III
(levels of will)	receptive	spontaneous	voluntary
(forms of cognition)	sensuous	intuitive	discursive
(forms of consciousness)	common consciousness	self-consciousness	memory
(acts of powers)	perception	synthesis	association
(names of powers)	primary imagination	secondary imagination	fancy

The table has three major features. First, columns I and II are very closely related. Both common consciousness and self-consciousness are self-knowledge, although knowledge of different aspects of the self. Common consciousness is or knows the self as agent. Self-consciousness is or knows the self as an act. Because will is never actually suspended (I, 77), 'receptive' (the 'relatively passive') and 'spontaneous' name differences in degree, not kind, of mental activity (cf. I, 202). Because all knowledge is the concurrence of subject and object, 'perception' itself is 'synthetic', albeit not consciously so. Yet the terms 'sensuous' and 'intuitive' are far less closely related. One is mediated, the other immediate; one is physical, the other spiritual.

This reveals the second feature of the table. All the elements in column I describe the mind's encounter with the sensuous domain; all the elements in column II describe the mind's encounter with itself. The table thus reflects the differences, and the similarities, between our knowledge of things and our knowledge of thoughts – a distinction with which epistemology begins (I, 65). The opposition between things and thoughts has already been observed at length in the differences between sensation-dependent fanatics, and geniuses, whose minds are 'affected by thoughts, rather than by things' (I, 20). In a highly characteristic way, Coleridge moves forward by delving beneath prior topics; he makes the implicit explicit; he moves background issues into the foreground. Yet notice as well that he does not tell us that this is what he is doing. He writes as if he presumes we will anticipate these epistemological issues as the next logical step. It is the logical progression only for one who makes much of the fact that fanatics' minds are passive, while geniuses' minds are active.

The table of distinctions at first accommodates the fanatic–genius, passive–active distinction by appearing to grant that minds *are* passive in their relation to the physical world. But as the table and the epistemology underlying it are developed, this appearance is gradually discarded. This development takes place in chapters V to IX, which are centrally concerned with the realities named in column III. The third feature of the table is the extent to which column III names the central issues in Coleridge's critical commentary on his own times – and on Wordsworth. Throughout the analysis of associationism, the speaker argues that Lockean philosophies do not explain the phenomena named in column II, those concerned with the mind's experience of itself. Materialist associationisms collapse the intuitive into the sensuous, the spontaneous into the receptive, and so on. The network of relations among these fifteen terms underlies Coleridge's contention that Wordsworth's attitude toward the landscape verges on an empiricism that is ultimately pantheist. Wordsworth, Coleridge contends, attributes to *things* what he ought to attribute to his own imaginative *thinking*. In his theory and in his poems, he sometimes exaggerates or mismanages all that column III represents, because he has been unduly influenced by the Lockeanism of the day. He, too, tends to represent the intuitive as the receptive ('the light reflected, as a light bestowed'), although – Coleridge insists – he knows better. Coleridge's own account of fancy explains that the poet's associative processes should be controlled by imagination's spontaneous impulses, not by the spacio-temporal forms of the landscape. He offers an imaginative, not material, account of associating.

The concept of will is the *Biographia*'s structural foundation because here Coleridge is centrally interested in discrediting the Lockean contention that the mind is a *tabula rasa*. The theory of imagination arises by contrast to this common but perniciously mistaken notion that the mind is passive. By asserting that the mind is active, he can account for the controversy over *Lyrical Ballads* by analyzing the intellectual passivity of fanatical critics. From the same standpoint, he can undermine portions of Wordsworth's theory by contending that Wordsworth's careless writing suggests that the mind is passive in its relation to the landscape. By analyzing the merits of Wordsworth's best poems, Coleridge can champion the moral and cultural value of Wordsworth's exemplary genius. He can restore the elements in column III to their proper place in our knowledge of human nature – to the dignity and value Wordsworth's best poetry so brilliantly portrays.

Despite – or perhaps because of – this structural centrality, the *Biographia* seems to explain the idea of will everywhere in general, but very few places in particular. It is a genuinely elusive idea, but one that Coleridge regarded as crucial for his philosophy.[1] In most rudimentary terms, the idea of will comes down to this: the mind is active. Most precisely, the mind *is* an act. It is not a blank slate on which the material world writes by means of the sense organs. 'The pith of my system', he is quoted as saying, 'is, to make the senses out of the mind – not the mind out of the senses, as Locke did' (*TT*, 25 July 1832). The pith of *Biographia Literaria*'s design is Coleridge's insight into the relation between literary value and moral value. He risks the abyss of pantheism because he must have ways, even interim ways, to link imaginative power as a literary fact to imaginative power as an epistemological fact. He must have this link because it is crucial to the proper evaluation of Wordsworth's poetry. The origin of great art, and the origin of moral insight, are one and the same: Wordsworth at his best is a great poet and a great thinker for one reason, not two reasons. Coleridge cannot prove the relation he sees between these two functions of imagination's power, but he endeavors to reveal to the self-consciously thinking reader that a poem's beauty and its truth elicit or require the same intellectual activity from its reader. By urging and helping us to think about our activities as readers, Coleridge elicits our consent to his new version of the old ideal, 'dulce et utile'.

Many critics have puzzled over the fact that both before and after *Biographia Literaria* Coleridge attributes to reason many of the epistemological functions that the *Biographia* seems to attribute to imagination. This is not quite the case, despite appearances: the *Biographia*'s account of will offers a very subtle and difficult distinction between secondary imagination and pure reason, which is the sheerly active pole that is one part of imagination's synthesis. Because this very subtle distinction supplies the crucial link between literary value and moral value, let me stop here to preview Coleridge's argument. Without such an outlook over the difficult terrain ahead, my own analysis will unduly recapitulate the baffling intricacies of Coleridge's own way.

One preliminary note: generations of scholars have described the *Biographia* as almost a pivot in Coleridge's career: before this, poetry; after this, religion. Before this, imagination; after this, reason. Beginning in a substantial way with McFarland's and Barfield's work in the late 1960s, this dichotomy has been increasingly challenged. From his early days as a Hartleyan to his last hours in Highgate, Coleridge was very centrally concerned with morals. His 'orthodoxy' – that usually scornful term – was no coward's shelter. His Christianity was subtle, imaginative, and intellectually daring. His literary theories cannot be understood properly in a radical isolation from his religious speculation, because they rest on an analysis of consciousness that cannot be formulated without recourse to religious concepts. Similarly, his religious inquiries and allegiances cannot be appreciated by one who fails to recognize the bold imaginative powers at work in his reaffirmation of classically Western moral values. In short, let me begin by positing the integrity of Coleridge's intellectual career, just as I began by positing the unity of his intellectual autobiography, because it permits me to gain a vantage-point from which this integrity can be more clearly seen and more objectively evaluated.

The scope and significance of this assumption becomes most fully evident if one contrasts this study with Kathleen Wheeler's *Sources, Processes and Methods in Coleridge's 'Biographia Literaria'*. Wheeler contends that 'There are passages in the *Biographia* which have an imaginative, "paganistic" originality and individuality which no formulations explicitly Christian could possibly allow' (p. 146). Later in his career, she explains, 'uncertainties . . . led Coleridge to have to suppress imagination and irony as uncontrollable elements foreign to his Christian philosophy' (p. 133). 'Immediately upon finishing the *Biographia* he retired into the safety of the mainland of ordinary conventional consciousness, and occupied much of his intellectual energy with untangling the issues within the Christian theological tradition' (p. 147). In representing Coleridge's Christianity as a retreat from full self-consciousness, from the burden of individual identity, and from the responsibilities coinherent in creativity, Wheeler portrays him as attempting to return to the dimness of sensation and enfeebled intellect characteristic of the deficient multitude. Because such a retreat is not psychologically possible, the act of denying one's own self-consciousness is profoundly self-deceptive. That is why Wheeler and those who share her view describe Coleridge's later career as signaling a radical personal failure – however scrupulously they avoid condemning him. The quality and influence of his theology offer, apparently, no amends; nor do the ways in which his inquiries challenge the orthodox *status quo*. Different ways of understanding Coleridge's career are important for the formal evaluation of *Biographia Literaria* as a discourse, because the *Biographia* includes many specific references to Christian beliefs. Those who regard such statements as irrelevant or contradictory change the *Biographia* no less radically than those who oppose Milton's God change *Paradise Lost*.

In the *Biographia*, Coleridge's arguments about Wordsworth's theories and poems presume the theory of imagination, which presumes the idea of will, which cannot be defined apart from the ideas of reason and faith that are its complements in his analysis of consciousness. Understanding the relations among reason, faith and will, and understanding the relation between this complex and the idea of imagination, are prerequisite to following the path of his argument about the relation between moral value and literary value. So let us look first at the relations among reason, faith and will; and then at the relation between will and imagination; and finally at the ways in which this relationship influences what imagination produces. This preliminary summary can do scant justice to the richness and philosophic complexity of these issues.[2] But let complexity wait for later, as the *Biographia* itself gradually engages these problems. What we need now is no more than a very plain, very general sense of direction.

Will, faith and reason together name the single, complex, highest power of the human mind; and the ideal union of literary value and moral value derives from the *singleness* of this power. When discussing only one of these three, Coleridge usually attributes to it the whole complex power.[3] He does so consistently in the *Biographia*, which focusses our attention almost exclusively on will. But when he defines all three together, he attributes to each a specific aspect of the single power: reason is cognitive, will is motive, and faith is the relation between the fullest operation of each.[4] The most elegant and lucid definition of this psychological trinity concludes the 'Essay on Faith'.

> Faith subsists in the *synthesis* of the reason and the individual will. By virtue of the latter therefore it must be an energy, and inasmuch as it relates to the whole moral man, it must be exerted in each and all of his constituents or incidents, faculties and tendencies; – it must be a total, not a partial; a continuous, not a desultory or occasional energy. And by virtue of the former, that is, reason, faith must be a light, a form of knowing, a beholding of truth. In the incomparable words of the Evangelist, therefore – *faith must be a light originating in the Logos, or substantial reason, which is co-eternal and one with the Holy Will, and which light is at the same time the life of men.* Now as life is here the sum or collective of all moral and spiritual acts, in suffering, doing, and being, so is faith the source and the sum, the energy and the principle of the fidelity of man to God, by the subordination of his human will, in all provinces of his nature to his reason, as the sum of spiritual truth, representing and manifesting the will Divine. (Shedd, V, 565)

In describing faith as both motive (the 'energy' of will) and cognitive (reason, a 'form of knowing'), Coleridge places himself approximately intermediate between Roman Catholic and Anglican Protestant doctrines.[5] The essential act of faith is fidelity to God. Yet this is simultaneously fidelity to the self, to one's own reason as the origin of individual identity and personality.[6] Such simultaneity is possible because reason knows the difference between right and wrong. Reason knows the difference because it knows God's will, or God as Absolute Will. In knowing the difference between right and wrong, reason itself participates in the motive aspect of faith: the entirely rational person will by definition not desire that which he knows to be wrong. Yet sin is precisely such a desire: it is the failure to subordinate desire (will) to knowledge (reason). By defining sin in this way, Coleridge portrays it as simultaneously inauthentic, psychologically diseased, and contrary to God's will. The well-formed conscience, in turn, testifies both to mental health and to morals: it reflects the unity or the disharmony of faith, will and reason.[7]

The 'Essay on Faith' emphasizes faith's role in this psychological trinity; *Biographia Literaria* emphasizes will's role. It describes *will* as the mind's power to *act*, and argues that the mind's essential act is *knowing*. Coleridge usually calls this essential cognitive act *reason*, and then distinguishes (in basically Kantean ways) between reason's cognition and the cognition of understanding.[8] But the distinction between reason and understanding very seldom appears in the *Biographia*. For clarity's sake, I will follow the *Biographia*'s usage, using *will* to name the mind's power to act, a power primarily evident in the power to know. In the *Biographia*, then, will is both cognitive and motive, and its highest form of cognition is the act of faith or the knowledge of God.

Let us turn now to the character of will's interactivity with imagination. Will is involved in 'each and all' human acts, from the most profound to the most trivial. Knowing is not a part of will, as an arm is part of a dancer. Rather, knowing is to human being as dancing is to the dancer *per se*. As chapter XII explains, the epistemologist examines the fundamental form of this human act, which is self-knowing or self-consciousness. By virtue of self-consciousness, all our other acts are different from the acts of unconscious nonhumans, just as by virtue of dancing all the movements of a dancer are (potentially, at least) more coherent, deliberate and beautiful than those of a nondancer. This turning inward of will, the self-consciousness, is the act of secondary imagination.

It is or requires the act of imagination because Coleridge here distinguishes knowing as such from the ability to dissolve and simultaneously to reconstitute the unity of consciousness. When Coleridge later in his career stops discussing imagination, it is at least in part because this distinction is not absolutely necessary to his principal arguments about reason itself. And later on he is more interested in determining how reason accounts for the richest development of human consciousness, rather than how imagination acts as an essentially necessary 'catalyst' for these supreme human achievements. The *Biographia*, however, does emphasize imagination's role in attaining self-consciousness because (*a*) imagination's access to the primal unity of will, faith and reason provides the link between moral value and the most perfectly achieved imaginative works, and (*b*) because self-consciousness is only one instance of imagination's power to dissolve and recreate. The process of composing poetry is another.

When will and imagination interact as self-consciousness (when will through imagination strives to know itself), will discovers the pure spirit or soul. It discovers its own being-which-is-knowing that Coleridge usually calls 'reason'. As we can and cannot tell the dancer from the dance, so we can and cannot distinguish our being from our knowing. The unity of being and knowing is an act, the act of self-knowing, which can be represented by the words 'I am'. The human power of knowing is an echo in the finite human mind of the infinite and absolute knowing that is God, 'the infinite I am'. One's ability through will to know one's own consciousness, to know the human being-which-is-knowing, is thus a knowledge of or an encounter with the absolute in a pure but relative form. It is consciousness of the human in the divine, or the divine in the human, or Christ within us, 'begotten not made, one in being with the Father'.[9] In short, it comes to this: will as cognition (the reason aspect of faith) knows God; it also knows itself as pure spirit, as pure knower, and thus as both free and immortal by virtue of its essential identity with or participation in the absolute knowing that is God.[10] It attains such knowledge only when or as it exerts the fullness of its cognitive power on the mind itself, and such self-consciousness requires an immensely powerful secondary imagination.

Will thus involves two paradoxes. The first is the possibility of an absolute in relative form. This derives from the mystery of the Incarnation, or the Trinity generally, about which the *Biographia* says almost nothing. The second is the paradoxical relation between the mind and the world: the world is both physically real and independent, and created for us through the act of knowing. Since knowing is such an important access to the divine, the contradiction may be capable of symbolic resolution. But, again, the *Biographia* says almost nothing, repeatedly deferring solution to the Logosophia. These two paradoxes underlie Coleridge's central contention that the greatest works of literature intimately synthesize moral insights with vividly particular portraits of all that we call 'reality'. Because the paradoxes are genuinely irresolvable, the argument about literature is an essentially rhetorical construct. Coleridge seeks to persuade us by appealing to 'inner experience' generally, and by specific appeal to the 'inner experience' of the meditative reading of poems. And this mode of argument is neither outrageous nor sly. Recognizing that 'proofs' of God can no longer be valid or meaningful, Coleridge sees further that 'proofs' of the cultural and moral value of literature are equally futile. We need, he recognizes, a new defense of poetry.

This account of the interactivity of will and imagination has emphasized the role of will so as to sketch the connection between imagination and the moral realm. Explaining the same interaction with an emphasis now on imagination can sketch the connection between imagination and literature. The imagination mediates between the mind's active pole (will) and its passive pole (sensation).[11] Imagination's own activity is synthesizing these two poles. This synthesis generates two sets of 'products'. The first set, produced through primary imagination, is common consciousness and perception. Common consciousness is the union of self-as-subject (will as act or as knowing) with self-as-object (will as agent or as being); it arises coinstantaneously and spontaneously with the act of perception. It can be represented by the phrase 'I am', whereby the 'I' is regarded or discovered as an entity distinct from its surroundings.

The second set, produced through secondary imagination, is philosophic or imaginative self-consciousness and poetry (in the highest sense in which poetry and philosophy are equatable). These products arise when the synthesis comprising common consciousness becomes itself an object of knowledge. Common consciousness can itself be known only by one who can simultaneously dissolve and reconstitute its union of being and knowing. Such self-consciousness or philosophic consciousness is the knowing of common consciousness both as a unity and as its parts.[12] Secondary imagination distinguishes the dancer from the dance, but in doing so realizes that the two *cannot be known in isolation from one another.* Imaginative self-consciousness discovers or generates suprasensuous knowledge because it directly intuits the will itself (the purely active pole) when it regards the unity of common consciousness as its parts. It 'dissolves, diffuses, [and] dissipates' not the object itself, but the relation between mind and object. I will explain more about imagination's direct intuition of will when we come to chapter XII.

The 'Essay on Faith' explains that faith as a product is knowledge, and faith as a process is will. The *Biographia* explains that poetry as a *product* is the union of universal (via will's self-scrutiny) and particular (via the senses) that Coleridge calls a symbol.[13] Poetry's moral and human value derives from these two links, first to God and secondly to the richness of human experience or reality as humanly known. Poetry as a *process* 'brings the whole soul of man into activity, with the subordination of its faculties to each other, according to their relative worth and dignity' (II, 12). By virtue of this whole involvement, poetry is both an intellectual and linguistic craft with its own rules, and an impassioned self-expression bounded only by the expressing self. Poetry as a process also achieves symbolic richness: it is both universal in its fidelity to rules derived from fundamental patterns of human consciousness, and particular in its presentation of both specific situations and the individuality of its author. We will see much more of Coleridge's ideas about the nature of poetry when we come to the *Biographia*'s second volume.

One final note about imagination. It is not directly cognitive. We have only two sources of knowledge: the relatively passive sense organs, and the will (or reason). The imagination – at either of its levels – can be called cognitive only because it synthesizes cognitive powers. It does not, itself, have access to objects as the senses do, nor to the suprasensuous as the will does. If it did, then the distinction between sensuous and suprasensuous would become very badly blurred; and this is likely to land us in pantheism. And yet we have no conscious knowledge of any sort without the imagination. Because it is not necessary in every context to specify that imagination 'knows' only in this qualified and indirect sense, Coleridge in the *Biographia* talks about imaginative knowledge or self-conscious knowledge when he wishes to contrast what may be known through sensation with what may be known through meditation. Such passages are highly condensed, or strictly adapted to local argument; but they are not contradictory. (They do, however, make it somewhat difficult to specify the relation between Coleridge's idea of imagination and Kant's.)[14] Coleridge's point, inevitably, is that imaginative knowledge arises from the synthesis or harmony of all human powers, both spiritual and natural. Its opposite is strictly empirical or sensory observation, which does not, finally, deserve the name 'knowledge'.

The *Biographia* says little about faith, and less about reason and understanding, because it is primarily concerned with the products of imagination, not with the full intricacy of the activity of imagination in concert with other powers. Coleridge defines only those parts of his full philosophy that he needs to establish the unity of truth, verbal precision and aesthetic power in great poems. As he says in chapter IX, he intends to offer an aid to judgment not – as later – an aid to reflection. Formal arguments concerning the exact activity of will, and its interactivity with imagination, are confined to one chapter – to the extraordinarily compressed summary and revision of Schelling's analysis of consciousness. But the practical or experiental aspects of will and imagination are worked out in a lucid and sometimes leisurely way in chapters V to XI, as the speaker gradually and simultaneously refutes materialism and recognizes the unity of being and knowing.

This refutation formally begins in chapter V, which begins with the 'table of distinctions' that we have just examined. Somehow it ought to be obvious that the three levels of will provide a basis for the philosophic inquiry projected in chapter IV. But the remarkable absence of will as a term and an explicit issue in most commentaries on the *Biographia* demonstrates that these valuable distinctions, especially as later elaborated, largely escape even careful readers.[15] This happens, I suspect, because Coleridge moves so rapidly to the summary of Mackintosh's lectures that he invites us to see the chapter's opening paragraph as no more than an introductory historical flourish. Furthermore, one who expects Coleridge to be always digressive and disjointed will be particularly willing to dismiss this paragraph because it does not immediately and intimately link chapter V to chapter IV. That expectation becomes self-fulfilling: the analysis of associationism appears largely irrelevant, and this misperception itself generates much subsequent confusion. The unity of the *Biographia* begins rapidly to unravel, especially for a reader who also discarded chapter II because of its equally off-handed opening. As a composition, *Biographia Literaria* is by far too fragile to resist and correct such readers.

I doubt that it is possible to apportion 'responsibility' or 'blame' for the reader's probable misdirection at chapter V: Coleridge's genuine clumsiness here is too complexly interwoven with the traditions influencing how we approach his works. I would point out only that autobiography offered Coleridge ample resources for the devising of a more helpful transition, resources that one must assume he ignores for conscious and unconscious reasons of his own. Regarded as autobiography, chapters V to VII refute the claims advanced in lectures by Sir James Mackintosh, who according to Coleridge asserted that Hobbes had advanced a new explanation of spontaneous mental activity, an explanation fully worked out by Hartley. The speaker sharply disagrees with Mackintosh's high praise for these two philosophers. Mackintosh's lectures are not linked to the sequence of influences recorded in chapters I to IV, although since Coleridge attended them in 1800 they might have been fitted in. Since Hartley was actually a quite major influence (a fact noted in chapter X), he, too, offers a means of linking these chapters to the first four.[16] But no autobiographical continuity links chapter V to what has gone before, until chapter IX describes the philosophers analyzed in these chapters as a sequence of studies the speaker had undertaken. This 'revision' establishes Mackintosh as a student and historian of philosophy opposite and equivalent to the speaker. It reflects helpful emphasis back to the table of distinctions, and to the question whether ancient or modern philosophers more accurately understood the spontaneous (i.e. imaginative) activity of mind. It is possible that the lack of immediate autobiographical linkage is intended to signal that *Biographia Literaria* is not simply or exclusively an intellectual autobiography, but also an inquiry into will and poetry. If so, then the principal chronological tie becomes the speaker's *present* intent to present his 'poetic creed' not as opinion, but as 'deductions from established premises' (I, 65): the autobiography takes the first of several leaps 'forward' into the speaker's present time.

Regarded as philosophy, chapters V to VII progressively develop the issues of earlier chapters: they define fancy, and distinguish it from imagination. In defining fancy, Coleridge asserts that association is governed not by things but by thinking. The spacio-temporal relations of objects matter less than the power of will to focus attention and thereby to control the clarity with which items are present or accessible within one's memory. The spontaneous operation of will (the secondary imagination) thus can govern the activity of fancy in associating elements linked by any notion or feature at all. Coleridge sketches this interaction of fancy and imagination in the densely metaphoric and analogic 'water-insect' passage late in chapter VII. These images and analogies reappear in the criticism of Wordsworth when Coleridge contends that Wordsworth attributes to the rural landscape a power to govern association that properly belongs to secondary imagination. This error, Coleridge claims, is evident both in Wordsworth's statements about rustics' language, and in his unsuccessful poems.

Let us begin with the definition of fancy, turning afterwards to the critique of materialist theories of association. Chapter V describes fancy objectively, from the perspective of things associated; chapter VI describes fancy subjectively, from the perspective of mental controls over this process. Chapter VII explores the consequences of mental control over fancy, and formulates the 'true practical general law of association' in a way that emphasizes fancy's subordination to will and imagination. Chapter VIII explores the metaphysical issues raised by this subordination; further inquiry into such issues will generate the formal definition of imagination in chapter XIII.

The objective account of what perceptions are associable begins from the same fundamental conservatism we have already noted: 'For many, very many centuries, it has been difficult to advance a new truth, or even a new error, in the philosophy of the intellect or morals' (I, 66). On this basis, the speaker prefers Aristotle to the moderns: 'In as much as later writers have either deviated from, or added to his doctrines, they appear to me to have introduced either error or groundless supposition' (I, 71). Yet, as Shawcross points out, the speaker emends Aristotle, who does not list the 'five agents or occasioning causes' of association (I, 72). Even this position is subsequently 'clarified' into something quite different. The five causes are summarized as variations on the *contemporaneity* of original impressions; the speaker later substitutes *continuity* to eliminate altogether any necessary temporal link (I, 87; cf. I, 70). Coleridge calls down the authority of Aristotle against the authority of the associationist tradition in English materialism, arranging and adding to Aristotle's rather sketchy remarks on the topic for his own purposes.

Aristotle's sketchiness very nicely deflates association from the complete theory of mind that it is in Hartley to no more than the name of one class of actions that the mind can perform. The speaker approvingly notes that Aristotle provides only 'a comprehensive survey of the different facts, and of their relations to each other without *supposition,* i.e. a fact *placed under* a number of facts, as their common support and explanation' (I, 72). Because Aristotle consistently distinguishes mental movement or activity from movement in space, the speaker claims that Aristotle supports his own major contention about fancy: association is controlled not by the physical relations of the objects whose impressions are associated by the mind but, rather, by strictly mental processes. Association is not a law governed by things, but a law governed by thinking – a process that the mind itself controls.

Chapter VI turns from this concern with the relations among associable objects to consider the mental processes by which fancy is directed. The speaker asserts that 'the will, the reason, the judgement, and the understanding' are the 'determining causes' of association (I, 76). If these higher powers failed to exercise such authority, then 'our whole life would be divided between the despotism of outward impressions, and that of senseless and passive memory' (I, 77).

There follows an example designed to support this very central contention. It begins with a verb in the imperative mood: 'Consider, how immense must be the sphere of a total impression from the top of St. Paul's church . . .' (I, 77). The reader who resists has demonstrated his control over association: he refuses to summon up the view associated with these words. The reader who cooperates would be swept into delirium if will did not control and limit the associative movement of mind. Either way, the speaker makes his point by eliciting the control that is at issue, rather than by constructing formal philosophic counter-arguments.

Because this strategy would probably not persuade a professional philosopher (especially a sophisticated empiricist), we have here fairly clear evidence concerning the kinds of reader Coleridge expected. This passage, like the footnote defining 'idea' (I, 69 n), or the explanation that both materialism and idealism can be traced back to the ancients (I, 66), or the footnote distinguishing objective and subjective forms of consciousness (I, 53 n), seems to suggest that Coleridge expected little formal sophistication. The argument is designed for one who shares the speaker's essential values – both his Christian ideas about the mind and about moral responsibility, and his attitudes toward inquiry. The long experiential arguments identify the speaker as a person more deeply concerned about practical consequences or moral issues than about formal proofs. We are to realize that, for this man, proofs without such practical bases and moral conviction are merely academic word-games – an abuse of language closely akin to that of anonymous critics (see I, 95–7; I, 178–9; cf. *CL*, II, 961). In effect, these experiential arguments define the powers of will as axioms, a status that never changed (see *AR*, 153–9). Personal agency is an unquestioned but well-examined fact from which Coleridge begins. The reader who is more interested in poetry and Wordsworth than in philosophy and Schelling might accept such a complex axiom. But such a reader is apt to be confused and annoyed when Coleridge suddenly shifts to a dense discourse that presumes a thorough knowledge of the implications of various philosophic formulae, as he does in chapters VIII and XII.

The professional philosopher who can read such chapters with relative ease will most likely object to the breadth of Coleridge's initial assumptions. The professional is more likely than the amateur to demand that Coleridge prove his idea of will, or argue formally on behalf of his concept of God. In the absence of such proofs and arguments, the professional might think that these illuminations are to be taken as proofs; and thence conclude that Coleridge is a bungler with no sense of formal argument, nor of the complexity of his issues. This misperception derives in part from the sharp wit that guides less experienced readers: Coleridge writes as if he has demolished his opponents' positions. His repeated statements of intent to supply formal proofs in another book should signal his recognition that such proof is necessary. Yet the confident tone, the unfinished Logosophia, and the irresolvable paradoxes leave Coleridge quite vulnerable to sharp professional attack.

And in all this it must be remembered that in the *Biographia* Coleridge explicitly refers to a class of readers to whom he expects to be almost entirely opaque: anonymous critics and their kind. Rather than leave his argument vulnerable to the confused apprehension of this powerful group, Coleridge's speaker periodically breaks off his discourse with a reference to the unspoken. Usually the unspoken is represented as the Logosophia or some other unwritten or unfinished work; occasionally, as in chapter VI, it is represented as a mystery that should not be revealed indiscriminately. As these references become more explicit, it gradually becomes evident that all refer to the relation between the creative powers of human cognition, and the power or activity that is God. The most famous reference to 'mysteries' is the chapter's second 'anecdote', describing the delirious serving girl. The story attributes to memory the passive recording falsely attributed to fancy itself, and asserts that *conscious* memory represents only a fraction of the total power. The girl's ravings reveal association without the conscious control of will. The story claims that even relatively passive mental processes rest not on material but on spiritual causes: 'all thoughts are in themselves imperishable', and their record is the 'dread book of judgement' (I, 79–80).[17] The concluding lines attribute the unity and permanence revealed by association operating as memory to 'the free-will, our only absolute *self*' (I, 80).

The passage from Plotinus links will to the aesthetic issues defined earlier. Before defining imagination, the speaker must solve several problems in epistemology and metaphysics. Because he solves them through religious meditation, moral issues often color chapters V to XIII. As a result, thematic unity demands coherent relations among morals, aesthetics, imagination and will. These relations are first defined here, when the speaker 'breaks off' a discussion of the moral implications of will to quote the following. It is 'profanation' to speak of such things, he explains,

> 'To those to whose imagination it has never been presented, how beautiful is the countenance of justice and wisdom; and that neither the morning nor the evening star are so fair. For in order to direct the view aright, it behoves that the beholder should have made himself con-generous and similar to the object beheld. Never could the eye have beheld the sun, had not its own essence been soliform,' (*i.e. pre-configured to light by a similarity of essence with that of light*) 'neither can a soul not beautiful attain to an intuition of beauty.' (I, 80 n)

Coleridge adds 'imagination' to the first sentence to adapt the passage to his own ends – a characteristic strategy.[18] The speaker literally asserts that he cannot continue this line of moral inquiry because not everyone will understand (another instance of the 'deficient multitude' theme).[19] In Coleridge's context, the passage from Plotinus implicitly equates imagination, aesthetic sensitivity, and consciousness of will. It also asserts a necessary connection between this psychological unity and the metaphysical unity of the Good, the True and the Beautiful. The speaker later substantiates this necessary connection through the analysis of will and consciousness (i.e. through the definition of imagination). The theory of imagination explains how the Good, the True and the Beautiful are evident in the most perfect instances of poetry.

In short, if the last paragraph of chapter VI is read as a transition – certainly what the reader expects in a last paragraph – one discovers both the unity of prior issues and a basis for understanding how the diversity of earlier issues will lead to a higher unity. Will interrelates imagination, beauty and the fanatic–genius opposition; the equation of imagination and the consciousness of will maps new ground. The 'breaking off' is merely stylistic, an odd and probably unsuccessful device to draw attention to the highly condensed and important integration of several central issues.

Chapter VII defines the ontological and metaphysical consequences of mental control over association. Its concluding definition of fancy both complements and supplants the 'Aristotelian' five causes by locating the real cause of association in the controlling power of will. The chapter is dense, quick, and tightly woven with the critique of Hartley; but every idea follows clearly from one central point: failure to recognize the agency of will destroys the ideas of consciousness, moral responsibility or personal agency, God, faith and causality.

As a philosopher (and a Christian), the speaker values final causes, as he explains in chapter IX: 'We learn all things indeed by *occasion* of experience; but the very facts so learnt force us inward on the antecedents, that must be pre-supposed in order to render experience itself possible' (I, 94). That is, we *ought* to be forced inward to final causes, by our own ontology. 'The facts' will only 'force' us if we establish certain standards for explanations. The speaker argues for the *necessary* existence of suprasensible realities. His argument centers on a complex of terms ('consciousness', 'will', 'self', 'soul') that are not entirely synonymous but, rather, aspects of basic human identity. This complex is closely linked to God, in part through the traditional associations of religious language, and in part for reasons only later explained (but discussed by me at the beginning of the present chapter).

The speaker first defends consciousness itself. According to Hartley's followers (including, once, Coleridge himself), 'consciousness [is] considered as a *result*, as a *tune*, the common product of [material] breeze and [bodily] harp[.] . . . [But] what is harmony but a mode of relation, the very *esse* of which is *percipi?*' (I, 81) To hear and to analyze the music made by the harp requires a third position, neither harp nor breeze but auditor. If consciousness were merely a product of the physical world and the physical body, then we could by definition never achieve the knowledge of consciousness that the image defines. 'Listening' requires the power to observe one's own mind. It requires self-consciousness. The power of self-observation is the single most central fact for Coleridge's philosophy generally; it is defined here for the first time through a metaphor. Coleridge's equation of poetry and philosophy must be taken very seriously by any student of his prose – or his poetry.

The second suprasensible is will itself, considered as moral responsibility or personal agency. If final causes are discarded, then 'the disquisition, to which I am at present soliciting the reader's attention, may be as truly said to be written by Saint Paul's church, as by *me*' (I, 82). The reference to St Paul's echoes the earlier reference to introduce another witty portrait of common-sense experience. The passage appeals to the experience of personal agency, rather than proving its 'objective' possibility. None the less, the paragraph strongly and successfully urges the irrationality of denying personal agency.

The denial or the defense of self-consciousness and personal agency leads directly to the denial or the defense of God. Our knowledge of our own will (i.e. self-consciousness) intimately involves a knowledge of God as 'an intelligent and holy will' (I, 83). Limiting all explanations to efficient causality necessarily leads to the 'degredation of every fundamental idea in ethics or theology' because these ideas depend on entities that are not knowable through the sense organs. Spinoza's denial of both personal agency and the personality of God stands silently behind the critique of associationism. The speaker refutes not the intent of Locke or Hartley, but the consequences of object-oriented philosophy as made evident by Spinoza.[20] By suggesting that the similarity of God and man rests on the power of will, Coleridge firmly anchors the relation between his moral and his aesthetic concerns: the activity of mind that generates art also leads to God.

Final causes must be distinguished not only from efficient causes, but also from necessary conditions (I, 85). The contemporaneity of objects (as stressed by Hartley's mechanism) is a law of matter, not of mind. The development of this idea introduces the first substantial explanation of the interaction of fancy and imagination: the famous 'water-insect' passage, followed by the formal definition of the law of association. This definition stresses the agency of will that the water-insect passage illuminates in greater detail.

> . . . the true practical general law of association is this; that whatever makes certain parts of a total impression more vivid or distinct than the rest, will determine the mind to recall these in preference to others equally linked together by the common condition of contemporaneity, or (what I deem a more appropriate and philosophical term) of *continuity*.

But the will itself by confining and intensifying the attention may arbitrarily give vividness or distinctness to any object whatsoever. (I, 87)

The substitution of 'continuity' eliminates the last traces of materialism from the law of association: continuity can link past and present, or objects here with objects there, on the basis of subjectively originating similarity. Most important, the recalled feature that triggers the associative leap depends not on physical conditions, but on the 'arbitrary' or selective focussing of attention on to particular features of a given perception. Thus, the operations of fancy are determined by habits of observation (what aspects are noted?), by the power of attention or concentration (how clearly are the aspects noted?), and by the subtlety with which resemblances are noted (are the relations crude or delicate?). The important qualities of fancy are determined not by the acuity of sense organs, but by the entire character of a person's relation to the environment – a relation established through primary and secondary imagination.[21]

This definition follows the water-insect passage; it partially explains how imagination, or the spontaneous level of will, can control the associative activity of fancy. Having looked at the definition first, we are better prepared to recognize how much more the metaphor suggests than the consecutive first reader may immediately recognize.

. . . contemporaneity (Leibnitz's *Lex Continui*) is the *limit and condition* of the laws of mind, itself being rather a law of matter, at least of phaenomena considered as material. At the utmost, it is to *thought* the same, as the law of gravitation is to loco-motion. . . . Let us consider what we do when we leap. We first resist the gravitating power by an act purely voluntary, and then by another act, voluntary in part, we yield to it in order to light on the spot, which we had previously proposed to ourselves. Now let a man watch his mind while he is composing; or, to take a still more common case, while he is trying to recollect a name; and he will find the process completely analogous. Most of my readers will have observed a small water-insect on the surface or rivulets, which throws a cinque-spotted shadow fringed with prismatic colours on the sunny bottom of the brook; and will have noticed, how the little animal *wins* its way up against the stream, by alternate pulses of active and passive motion, now resisting the current, and now yielding to it in order to gather strength and a momentary *fulcrum* for a further propulsion. This is no unapt emblem of the mind's self-experience in the act of thinking. There are evidently two powers at work, which relatively to each other are active and passive; and this is not possible without an intermediate faculty, which is at once both active and passive. (In philosophical language, we must denominate this intermediate faculty in all its degrees and determinations, the IMAGINATION. . . .) (I, 85–6)

The passage opens with a reference to gravity which, like the earlier reference (I, 30 n), asserts the *relative* opposition of two forces between which imagination mediates. The passive aspect is sensation, which obeys laws of matter such as contemporaneity. The purely active pole is pure will (or pure reason). Despite the vivid sensual detail of the insect and its shadow, the description emphasizes not the creature itself, but its activity. It is easy to enjoy Coleridge's metaphors as rich ornament, but one dare not stop there.

As the swimming insect or the leaping person demonstrates, genuine synthesis requires that imagination share essential features with the active will and the relatively passive sense receptors. That is, the leaping body has both mass *and* the capacity to resist gravity by virtue of the same essential property: muscle, skeleton, and nervous organization. In the same way, imagination's mediation cannot be a merely mechanical switching back and forth from activity to passivity, because then imagination would be no more than a title for the alternative dominance of one or the other over consciousness. Nothing so crude could possibly account for the delicately balanced unity that characterizes both geniuses' psyches and their works.

How does the imagination achieve its mediation between the active and passive aspects of mind? That is the question with which the consecutive first reader is left – that, and the image of progress via synthesis. This strategy provides a framework or a niche for the definition of imagination. This definition develops quite slowly until the image of synthesis reappears in the relative definitions of 'subject' and 'object' in chapter XII.

Let me once again pause to preview Coleridge's answer to the question poised at this point. As I have already explained, imaginative synthesis consists partly in the relative passivity of primary imagination as perception, and partly in the activity of secondary imagination as it dissolves and reconstitutes perceptual unity and common consciousness. The whole issue arises in chapter VI because the imagination's synthesis *per se* depends on the fancy's power to collect perceptions that have features in common, to assemble 'material' capable of synthesis into a whole by virtue of its fundamental interrelations. But, as the law of association points out, fancy cannot collect coherently except under specific direction. The other two analogies in this passage make the process quite clear. In trying to recollect a name, one summons to preconsciousness many scattered memories all of which have some bearing on the sought-for name. The secondary imagination seeks or creates the pattern in the memories that will reveal the name. Yet this creating is only theoretically distinguishable from the imagination's control of the re-collecting or assembling performed by fancy, because the synthesis gets under way as soon as there is more than one 'datum' present. The 'Essays on Method' explain this more fully (*F*, I, 448–524).

The process of composing demonstrates the same inseparable cooperation. Assembling materials can be mechanical and dull, yet clearly it is crucial. In any substantial investigation, knowing what to gather and where to look depends partly on logic and experience, but more centrally on intuition. The act of composing requires that one discover the pattern one has created, the pattern implicit and buried in the reams of notes. For this process to succeed, the writer's genius (that is, both imagination and, in the old sense, guiding spirit) must both fuse with and stand critically aside from what has been gathered. As many scholars have testified, one delight of the work is in discovering how central one's whimsical quests can prove to be. Such experiences would be far from delightful were it not for confidence that such whimsy is not blind chance but preconscious purpose. Whether poetry or prose, literature or literary criticism, imaginative works of any kind both resist and imitate the material world by means of the extraordinary care exercised by imagination through fancy in the selection of appropriate materials.

My point is that when Coleridge suggests, 'let a man watch . . .,' he expects that we will. Although fancy and imagination are distinct, imagination cannot operate without fancy any more than fancy can operate coherently without the focus or motive that will provides. This focus need not be imaginative, but it certainly can be. As Coleridge is quoted as saying, 'Genius must have talent as its complement and implement, just as, in like manner, imagination must have fancy. In short, the higher intellectual powers can only act through a corresponding energy of the lower' (*TT*, 20 August 1833). By interposing the activity of the water-insect and the other analogies in the definition of fancy, Coleridge sketches the interaction of fancy and imagination through images for it. The images function analogously to a statement of intent, yet only for the reader who knows to take them this seriously, and who is capable of carrying forward the cognitive range of a metaphor.

The definition of fancy as partial and dependent provokes curiosity concerning the powers that control fancy. This curiosity would have been even more keen for the sympathetic contemporary reader. By attributing all association to fancy, and then defining fancy as he does, Coleridge prepares ground for his own ideas about the mind. These begin to come to the foreground in chapter VIII.

But, before proceeding to chapter VIII, I should summarize one aspect of the issues in question. When Coleridge demotes 'association' from the title of an adequate philosophy to the name of one class of mental acts, he reopens the questions this popular philosophy had answered: What is perception? and What is thinking? One option is to reverse Lockean mental passivity, but this generates other, equally severe problems. The mind is neither absolutely active nor absolutely passive: as chapter VII concludes, there is the 'intermediate' or synthetic power of imagination – the spontaneous movement of mind that Mackintosh claims Hartley had explained. Chapter VIII's emphasis on dualism may seem tangential, because this word has not previously appeared. Yet Coleridge does not depart from his topic. He again delves beneath it, to the fundamental issue that has been shaping his counter-arguments all along: What is the relation between mind and external reality? He must answer this metaphysical question before answering the psychological ones; his fundamental disagreement with associationism is as much metaphysical as psychological.

But Coleridge himself had not yet answered the metaphysical question in strictly philosophical terms. (As McFarland has explained, a rigorous solution is not possible.[22]) In the *Biographia*, Coleridge does not attempt to close his system or to complete his argument formally. Completion is repeatedly deferred to the Logosophia, as we see for the first time in chapter VIII. As we shall see, in chapter X he offers instead a pair of assertions about faith and cognition: through the activity of faith, we have immediate knowledge of both a personal God and a real world of physical objects immediately known. Beyond these assertions, one finds only hints toward a philosophical construction. As these suggestions become more explicit, claims about the relative completeness of the Logosophia become more explicit as well.

In chapter VIII these hints are not very specific. The first two depend on Coleridge's prior critique of anonymous critics and the reading public. The speaker describes the possibility that body and spirit '*may* without any *absurdity* be supposed to be different modes, or degrees in perfection, of a common substratum', but explains that this possibility was not 'the fashion' (I, 88). Yet fashion is hardly a reliable guide to philosophic truth. As Coleridge remarks elsewhere, 'From a popular philosophy and a philosophic populace, Good Sense deliver us!'[23] A second, rhetorically similar hint emerges later: 'Leibnitz's doctrine of a pre-established harmony . . . was in its *common* interpretation too strange to survive the inventor – too repugnant to our *common sense*; (which is not indeed entitled to a judicial voice in the courts of scientific philosophy, but whose whispers still exert a strong secret influence)' (I, 89). As he elsewhere explains, philosophic arguments 'can be of no permanent utility, while the authors themselves join in the vulgar appeal to common sense as the one infallible judge in matters, which become subjects of philosophy only, because they involve a contradiction between this common sense and our *moral* instincts, and require therefore an arbiter, which containing both (*eminenter*) must be higher than either' (*LS*, 110). Coleridge uses the accumulated pressure of his critique of 'popular' thinking to identify two philosophic ideas as viable: Leibnitzian pre-established harmony, and the common substratum of being and knowing.

The third hint is somewhat more difficult to explain. On the narrative level, as we shall see shortly, Coleridge in these chapters examines philosophy since Descartes and Hobbes as described by Mackintosh. Chapter VIII returns to Descartes. It briefly describes attempts to correct Descartes' erroneous supposition that mind and matter are absolutely heterogeneous, dividing these attempts into the unsuccessful and the unfashionable. This strategy delivers the speaker to an apparent dead end.

No prior philosopher seems able to explain the relation between mind and physical reality. Yet he perseveres.

> But it is not either the nature of man, or the duty of the philosopher to despair concerning any important problem until, as in the squaring of the circle, the impossibility of a solution has been demonstrated. (I, 89)

This statement shifts our attention from particular philosophies to the logical form of basic philosophic questions. It allows the speaker to formulate the question about mind and matter that 'the philosopher' seeks to answer, and thus to determine the necessary form of all possible answers. His formulation changes the question in crucial ways.

> How the *esse*, assumed as originally distinct from the *scire*, can ever unite itself with it: how *being* can transform itself into a *knowing*, becomes conceivable on one only condition; namely, if it can be shown that the *vis representativa*, or the Sentient, is itself a species of being; i.e. either as a property or attribute, or as an hypostasis or self subsistence. The former is, indeed, the assumption of materialism; a system which could not but be patronized by the philosopher, if only it actually performed what it promises. (I, 89–90)

By shifting the inquiry from mind and matter to knowing and being, Coleridge tries to sidestep the insolvable problems that radical dualisms pose. His answers represent one position – the 'hypostasis or self subsistence' of being and knowing – as the only remaining viable alternative.

He also reaches back to gather in the 'unfashionable' possibilities: these three hints tend in a single direction. Hypostasis or self-subsistence or common substratum (etymologically and historically related terms, generally speaking) all point to a pre-existent harmony between being and knowing. Chapter IX consolidates and clarifies the basic point Coleridge has asserted:

> The term, Philosophy, defines itself as an affectionate seeking after the truth; but Truth is the correlative of Being. This again is [in] no way conceivable, but by assuming as a postulate, that both are *ab initio*, identical and coinherent; *that intelligence and being are reciprocally each other's substrate.* (I, 94; my italics)

As the reference to hypostasis suggests, this is potentially a Neoplatonic and pantheist answer to the metaphysical question. But only potentially. 'Hypostasis' also translates into Latin and then English as 'person', and figures in theories of the Trinity. The subsequent reference to the Logosophia leaves no doubt about Coleridge's intention, although it provides no explanation of how this intent will be realized.

The strategy is designed to lead us to accept the substantial unity of being and knowing as both an orthodox and a necessary solution. He defers to the Logosophia only the proof for that which we should see as logically necessary. However irking for those who share Coleridge's interest in the philosophical grounds of literary theory, such a tactic is not formally unreasonable in a book with the *Biographia*'s declared intent. Not every author is bound in every circumstance to trace the grounds of his argument back to first principles in metaphysics. Yet, because the speaker has rigorously examined Mackintosh's claims, we expect and demand equivalent rigor when he advances his own, alternative philosophy. We might tolerate the missing metaphysics had the speaker not already engaged metaphysical issues with such passion and in such detail. That earlier detail supplies the necessary grounds for the speaker's claim that his ideas are the only remaining viable ones, but the imbalance *per se* threatens his credibility.

The reader is also apt to be disappointed by chapter VIII's brevity. Coleridge's prose is often highly condensed, because he richly utilizes the semantic powers of sentence structure and etymology. Such condensation merges with the genuine difficulty of his ideas and arguments to generate a stylistic surface that has been judged cryptic, or obscure, or impenetrable. Recent scholarship has sufficiently undercut those accusations: the need for generalized defense is past. What needs to be noted here is how Coleridge's *departure* from his usual standards both provokes and justifies charges of obscurity. In chapter VIII undue brevity replaces condensation. The so-called hints tend to accumulate rather than develop; one finds redundance, not richness.

One easy explanation would suggest that the unusual brevity immediately reflects anxiety generated by pantheism and unresolved metaphysical questions. In reply, I would point to later places – to be examined in detail – that are far more pantheistic and yet masterfully managed.[24] I prefer another explanation, if explanations be necessary. Coleridge appears to have lost for a time his concentered attention to a particular audience, because basic comprehension of the chapter requires recognizing the metaphysical and theological issues signaled by 'substratum', 'subsistence' and 'hypostasis'. Such is not the case generally in *Biographia Literaria*. Coleridge writes for an astute and attentive reader, but not one particularly learned in the history of philosophy and theology.

This lapse also reveals what I take to be a fundamental uncertainty underlying Coleridge's idea of his most probable audience. I have said that Coleridge writes for someone who firmly but unreflectively accepts the dominant Lockean psychology and metaphysics of his day. This expectation makes a sort of 'demographic' common sense, I grant: surely the majority of his contemporaries did accept this world-view; Wordsworth's poetry can strongly appeal to thoughtful empiricists (witness John Stuart Mill). But I wonder how likely it is that one who is *naïvely* empiricist will prove capable of thinking with the energy and rigor that the *Biographia* demands. If one's own experience has never prompted dissatisfaction with Locke, will one possess the imaginative energy such thinking requires?

And if one's experience has prompted dissatisfaction, then it is plausible that one will have read some other philosophy somewhere along the line, or that one will not be quite so persuadable as Coleridge seems to desire. Perhaps Coleridge's lapses into philosophically dense argument reveal a wavering doubt that there can exist a readership of capable, philosophically naïve minds. It is as if he is just not sure how much philosophic sophistication to expect from his 'good readers', which may in turn reflect a reasonable fear that the right audience does not in fact exist. Perhaps his audience is as much an artful construct as his 'speaker'. Haven remarks that 'In the development of Coleridge's thought, the problem posed by the confrontation of Mariner and Wedding Guest is as important as the Mariner's experience itself'.[25] This may prove true not only for Coleridge's thought, but also for his works. The ideal reader – the perfect Friend of the Friend – will both understand the technicalities and tolerate the postponed proof because he understands that symbolic realities cannot be demonstrated.

Coleridge's problem in imagining the right audience is no doubt a thorny one, given his times, and given the formally incomplete argument he has chosen to write. But abrupt changes such as chapter VIII must still be accounted serious flaws; he has entirely lost control of the useful contrast between good readers and Lockean blockheads. Some good readers will be perplexed by the chapter; others will find that it raises confusing questions about what level of philosophic rigor they should expect of this book generally. In his art as in his life, perhaps, Coleridge understood very little about how to elicit and to satisfy consistent, reasonable expectations from those around him. Or, conversely, disappointing expectations served some subterranean purpose of its own.

The major flaws of chapter VIII are recouped in the second paragraph of the next chapter, where Coleridge more solidly forges the link between Christian orthodoxy and the unity of being and knowing. Whatever its flaws, chapter VIII could not have been simply deleted: it summarizes materialism's failure, so as to close the preceding three chapters and to clarify those points on which future development depends. Preserving this numbered summary would have meant substantial rewriting of chapter VIII. Rather than rewrite, Coleridge repeats before proceeding, addressing once again the reader to whom earlier chapters have been addressed. Such repetitions are not at all characteristic, and may signal his recognition that chapter VIII is genuinely obscure.

As we have seen, the long discussion of fancy serves in part as a critique of contemporary associationist psychologies. This aspect of chapters V to VIII comes more fully into view if we examine them from the perspective of narrative continuity. Mackintosh's four claims reflect the speaker's perception of the philosophical *status quo* in England. Given his early allegiance to Hartley, and the opening paragraph of chapter IX, these chapters also recount the first stages of his own philosophical development.

Let me list Mackintosh's claims, for easier reference later.

1 the 'law of association as established in the contemporaneity of the original impressions, formed the basis of all true psychology'
2 'any ontological or metaphysical science, not contained in such (i.e. empirical) psychology, was but a web of abstractions and generalizations'
3 Hobbes is 'the original *discoverer* of this great law', while Hartley offers 'full application to the whole intellectual system'
4 association is to the mind what gravitation is to matter (I, 67).

These objections, listed here in the order presented, are refuted as a group rather than individually. The only Mackintosh claim contextually emphasized concerns Hobbe's originality. One does not necessarily expect any further refutation of Mackintosh. Nor, more importantly, is it particularly evident in chapter V that the speaker fundamentally disagrees with associationism. His principal methodological criticisms could just as easily have led to a new and better associationist psychology.[26] Although one might charge that Coleridge inadequately introduces the scope of things to come, what he introduces and how he begins suggest a reasonable respect for the power accruing to the ideas he would discredit.

His intent is not primarily to discredit Hobbes or Hartley or Mackintosh, but to discredit the domination of the material world over the mind by means of the sense organs, as advocated by the English empiricist tradition generally. His critique is not primarily ontological, not the argument that it is naïve or inadequate to see reality as comprised of discrete independent objects impinging on passive human consciousness to generate our knowledge of things. On the contrary, this real world of independent objects immediately (but not passively) known remains a very English cornerstone in his system. The critique instead depends on an analysis of ordinary mental experience. As we have seen already, he consistently appeals to our knowledge of our minds rather than to our knowledge of things.

Hobbes is fitted into the table of distinctions through Mackintosh's claim that psychological association accounts for the *spontaneous* activity of mind. But, as the speaker shows, Hobbesian theories deny genuine spontaneity by defining the mind as passive. When the speaker describes the imagination as spontaneous, he integrates himself into the table, and further clarifies his rivalry with Hobbes *et al.* Hobbes surrenders originality to Descartes and accuracy to Aristotle; the speaker credits him only with inventing a physiological mechanism that has no basis in fact and no power to account for the complexity of association *per se.* As Mackintosh, Shawcross and the family editors point out, this is hardly fair to Hobbes; but Coleridge may have quite complex motives here.[27]

Coleridge refutes Hobbes so as to reshape the contemporary view of psychology. He wants to shift attention away from the popular (and persistent) misconception that psychology will achieve the spectacular practical results of the physical sciences by equating the real with the quantifiable or the visible, by making itself into a subordinate branch of mechanics or astronomy. By insisting that association has long been studied by philosophers, Coleridge focusses attention far more sharply on the specific recent innovations: physiological mechanisms. By discrediting the mechanisms, he can discredit associationism as a total psychology without denying its power to account for substantial areas of mental experience.

Hartley's mechanism is analyzed in a way that discredits any strict physiological mechanism: if they are strict or consistent, they deny will. By refuting Hartley's theory logically, experientially and morally, the speaker again asserts his criteria for philosophy. The logical refutation demonstrates well the Coleridgean difference between the conceivable and the visible (I, 74–6). If you visualize Hartley's mechanism as the balls on a billiard table, everything works beautifully. But if you realize that two different sensations must be two different vibrations, then it becomes impossible to understand how one vibration could ever directly propagate another vibration different from itself. Thinking of *acts* (vibrating) as *things* (billiard balls) leads only to mayhem. Coleridge refutes the mechanism by appeal to the distinction between visual and conceivable so as to prepare the reader for his own philosophic method: analyzing the *act* of perceiving rather than the *things* perceived. The difference proves crucial.

I have already discussed the experimental refutations: the speaker denies the mental passivity inherent in Hartley's philosophy by appeal to the experience of psychological self-control, and the experience of personal agency. The refutation on moral grounds consists partly in the experiential appeal to personal agency, and partly in the argument that Hartley's apparently strict empiricism disallows any nonmaterial God. Moral values lose any ground but observable utility: doing good for its own sake loses meaning.[28] Hartley's evident piety allows the speaker to renew the contrast between himself and anonymous critics: he distinguishes between the system's morality and the man's (I, 83–5). The distinction serves another purpose as well. It enforces the speaker's claim that bad ideas mislead good men. It underscores England's need for correct philosophy – a need argued at length in chapter X.

We have seen how the speaker responds to Mackintosh's first and third claims, concerning the validity of associationist psychology and the importance of these two figures. The speaker refutes Mackintosh's second claim by experiential arguments that turn the same charge against Hartley: his metaphysics is but 'a web of abstractions and generalizations' that both morals and concrete experience disprove. The fourth claim (association: mind::gravity:matter) restates the second claim within a different metaphor, one that emphasizes again Coleridge's disagreement with a falsely grounded imitation of physical science in the sciences of mind.[29] A law of the mind will be found in the mind, not in the relations of material bodies: philosophers must remember the difference between things and thoughts.

A law of mind will also not be found in the relations between the central nervous system and its environment. Chapter VIII highlights this underlying disagreement with the English tradition, which to the speaker represents one set of attempts to amend Descartes' erroneously absolute distinction between mind and matter. As we have seen, the chapter's first two paragraphs divide emendations into the unsuccessful and the unpopular. The speaker proposes instead that the question be located within the mind, as the relation of being and knowing, rather than outside the mind, as the relation of mind and matter.

Materialism generally – and mechanist associationism in particular – may at first appear to locate the question properly, because it regards knowing as an attribute of being. But the speaker argues that this is not the case. Consistent materialism replaces dualism with monism, but it is an object-dominated monism. Everything is absorbed in the material; the mind is reduced to passive neural mechanisms. This amounts to a denial of real individual existence, a denial logically prior to the denials of moral responsibility and suprasensible realities that we examined earlier. As commented earlier, Spinoza stands in the shadows. It was he who demonstrated the necessity of these consequences from materialism; 'hylozoism was Cudworth's veiled term for the argument of Spinoza's *Ethics*.[30] A McFarland's *Coleridge and the Pantheist Tradition* so persuasively argues Spinoza's importance to Coleridge cannot be underestimated. Spinoza informs and enlivens Coleridge's opposition to the English materialist tradition – an opposition everywhere present in *Biographia Literaria*.

The chapter concludes with a numbered list of objections to any associationist psychology that is dependent upon a materialist epistemology (I, 92). These objections reflect and counter-balance Mackintosh's claims. They also concenter reader attention on the problem of perception. What is it? How is it possible? What may be known? These are the questions taken up in chapter IX as Coleridge begins to define the most fundamental synthesis achieved through imagination: the synthesis of being and knowing in perception and common consciousness. The complexity and apparent indirectness of chapters IX to XI derive from his attempt to describe this synthesis within the context of issues we have seen to this point: the contrast of geniuses and fanatics, with all that involves the various activities or 'levels' of will, and how they are coordinate; the moral and ontological consequences of suprasensible will; the cultural conflict between true philosophy and its 'popular' counterparts. These issues remain so much in the foreground because the formal definition of the unity of being and knowing, and in particular *how* that definition unifies his positions on these issues, will be repeatedly deferred to the Logosophia. It is only by interweaving these issues that the speaker can explain the unity of being and knowing without verging into formal metaphysics. We see more of the practical consequences than of the theoretical bases. *Biographia Literaria* is an unrelentingly practical book.

4 Imagination's Synthesis of Being and Knowing

> Truth is a good dog; but beware of barking too close
> to the heels of an error, lest you get your brains kicked
> out.
>
> *Table Talk*, 7 June 1830

Coleridge often relies on such symmetries as the contrasts of genius and fanatic, or objective and subjective aspects of an issue. As one recognizes his favorite symmetries, the prose works become easier to follow. Chapters IX, X and XI demonstrate how such symmetries are multiplied as the *Biographia* progresses. Yet many readers find these chapters inconsequent. Such judgments arise, I suggest, not from a lack of unity and relation, but from an excess.

In chapters V to VIII the speaker criticizes philosophies he does not accept; in chapter IX he praises those he does. The earlier chapters contrast the methods of ancient and modern philosophers; the later chapters renew the contrast to define the true modern heirs of ancient wisdom. Chapters I to IV contrast genial poetry and pseudo-poetry, with passing reference to the qualities shared by genial poetry and genial philosophy (see, e.g., I, 59–60). Chapters V to XI contrast genial and pseudo-philosophy (whether political philosophy, philosophy of mind, or philosophy of religion), with passing reference to qualities shared by genial poets and genial philosophers (see, e.g., I, 140). Chapters X and XI also develop the contrast between geniuses and fanatics. The earlier chapters principally contrasted their personalities, with secondary emphasis on their works. These later chapters reverse the emphasis. The genius imaginatively synthesizes the relatively active and relatively passive aspects of human nature to arrive at permanent principles, the foundation of true national harmony and well-being. The fanatic exists always at an extreme, provoking repression and revolution, because his dependence on sensation generates political notions as inadequate as the philosophic notions criticized in chapters V to VIII.

This abundance of relations can be confusing because the issues are not arranged in a distinct system. Instead, particular issues relate to each other primarily through a common relation to Coleridge's central contention that the mind is active. Although that contention is closely related to his argument about imagination, and imaginative power is crucial for insight of any sort, Coleridge provides relatively few direct links between imagination and these autobiographical anecdotes. He seems to expect that his readers will share something of his own extraordinary gift for seizing immediately the generative idea underlying any argument or any illustration, however elaborate. Yet the length and associative flow of these chapters can make that a difficult task. The readers most seriously interested in Coleridge's ideas may grow impatient with the loquacious speaker, however entertaining he may be at times. But, once having grasped the idea of will in its relation to imagination, the *Biographia*'s reader principally needs a memory tenacious enough (or a notebook large enough) to keep track of all the issues that this idea shapes. Let me begin by collecting and interrelating the major ideas of these chapters, so that I can, later on, show how the funny stories and widely ranging illustrations are designed to explain, to justify and to emphasize these ideas.

The first of these is Coleridge's idea of philosophy. The opening paragraph of chapter IX restates and develops the speaker's encounter with an apparent dead end so as to extend his redefinition of the philosopher's central question into a redefinition of philosophy itself. Limiting inquiry to empirical procedures – observe, collect, classify – would be a 'wilful resignation of intellect' that results in the destruction of all ideas of cause and effect (I, 93–4). Causality has already been featured as a principal moral concern: without valid causality, there is no valid moral responsibility (I, 82–3). If we are to understand experience, and intelligibly defend or ground our belief in personal agency, we must (like Kant) discern and study 'the antecedents, that must be presupposed in order to render experience itself possible' (I, 94).

But philosophy is not just the science of antecedents to experience. It is also 'an affectionate seeking after the truth' (I, 94). It engages both intellect and passions. Philosophy, like poetry, is the work of the whole person. This fact requires or generates another postulate, that 'Truth', or knowing, and 'Being . . . are *ab initio*, identical and coinherent; that intelligence and being are reciprocally each other's substrate' (I, 94). As I noted in the last chapter, this postulate resolves the major problems posed in chapter VIII; being can transform itself into knowing because the *esse* and the *scire* are not originally distinct but, rather, originally identical and coinherent.

Coleridge's justification for this postulate assimilates scholastic theology, neoplatonism, Descartes and post-Kantean analyses of consciousness. All of these point to the truth, '*Cogito quia sum, et sum quia cogito*'. That is, in consciousness itself, or as the basic act of consciousness, we find affirmation that knowing and being are one. (Here, and more emphatically later, Coleridge differs from Schelling in closely linking the psychological or human union with the simultaneity of knowing and being in God.) The remainder of chapter IX and all of chapter X explain how the unity of being and knowing in consciousness is evident in various human activities:

philosophy itself, politics, journalism, history and religion. Only when these practical consequences have been presented – and copiously illustrated – does Coleridge attempt a formal derivation of the unity. As he does in chapter VIII, Coleridge presents this derivation as a partial and incomplete proof of something already known to be true.

Coleridge most forcefully urges the necessity of this psychic or moral unity in philosophy itself. Unless philosophy engage the whole person, unless it be true to the union of being and knowing that it would explore, philosophy reduces itself to academic word-games. (And, unless this integrity be noted and remembered in Coleridge's own writing, he appears to be a pantheist, a submerged materialist and atheist – as he undoubtedly realized.) The speaker praises ill-educated but imaginative mystics in part to make this point: despite their inadequate explanations, these men possessed truths that academicians did not. The writings of mystics 'acted in no slight degree to prevent [his] mind from being imprisoned within the outline of any single dogmatic system. They contributed to keep alive the *heart* in the *head*' and to lead him to the intuition that 'all the products of the mere *reflective* faculty [i.e., understanding] partook of DEATH' (I, 98). Because the existence of will cannot be formally or logically proven, no strictly logical or 'closed' or 'dogmatic' system can include it. Yet a philosophy that denies or neglects will also denies or neglects our spiritual nature. All logically self-contained philosophic systems are pantheist:

> The inevitable result of all consequent Reasoning, in which the Intellect refuses to acknowledge a higher or deeper ground than it can itself supply, and weens to possess within itself the center of its own System, is – and from Zeno the Eleatic to Spinoza and from Spinoza to the Schellings, Okens, and their adherents, of the present day, ever has been – PANTHEISM under one or another of its modes. . . . (*F*, I, 523 n)

The most a philosophic system can do is demonstrate, more or less as Kant did with the categorical forms, the necessity of postulating such a power. None the less, the actual necessity of postulating will derives not from abstract logical argument, but from the fabric of mental and physical experience. The Logosophia was to supply a very important proof, but not the crucial one. The logically *and morally* prior demonstration of the need to postulate will derives from an examination of ordinary experience. Coleridge provides this partly in *Biographia Literaria*, and more formally in *Aids to Reflection*.

To summarize: philosophy engages the whole person, and postulates both the twelve categorical forms and the unity of being and knowing. The revision of the *cogito* and (in reference to Fichte) the assertion that philosophy must begin 'with an *act*, instead of a *thing* or *substance*' (I, 101) suggest that the act in question is 'the mind's self-experience in the act of thinking' – the act of imagination (I, 86). In self-consciousness, the act of knowing and the state of being are simultaneous and identical. Coleridge has already urged that we take our consciousness of personal agency as evidence that causality is no chimera: the categorical forms are evident in consciousness or thought, not in things.

The second major idea defined in these chapters concerns the value, and the imaginative origins, of principles. Coleridge begins by accommodating his sketchy definition of imagination both to the definition of truth and to the union of being and knowing that were outlined in chapter VIII and the first part of IX. By defining imagination as '*esemplastic*', Coleridge frees the term from its usual place in aesthetic theories derived from Locke.[1] The subsequent discussion of pedantic expressions provides some vocabulary for distinguishing the relatively active from the relatively passive, or our knowledge of thoughts from our knowledge of things.

Knowing	*Being*
the thought, or act of thinking	a thought, or the object of reflection
intuitive	sensuous
subjective	objective
perceiver	perceived
Reason	Understanding

These are the relatively opposite powers and aspects of experience that imagination fuses into the unity of common consciousness, and the unity of perception.

This table underlies chapter X's discussion of principles because it amplifies the defiinition of truth as the union of knowing and being, or – more concretely – as the union of perceiving mind and perceived thing or situation. Truth, like consciousness, is a mode of relation whose *esse* is *percipi*: to speak of the true and the false (as distinct from the actual and the nonexistent) is to define a relation between perceiver and perceived. Principles as well as poems thus depend upon the synthetic activity of imagination.[2] Genial inquiry derives from principles not opinion, or it seeks to establish principles where opinion had held sway. Anonymous criticism is unprincipled in both senses of the word: it derives from opinion, politics and personality; and it seeks pernicious and sometimes immoral ends. The ongoing contrast between philosophic inquirers and anonymous critics rises again into the foreground in these chapters: auto-biography proceeds side by side with a sustained account of imagination's role in various aspects of philosophic quests of several kinds.

Finally, in these chapters the speaker defines the major idea of his own epistemology: under certain circumstances, the fact that something is *perceived* must be taken as evidence that it *is*. Under certain circumstances, the unity of being and knowing in consciousness extends to an analogous unity between human knowing and independently objective being. The circumstances? That the realities perceived are not objects of the senses, and that there is 'the absence of all motive to doubt' (or that 'the law or conscience peremptorily commands' belief in) the reality thus asserted (I, 133, 135).

The speaker defines only two elements of this set: things in themselves, and the personality of God (I, 132–6). Coleridge here assimilates the epistemological and metaphysical problem of things in themselves to the theological problem of God's personality, so as to draw on religious traditions in support of his position. As a result, however, conscience bears an enormous philosophic burden: the theoretical ground for material reality becomes the judgment by conscience that the doubt is contranatural ('wrong' in both senses).[3] In short, the imaginative synthesis of being and knowing provides direct access both to God and to the real world. It establishes the twin poles of Coleridge's philosophy, the 'I am' and 'it is'. Yet, since logic cannot prove the reality of these two poles, imagination assumes another crucial task. It is also the power whereby the philosophic mind recognizes this state of affairs. That is, primary imagination knows God and the real world: secondary imagination knows that such knowledge is the work of imagination (not of the senses alone), and knows further that it is valid although not subject to logical proof.

Let us step back for a moment, to see where we have come. Six chapters ago, at the end of chapter IV, the speaker resolved to understand and to explain imagination as Wordsworth had revealed it. True to his character, he begins by investigating answers others had found. These progressively sharpen his sense (and ours) of the answer he is seeking. Chapters VII, VIII and IX begin to formulate this answer: knowing and being are originally identical and coinherent; relatively to each other they are active and passive; this coinherence requires a faculty both active and passive that synthesizes the two into the unities of thought and thinking, or perception and consciousness. This is conceivable as a psychology, but will it do as a metaphysics? As we have just seen, the speaker discovers that genuine philosophy itself requires imagination. It takes imagination to understand imagination. The scheme works as a metaphysics only if we can give equal weight to sensuous and suprasensuous knowledge, if we can both allow *and* allow *for* the differences between the two kinds of knowledge.

Coleridge's philosophic and rhetorical strategy here needs to be examined closely. In accordance with the autobiographical character of *Biographia Literaria*, the speaker's experiences and recognitions are given. Intuitive certainty concerning God and things in themselves is explicitly such a personal recognition, and no more: the speaker realizes that 'this must be the case', but offers no supporting argument. At most, he draws on the Bible and Christian tradition to suggest that such a resolution has long been available within Christianity, or that he has just recognized the need for a truth long taught by the Christian churches. But he presents this as no more than a brief demonstration of consistency with received doctrine, not as a proof. When the Christian God and things-in-themselves reappear in chapter XII as facts, they are presented as conclusions from a proof to be presented in the Logosophia. This strategy – or sleight of hand – clearly reveals the artifice of the *Biographia*'s autobiography. Coleridge can be intimately personal in his self-revelations when these serve his argument; less 'useful' personal facts from his complex experience are not included. Only an autobiographical form could have allowed two major assertions to be so distinctly limited without the limiting itself suggesting either authorial uncertainty or a mindlessly passive acceptance of religious doctrine.

On philosophic grounds, it is true that observation cannot, by definition, prove the existence of a material reality correspondent to sensation. An epistemology that begins with a rigorous distinction between the thing as we know it and the thing itself has generated a philosophical Humpty Dumpty. And theology has discarded formal proofs of God as incompatible with genuine faith.[4] As McFarland has argued at length, these two great poles of human experience – the real conscious spirit and the real natural world – are always initial assumptions. Whether or not one accepts a philosophy so explicitly grounded in such complex forms of these assumptions, one cannot dismiss Coleridge's position as facile or amateur. Coleridge argues that faith nourishes the rational understanding, and that spiritual knowledge follows from natural knowledge, but this does not mean that all humanly important truths are capable of logical proof.

The philosophic argument of chapters IX and X is not difficult when its major ideas are separated like this from the wealth of anecdote and history. Yet this raises a question more or less submerged until now: how does the narrative aspect of *Biographia Literaria* complement the philosophic aspect? More specifically, how does narrative chronology direct the reader's attention to these scattered philosophic points? The narrative successfully modulates emphasis through the consistency of the speaker's character, as this informs his relations with other thinkers and with his contemporaries.

The clearest instances are in chapter IX, where the speaker once again gratefully attributes to others the ideas that ground his theory of imagination. Once again, such attributes are paired with strong claims about the truth or value of the acquired insight. The elder speaker is more critical of his 'teachers' than the younger man had been: his evaluative comments about mystics and German philosophers interrelate the ideas he learns from each of them.

As we have seen, the first two paragraphs make explicit the philosophic basis of the speaker's position in chapters V to VIII. The inadequacy of strict empiricism demonstrates the need to postulate suprasensible realities such as causality, and thereby leads the speaker to accept Kant's explanation of the categorical forms and the function of understanding.

The host of major philosophers who 'all contributed to prepare [his] mind for the reception and the welcoming' of the substantial unity of being and knowing (both in consciousness and in God) reinforce the traditional authority and thus, for the speaker, the validity of this idea. Earlier he had recognized it only hypothetically, but now further study confirms his belief.

The remainder of the chapter explores the proper relation of knowing (reason, or self as act) to being (understanding, or self as agent) through commentary on the degree of balance achieved by the mystics, Kant, Fichte and Schelling. Both Fichte and the mystics, unlike either fanatics or professional academicians (always a suspect group, especially in *Biographia Literaria*) penetrate to important truths about reason; directly or indirectly, both are described as imaginative. Yet both neglect understanding and the beautiful physical world that it knows – the mystics through lack of education, Fichte through an inability to synthesize his knowledge of intuitive reason with an equally sophisticated knowledge of perception. Attention to the terms of praise reveals both the priority of reason (or will) and the philosophic importance of recognizing its priority. The intuitive reason is 'the inmost centre, from which all the lines of knowledge diverge to their ever distant circumference' (I, 96). It is the foundation on which all certain knowledge ultimately rests. Furthermore, only a philosophy recognizing this fact will be 'truly systematic: (i.e. having its spring and principle within itself)'; only such a system will be 'truly metaphysical' rather than heartless and 'dogmatic' (I, 101, 98), progressively unfolding the richness of its central idea or symbol. By praising Fichte's beginning with an act, not a thing or substance, the speaker contradistinguishes him from materialists who reduce everything to substance and deny the possibility of genuine mental activity (or will). This, too, identifies Fichte's position with the speaker's. The commentary on Fichte and the mystics directs the reader to essential features of Coleridge's philosophy, provided one has learned how (and why) the speaker judges and expresses his judgments.

This is more emphatically true for the commentary on Kant. Kant 'at once invigorated and disciplined [his] understanding'; the speaker was awed, among other things, by 'the adamantine chain of the logic' (I, 99). Such praise elevates Kant's analysis of the constitutive powers of understanding to a point beyond question: this is true; this is the defense of causality so necessary for a coherent and moral world-view. The speaker also argues that Kant's work on morals 'assume[s] a higher ground (the autonomy of the will) as a POSTULATE deducible from . . . the conscience' (I, 99), thereby claiming that Kant recognized (the speaker's views concerning) the cognitive and epistemological significance of will and conscience. Such a position is not clearer in Kant's works, the speaker explains, because a justified fear of persecution by fanatics led him to write '*mythically* or equivocally' (I, 100). This strategy allows the speaker to draw on the authority of Kant in support of those ideas which distinguish his own beliefs from a Schellingean pantheism. Kant's role is analogous to Aristotle's: he is a revered authority whose ideas the speaker 'clarifies', praises and assimilates.

The praise of Schelling is as unqualified as the praise of Kant or Aristotle, and once again based on major reinterpretation or adaptation. Like Schelling, the speaker proposes to complete Kant's work, to explain what Kant knew but dared not say. Yet this completing belongs to Logosophia, not *Biographia Literaria* (see I, 102): the unity of being and knowing as a metaphysical issue deserves separate study. The speaker's intent is more practical: 'To me it will be happiness and honor enough, should I succeed in rendering the system itself intelligible to my countrymen, and in the application of it to the most awful of subjects for the most important of purposes' (I, 104). To this end, we need only know that a correct analysis of being discovers the need to postulate spiritual knowledge, and that a correct analysis of knowing discovers the need to postulate a real world immediately known, to avoid a 'hyperstoic hostility to NATURE' (I, 102). Such studies have shown the speaker that imagination's synthesis must be faithful both to God and to nature – and thus to man. The 'voluntary' at chapter's end reminds us that such genuinely imaginative inquiry must expect a small audience (I, 105–6).

Chapter X divides the years from 1796 to roughly 1804 into five periods demarked by both geographical moves and changing endeavors: *The Watchman*; Nether Stowey and poetry; 'a cottage in Somersetshire'[5] and morals; Germany and German literature and philosophy; and finally London and the *Morning Post*. In the first period, the tales of his campaign for subscribers enforce again the speaker's diminished sense of self and self-importance, his imprudence, and his devotion to duty. The 'exemplary old clergyman' story renews the contrast between the serene, learned philosopher and the irascible ignorant reviewer. The speaker fails at magazine writing himself, because he refuses to swear absolute allegiance to either political extreme. He watches his efforts literally go up in smoke, and wryly concludes that he is not a popular writer. Although *The Watchman* is portrayed as a madcap adventure doomed from the start, its fate demonstrates the social power of fanatical party spirit.

As the stories of the second period illustrate, fanaticism does more than squelch small moderate periodicals: it also threatens the liberties of Englishmen. Both English and Continental history further demonstrate the violence elicited by fanatics. Yet the innkeeper and, ultimately, even Spy Nozy himself reveal the fundamental decency of ordinary people. Fanaticism, however dangerous, is an aberration of the powerful, not a character of the English people. Despite the delightful comedy of the speaker's stories, England's present relative tranquility is a fragile thing for which substantial thanks are due to Edmund Burke.

In such a context, the fact that the speaker's intellectual maturing culminates in his own advocacy of principles (in the fifth period) should be taken as clear evidence that he, too, has some measure of genial power.[6] The evidence from personality in the earlier chapters is matched here by more substantial proof. His persecution, like that of the genial figures in chapter IX only further demonstrates the dangerous ascendancy of the least capable minds (see especially I, 31–2; I, 148–51). The speaker's grim recognition of this ascendancy triggers a crisis in the third period, 'and it was long ere [his] ark touched on an Ararat, and rested' (I, 133). This crisis – doubting not only God, but also any substantial reality – leads him to recognize that fundamental truths in morals (and in epistemology) cannot be 'wholly independent of the will' (I, 135). Absolute proof is not possible. The frustrations, failure and political violence recorded in the chapter's anecdotes and histories sharply focus our attention on this crisis and its resolution because the hapless, good-hearted speaker naturally wins our sympathy.

In chapter XII the speaker neatly summarizes his conclusions from such experiences:

> But it is time to tell the truth; though it requires some courage to avow it in an age and country, in which disquisitions on all subjects, not privileged to adopt technical terms or scientific symbols, must be addressed to the PUBLIC. I say, then, that it is neither possible or necessary for all men, or for many, to be PHILOSOPHERS. (I, 163–4)

The speaker pleads that we defer judgment until we understand what he is trying to explain; yet paradoxically the *Biographia*'s most difficult philosophy is his subsequent analysis of self-consciousness to explain why it is rare, and why important. His descriptions in chapter XII of the unconscious multitude who will not comprehend his philosophy summarizes all the accusations previously made about their materialism, and their generalized hostility to abstract and rigorous thought (I, 160–4; I, 188–94). The speaker thus strives to protect himself from the kinds of criticism and miscomprehension that were his lot during the years described in chapter X: he gives up on one set of readers to appeal exclusively to the 'good reader' who has been postulated all along as the sympathetic audience to his complaints about the times.

Chapter XI is addressed to young male members of this properly attentive and thoughtful audience. The chapter focusses the two related contrasts, speaker–populace and speaker–fanatic. The supposed audience the chapter advises are the kind of men who supported and understood the speaker's fruitless endeavors as recounted in chapter X. They are the ones who should read chapter XIII, had the overwhelming numbers of thoughtless readers not effectively 'prevented' its publication. Such astute readers, like the speaker himself, form a culturally invaluable bulwark against fanaticism: the speaker advises that young men in this group avoid his imprudent ventures into journalism, and accept positions in the Church of England. Chapter XI's description of the good they may accomplish reappears later in *On the Constitution of Church and State* (pp. 42–76); the need to protect the people at large from fanaticism's influence remains a major concern of Coleridge. Even in the *Biographia*, the contrast between the genius and the fanatic is developed in far more detail than the theory of imagination alone requires. The conflict over *Lyrical Ballads* is but one sign of a most serious national *malaise*.

The chapter's advice to serious writers – 'drawn from my own dear-bought experience' – draws imagination's *spontaneity* into the foreground again (*CL*, IV, 633). The writer who tries to force the Muse, and the writer who reads and thinks only to publish, will both benumb their creative powers, because the end of imagination is comprised in the means. Imagination is an act, not a tool. Chapters VIII to X have emphasized imagination's synthesis more than its spontaneity, but this aspect of imagination comes again into the light in chapter XII.

5 Imagination, Philosophic Consciousness and the 'True and Original Realism'

> But what are my metaphysics? merely the referring of
> the mind to its own consciousness for truths indis-
> pensable to its own happiness! To what purposes do
> I, or am I about to employ them? To perplex our
> clearest notions and living moral instincts? To deaden
> the feelings of will and free power, to extinguish the
> light of love and of conscience, to make myself and
> others worthless, soul-less, God-less? No! to expose
> the folly and the legerdemain of those who have thus
> abused the blessed machine of language; to support
> all old and venerable truths; and by them support, to
> kindle, to project the spirit; to make the reason spread
> light over our feelings, to make our feelings, with
> their vital warmth, actualize our reason: – these are
> my objects, these are my subjects, and are these the
> metaphysics which the bad spirits in hell delight in?
>
> *The Friend*, I, 108

Chapters XII and XIII are the most difficult in the *Biographia*. They are
the most dense philosophically, the least conventional rhetorically, and the
most controversial. Chapter XIII's 'letter from a friend' and its 'missing'
philosophical construction have angered or frustrated even the most
sympathetic readers. They seem incontrovertible evidence that the
Biographia is a fragmentary failure. Although the chapter is undeniably
peculiar, and in many ways unsuccessful in achieving its rhetorical goals,
the 'missing' construction does not directly and absolutely destroy the
integrity of the work as a whole. And even more mystifying than this 'gap'
is Coleridge's rewriting of extensive passages from Schelling, as he bends
Schelling's arguments and methods to his own, different ends. Elinor
Stoneman Shaffer has studied these changes in great detail, and I am
indebted to her lucid and graceful explications of the complex technical
issues involved.[1] As Kathleen Coburn has observed in her notes to the
notebook drafts and translations that also underlie the chapter, much work
remains to be done on Coleridge's debt to and divergence from Schelling in
these pages.[2] My premise in explicating the design of these two chapters
has been that the study of their contexts in the *Biographia* itself is

reciprocally necessary to comparative studies, and yet – for practical reasons of coherence and readability – a distinct endeavor at this stage.

Yet a few remarks are in order. Many discussions of Coleridge's debt to Schelling in these chapters refer in passing to changes and deletions, as if these were insignificant overall, or as if they represented little more than his misunderstanding of the German philosopher. But such is not the case. Philosophical argument is a delicate thing: small changes can have large consequences. And some of Coleridge's changes are far from minor. As Shaffer demonstrates in detail:

> The fact that [Coleridge] often adopted whole phrases and passages literally is deceptive; the spirit, if not the letter, has been altered. So in this instance: while quoting, compressing, and summarizing Schelling, Coleridge criticizes him in essential respects. The scandal of these pages in the *Biographia* is not that they are based on Schelling, but that to a reader unacquainted with Schelling's treatise they must remain obscure, if not totally unintelligible. . . . Read against his texts in Schelling, Coleridge's Chapters XII and XIII appear as a cunning reduction of Schelling's elaborate *System*, and a sturdy dissent from it. ('Coleridge's aesthetics', p. 4)

Coleridge himself later judged these chapters 'unformed and immature'. They contain, he said, 'the fragments of the truth, but it is not fully thought out' (*TT*, 28 June 1834). Substantial portions are revised and incorporated in later works; the changes inevitably clarify, and sometimes develop, but never change the principal idea.[3]

The general tendency of Coleridge's dissent from Schelling can be explained briefly (see 'Coleridge's aesthetics', pp. 50–1). Schelling's *System des transzendentalen Idealismus* traces the stages whereby the Ich creates the entire world of objects through its knowledge of itself. Schelling justifies our certainty that there exists a real world by trying to prove that the proposition 'things exist' is ultimately identical with the proposition 'I am'. But, according to Schelling, we know only sensations, not things themselves – a position with which Coleridge sharply disagrees (I, 92–3, 178–9, 100). He also disagrees with Schelling's collapse of the world into the self: for Coleridge our certainty that things exist is independent of, not grounded in, our certainty of self. Shaffer summarizes Coleridge's disagreement well: 'The belief in the external world . . . is an assumption required by the nature of consciousness or the "I am" itself. It is, equally with the self, groundless because it is fundamental' ('Coleridge's aesthetics', p. 26). In short, although Coleridge incorporates parts of Schelling's explanation of the mind–world relation, he defines this relation in a substantially different way. He also avoids the dialectical logic whereby Schelling demonstrates the identity of the two propositions, an argument Shaffer judges 'highly dubious' ('Coleridge's aesthetics', p. 33). Schelling invents a special faculty capable of knowing the identity of these two propositions; Coleridge rejects this, too, asserting that the philosophic or secondary imagination differs only in degree from powers possessed by all people, and that conscience demonstrates the capacity for such imagination in everyone. Finally, Coleridge transforms Schelling's 'self-consciousness in general' to God. The consequences of that change are evident less in this local argument about things themselves than in the *Biographia*'s larger concern with the nature and value of poetry.

Given these substantial differences, what attracted Coleridge to the *System*? Why bother struggling to rewrite a philosophy so profoundly uncongenial? One aspect of Schelling's view of art deeply attracted Coleridge. Schelling's work implies that 'a successful piece of philosophy must itself be a work of art, or carry no conviction: its intuitions will be doubted. A piece of art must in turn illustrate intuitions worthy of philosophy. "Philosophic criticism" had indeed come into its own, and art achieved a staggering dignity' ('Coleridge's aesthetics', p. 16). For Schelling, a work of art most translucently reveals the mind's range of powers: artistry is the highest human act, and the greatest human achievement. It is not pleasant escape from sterner labors, but the most profoundly important of our endeavors. Furthermore, Schelling's insistence on the 'act of freedom' underlying the identity of the two propositions easily merges with Coleridge's idea that the conscience testifies to our moral freedom – thus linking art not only with philosophy, but also with religion.[4] Thus, Schelling's philosophy reaches a point Coleridge sought, but by means Coleridge rejected.[5] The incorporations and revisions in chapters XII and XIII seek the same ends by less radical, less pantheistic means, in part by introducing the ancient mystery of the one and the many in a Christianized form.

In design, chapter XII is a long parenthetical remark. The speaker explains why the multitude whom popular authors address will find chapter XIII incomprehensible, but in doing so he defines the core of his own epistemology in an unrelentingly technical and abstruse argument. Yet, despite the chapter's difficulty, it offers very few new ideas. Principally it summarizes the philosophical arguments of the first eleven chapters, defining or making explicit the relations among ideas presented earlier. Understanding the chapter requires no unravelling of peculiar structures or ineffective transitions but, rather, continually monitoring its allusions and relations to the earlier chapters – connections without which its minimal comprehensibility slides back into utter obscurity.

Before examining the chapter in detail, let me again preview Coleridge's argument. The chapter can be divided into four parts. The first (I, 164–74) explains that only some individuals can attain self-consciousness, although the capacity is at least latent in all. Self-consciousness is identified as intuitive, imaginative and the basis for the certainty of all knowledge; it is the proper domain of pure philosophy. Complex geometrical metaphors, delicately rewritten from Schelling, reveal that self-consciousness results from the 'spontaneous' level of will's operation.

The second section (I, 174–80) asks again what chapter VIII asked: how is perception possible? It establishes a context for this question by defining 'subjective' as essentially active and conscious, and 'objective' as essentially passive and without consciousness, and by defining a correlative distinction between pure philosophy and natural philosophy. In a cryptic and stylistically tangled paragraph, the speaker asserts the central assumption of his transcendental philosophy: perception is possible because our knowledge of external reality is 'unconsciously involved' in our knowledge of ourselves. This is but another formulation of chapter VIII's hypothesis that knowing and being are originally a unity; this new formulation emphasizes that perception must be the work of imagination, just as self-consciousness is. Not until chapter XIII, however, does Coleridge distinguish these two functions as 'primary' and 'secondary' operations of imagination. The speaker explains that the Logosophia will provide 'the demonstrations and constructions' of this philosophy. For his present purposes – defining 'the principles of production and of genial criticism in the fine arts' – explanation not demonstration will suffice (I, 180).

In the third section (I, 180–1), the ten theses attempt to offer this explanation. Most of them do little more than collect and summarize points made in earlier chapters, fitting these ideas into the general framework provided in the first two parts of chapter XII. We reach the heart of the matter in Thesis VII. If it could be proved that the certainty of all knowledge must derive from the certainty of the logical identity 'I know me' – i.e. from the imaginative act of self-consciousness – then we could be assured of the certainty of all genuinely immediate, intuitive, suprasensuous knowledge. We could be thus assured because all intuitive knowledge is knowledge of the fundamental unity of knowing and being. This does not, of course, *solve* the problem of perception: it does not proceed beyond chapter X's point that the 'constitution of the mind' renders it morally impossible to doubt the existence of a real world correspondent to sense-impressions (see I, 132–6). Only the Logosophia is to attempt to prove what the *Biographia* awkwardly and provisionally sketches.

Thesis VII is as cryptic and tangled as the central paragraph of the second section: Coleridge is trying to revise Schelling's account of 'unconscious involvement' into something sharply different. Schelling's argument depends upon an esoteric faculty that none the less provides us – the incapacitated, ordinary intellects – with our only accurate information about the fundamental character of reality. Coleridge's imagination, on the other hand, is a power that all possess at least potentially. Thesis VII merely validates or provides the means to validate the 'true and original realism' that is 'common to mankind' by grounding it in an equally traditional Western theism. It is tempting to sidestep the tortuous intricacy of Coleridge's prose by assimilating it to the cool clarity of its sources in

Schelling but, as Shaffer demonstrates, this seriously falsifies Coleridge's position. As René Wellek has argued in so many places, it is dishonest to credit Coleridge with particular statements or specific detailed arguments that he has copied from someone else; in this instance, confusing Coleridge with Schelling places Coleridge among the originators of an isolationist and radically formalist tradition in poetics to which he does not belong.

The fourth section (I, 188–94) is a Coleridgean 'miscellany' that ties the chapter's many loose ends to various major themes in the *Biographia* generally. Viewed retrospectively, the chapter's main contention looks back to the opening paragraphs of chapter IX: philosophy is possible as a science because the certainty of all knowledge derives from the imaginative act that is self-consciousness. In self-consciousness, as in God himself, being and knowing are '*ab initio*, identical and coinherent' (I, 94). The Logosophia will provide this science, but meanwhile we have the major practical result of literary interest: imagination is the faculty whereby we know who we are as moral beings, and what the world's order really is. From this follow two ideas that permeate the chapters on poetry and on Wordsworth. Because imagination is also the origin of great art, it is reasonable to expect the very best art to offer profound insight into the human condition. And, secondly, the origin and thus to some extent the particular character of poems will be intimately involved with the poet's self-consciousness.

I

In the chapter's first part, a complex geographic image for the relation between common consciousness and philosophic consciousness develops the contention that not all men are philosophers into an explanation of the philosophic role of imagination. Most men believe that empirical knowledge is the only knowledge: they cannot distinguish *knowing* from knowing *things*, and will not give credence to those who can (cf. I, 64–5, 73–4, 105–6, 149). Such 'valley-dwellers' can never attain absolute and spontaneous affirmation of immediate (suprasensuous) knowledge. The 'rivers' that carved the 'valley' define the relation between sensuous and suprasensuous knowledge:

> . . . in all ages there have been a few, who measuring and sounding the rivers of the vale at the feet of their furthest inaccessible falls have learned, that the sources [of the rivers] must be far higher and far inward; a few, who even in the level streams have detected elements, which neither the vale itself or the surrounding mountains contained or could supply. How and whence to these thoughts, these strong probabilities, the ascertaining vision, the intuitive knowledge may finally supervene, can be learnt only by the fact. (I, 166)

Sensuous and suprasensuous interpenetrate.[6] The stream of (common) consciousness reveals its origins in the pure spirit.[7] They only are qualified as philosophers who can intuit spiritual (suprasensuous) realities, as the speaker does in chapter X. In both instances, Coleridge insists that the intuition is spontaneous: ideas about spiritual realities cannot be demonstrated from without (like 'the truths of abstract science', I, 135); nor can they be elicited strictly by choice (I, 167, i–viii).[8] References to the 'direction' of the streams of consciousness sustain the geographic metaphor throughout the chapter: 'the common consciousness itself will furnish proofs by its own direction, that it is connected with master-currents below the surface' (I, 167; cf. I, 76–7). It will prove crucial to remember that the 'direction' of consciousness is both its contents and its activity regarded as a unity originating in the suprasensuous. It is quite characteristic of Coleridge to provide an image for so complex an idea.

Having explained that the subjective basis of transcendental philosophy is the philosopher's imagination, the speaker explains that its objective basis or its character as a system is constructions from postulates.[9] The 'direction' of consciousness is compared to the direction of the geometer's point moving in space. The geometer's point can be self-directed (indeterminate motion), directed from without (a straight line), or both, that is undirected externally but directly internally (a circle). These options exactly recapitulate the three levels of will: the voluntary or directed from within; the receptive or directed from without; and the spontaneous or intermediate. As J. B. Beer points out, the circle is one of Coleridge's favorite images for imaginative activity; it appears elsewhere in the *Biographia* as well.[10]

The geometer can literally construct or draw his point in motion, so as to demonstrate his idea in a physical form. The philosopher cannot. How, then, can he distinguish among the directions consciousness may take? The distinction rests on a moral (not sensuous) embodiment of the ideational or spiritual reality:

> . . . the inner sense has its direction determined for the greater part only by an act of freedom. . . . This more or less betrays already, that philosophy in its first principles must have a practical or moral, as well as a theoretical or speculative side. (I, 172–3)

As the geometer progresses by means of his constructions to a clearer intuition of space, so the philosopher progresses in his knowledge of consciousness by attending to the manifestations of moral freedom – the imperatives of conscience.[11] Thus it is, the speaker concludes (pointing again to problems posed by his contemporaries), that those unable to intuit consciousness directly will condemn discussions of its 'directions' as metaphysical moonshine. For such readers, a text in transcendental philosophy 'is groundless and hollow, unsustained by living contact, unaccompanied with any realizing intuition which exists by and in the act that affirms its existence, which is known, because it is, and is, because it is known' (I, 173). Such a self-confirming truth, or absolute, is necessary not only for any science of knowing, but also to guarantee certainty in general (see I, 168, xiv–xix). Those who cannot or – worse – who will not engage any issue involving abstract or purely intellectual truths stand on treacherous and uncertain ground even in their knowledge of objects. That is why anonymous critics and their kind are unreliable guides on *any* issue.

II

This transcendental philosophy that so few will understand is the analysis of philosophic consciousness as the ground of all knowledge. The chapter's central section (I, 174–80) defines the major question answered by the ten theses: how is it possible that we have immediate intuitive certainty concerning our knowledge of objects external to ourselves? Or, to use the less technical form of the same question from chapter X, 'what proof . . . of the outward *existence* of anything? Of this sheet of paper, for instance, as a thing in itself, separate from the phaenomena or image in . . . perception?' Chapter X answers, 'the existence is *assumed* by a logical necessity arising from the constitution of the mind itself . . .' (I, 133). The ten theses analyze that constitution to define the power and importance of secondary imagination.

This second section defines the metaphysical problem of mind and world from two perspectives. Natural philosophy assumes the priority of the objective (or being): inquiry moves from observation to theory. Ultimately, 'nature' refers both to the system of laws comprising the theory, and to the profusion of particulars that the theory encompasses. In the hypothetical 'completion' of science, when theories account for all observable particulars, 'the heavens and the earth shall declare not only the power of their maker, but the glory and the presence of their God' (I, 176). Nature will be revealed as truly 'the language of God', as his text but not as God himself.[12] Scientific inquiry, in its progress from being to the 'equatorial' unity of being and knowing, goes from creation to God. Only a *self-conscious* intelligence can perceive the unity of idea and law that underlies theory: to transform observations into theories is to transform 'nature' from particulars to relations – to intelligence or knowing. Science at its best is as imaginative an activity as poetry.

Transcendental philosophy attains the same equatorial point from the other side: 'We begin with the I KNOW MYSELF, in order to end with the absolute I AM. We proceed from the SELF, in order to lose and find all self in GOD' (I, 186). But the transcendental philosopher's immediate concern is the movement from self (knowing) to things (being), just as the scientist's immediate concern is developing and testing theories about material reality. Coleridge sketches the movement of transcendental philosophy hypothetically (I, 178) before deriving it formally (Thesis VII). This development from hypothesis to formal assertion exactly repeats the strategy we saw at the end of chapter VIII and the beginning of chapter IX: the speaker proposes no more than a formal explanation of what we already intuitively recognize must be the case.

The transcendental philosopher's scientific scepticism uncovers two ineradicable beliefs, two products of imagination: that I exist (the *I am*) and that the world exists (the *it is*). The *I am* 'is groundless indeed; but then in the very idea it precludes all ground, and separated from the immediate consciousness loses its whole sense and import' (I, 178). But the *it is* retains its meaning even when separated from the philosopher's consciousness of its certainty: if *it* really *is* then *it is* regardless of whether I am thinking about it. This state of affairs engenders the philosopher's hypothesis concerning the relation between self-consciousness and things. He intuits

> that the former ['the existence of things'] is unconsciously involved in the latter ['the existence of our own being']; that it ['the existence of things'] is not only coherent but identical, and one and the same thing with our own immediate self-consciousness. To demonstrate this identity is the office and object of his philosophy. (I, 178)

The first clause asserts that the basis of our knowledge of our own existence encloses or includes the basis of our knowledge of the existence of things. The second clause asserts that self-consciousness is the same as the *existence* of things without us (not the same as these *things*, but the same as the *existence* of these things, the same as their *being*). Yet self-consciousness is an act. It follows that the being of things without us is ultimately an act, and, further, that the being of all realities – conscious or not conscious, subjective spirit or objective nature – is knowing.

The hypothesis suggests that there are acts that we know *as acts*, as the various manifestations of our power to know. And there are acts that we know *as things*, as *beings*. Yet things are objects – passive, material, without consciousness. If they are acts, they are not human acts, for that would contradict our absolute certainty of their independent existence. They must therefore be acts of God, as no third possibility exists. God must, then, be the ground of their being – a familiar and orthodox idea. Coleridge's point is that our self-grounded knowledge of being (our own, or objects') exists in some important and intimate relation to God. Human knowing must somehow reflect the Supreme Being. Theses VI and VII later develop and substantiate what this earlier paragraph merely proposes.

The speaker strongly asserts that this hypothesis accounts for

> the realism common to all mankind[.] . . . It is the table itself, which the man of common sense believes himself to see, not the phantom of a table,

from which he may argumentatively deduce the reality of a table, which he does not see. . . . It is to the true and original realism, that I would direct the attention. This believes and requires neither more nor less, than [that] the object which it beholds or presents to itself, is the real and very object. In this sense, however much we may strive against it, we are all collectively born idealists, and therefore and only therefore are we at the same time realists. (I, 179)

He explains that this hypothesis will be formally established in the forthcoming Logosophia; but, as we have seen before, the Logosophia can do no more than argue formally and rigorously for that which we already realize must be true. Because the hypothesis involves knowledge of spiritual realities, no strict logical proof will be possible: logic can do no more than justify the necessity and consistency of this belief. Shaffer says it well:

> Coleridge's objections [to Schelling] are not those of mere 'common sense.' There is simply no alternative to beginning where our consciousness begins: with 'sense certainty' of both the self and the external world, of subject and object alike. Such certainty does not constitute proof; of these fundamental assumptions there can be no proof. It is in this sense that our certainty is not prejudice, but 'faith.' All our knowing is indeed transcendental, in that it revolves on itself and depends on the system of our fundamental, necessary assumptions. We cannot escape from the mode of operation of our minds. But just for this reason we are bound to consider its natural results as real. There can be no other reality. ('Coleridge's aesthetics', p. 28)

Such fundamental assumptions cannot be transformed into conclusions without substituting some other idea as the fundamental starting-point. Coleridge insists on both beliefs, and on the primacy of both.[13]

III

In the chapter's third section, the ten theses recapitulate major conclusions from the analysis of spontaneous knowing that began in chapter V but without the accompanying illustrations and history (personal or philosophic). Coleridge is trying to be exclusively abstract, keeping illustrations to a bare minimum and even then relegating them to scholia and to footnotes. I suspect that the attempt ran contrary to his particular genius: the theses have an odd objective clarity without conveying his meaning as effectively as the earlier formulations of the same ideas.

The first six theses primarily assemble earlier points into the argument that self-consciousness is the single absolute first principle of transcendental philosophy.[14] For knowledge to be a system, there must be some one principle that is true because it is known, and known because it is true; Thesis VI identifies this absolute as the *I am*, or self-consciousness.

Yet the Scholium to VI adds an important qualification that the appended note on Descartes explains in more detail: to affirm of the *I am* that it is true or self-evident does not necessarily imply that it exists. (It is self-evident that a circle is equi-radial, but that does not imply that there exists – physically exists – an absolutely genuine circle.) Yet, unless absolutely genuine self-consciousness exists, knowledge is not possible as a system, and therefore certain knowledge of any kind is not possible. Although the ground of being is not properly part of the science of knowing, the scholium points out that the ground of the *existence* of self-consciousness is God, 'the absolute self, the great eternal I AM, [in whom] the principle of being, and of knowledge, of idea, and of reality; the ground of existence, and the ground of the knowledge of existence, are absolutely identical, Sum quia sum' (I, 183).

Thesis VI asserts that the absolute principle of transcendental philosophy is the unity of being and knowing in self-consciousness. Thesis VII asserts that from the identity 'self-knowing knows the self' we can conclude the 'immediate certainty of all intuitive knowledge' (I, 184). Yet how does the certainty of self-knowledge accrue to the intuitive (not sensuous) knowledge of objects themselves? Thesis II points out that if A is certain, and B is the same as A, then B is certain. So let me rephrase the question: in what way is our knowledge of our own being the same as our knowledge of external being? Both are known by the pure spirit, not the senses; yet the spirit knows only itself (I, 184, ix); so the *knowledge* of the being of the self and of the being of the world must ultimately be the same knowledge. For this to be so, human being, and the being of the world, must have a single basis: the Supreme Being of God, in which human being *consciously* participates via the triunity of will, faith and reason.

As I said before: Coleridge's argument here possesses a certain odd logical clarity despite its essential opacity. The principal obscurity in the ten theses derives from the slippery meaning of 'spirit'. This confusion is deepest when, after defining 'spirit' as 'self-consciousness' (I, 183, iii), Coleridge speaks of 'the self-consciousness of a spirit' (I, 184, iii). In doing so, he slides from a specific limited use of the word to his more usual, broader, traditional use. I suggest that by 'self-consciousness of a spirit' he means the self-knowledge of one who possesses reason, because reason is the cognitive faculty whereby we possess spiritual or suprasensuous knowledge, and thus our own identities as essentially suprasensuous entities (souls or spirits who are both free and immortal). And, as I explained in chapter 3, in a fully developed, imaginatively activated self-consciousness, the reason – pure knowing – discovers its immediate, intuitive, suprasensuous knowledge of God's being, and human being (free and immortal) and the world's being (real objects correspondent to sense data).

With at least this much clarified, it becomes possible to see that Thesis VI and its Scholium, and Thesis VII together say that pure knowing (the divine absolute in a pure but relative form) encounters pure being (God) in which all other being (including its own) participates, or by which all other being is sustained. Ergo the certainty accruing to the identity 'I know me' also accrues to the statement 'I know the table itself' because both statements are purely spiritual acts. And pure knowing or philosophical self-consciousness – the highest spiritual act – is one act not several. The certainty of all human knowing about realities other than itself depends upon God; in *Biographia Literaria* this spiritual act is attributed to will, although elsewhere Coleridge attributes it either to faith or to reason as his particular argument warrants.

One's faith – the only correct name for it – one's faith in the existence of a real table is not to be confused with one's physical perception 'table over there'. The faith is in the reality of an object *correspondent to* perception; it is not, very strictly speaking, a faith in the complete reliability of fragile sense organs, nor in the adequacy of sensation as the sole basis of knowledge about physical realities. But when my hands and eyes and brain are operating 'normally', then my confidence that the table *is* there is just as valid as my confidence that I *am* here: in both cases, the confidence derives not from logical proof, but from the way normal healthy minds work. Let me cite again Coleridge's clearest statement on this matter:

> For wherein does the realism of mankind properly consist? In the assertion that there exists a something without them, what, or how, or where they know not, which occasions the objects of their perception? Oh no! This is neither connatural nor universal. It is what a few have taught and learned in the schools, and which the many repeat without asking themselves concerning their own meaning. . . . It is the table itself, which the man of common sense *believes himself to see*, not the phantom of a table, from which he may argumentatively deduce the reality of a table, which he does not see. (I, 178–9; italics mine)

Neither argumentative deductions nor, again more recently, skeptical critiques of such arguments can discredit this 'true and original realism' because it is an act of faith not a logical conclusion. As Thesis VII concludes, 'The self-conscious spirit therefore is a will; and freedom must be assumed as a *ground* of philosophy, and can never be deduced from it' (I, 185). Coleridge's emphasis here on free will rather than reason reveals again the *Biographia*'s central interest in the moral implications of the idea 'imagination'. We believe some things because we choose to, because the alternatives all lead to solipcism – the dead end Coleridge describes in chapter VIII. These issues arise in the *Biographia* because the genuinely great poet thus possesses intuitive knowledge of the moral realities sketched in Theses VI and VII. Thematic ties between chapter XII and other, more directly literary chapters appear much more clearly when one realizes that full self-consciousness so intimately requires (secondary) imagination that Coleridge legitimately uses the terms interchangeably.

Note that, throughout the argument to this point, Coleridge has been talking only about the certainty of beliefs – not their objective validity. His strictly limiting the domain of transcendental philosophy is to prevent us from translating his conclusions about the certainty of our knowledge of being into statements about the nature of being itself. Such extensions – any study of the full unity of knowing and being – belong only to the total philosophy in which religion subsumes both transcendental and natural philosophy. The transcendental philosopher accepts as axiomatic that we have real knowledge of external realities, and simply asks *how* this is so – not whether it is valid.

Although transcendental philosophy does not ask about being, we can – and probably must – because the real independent existence of things is one of Coleridge's major practical divergences from his sources in Schelling. Does thesis VII contradict Coleridge's earlier insistence on the 'true and original realism'? Does the identical ground of *knowledge* of being imply that spirit and objective nature are ultimately indistinguishable? No: to say that two things are known in the same way is not to say that they are the same. The chapter's several references to the Christian God suggest an orthodox interpretation instead: God creates, sustains and relates the being of both human minds and the natural world, but yet generates and maintains the necessary distinction between the two by creating the human as essentially subjective or active, and nature as objective *relative to man* (see *PhL*, 523–4). As Coleridge often insists, the essential difference between persons and things is the foundation of morals.

Thesis VII prompts another question as well. What about other instances of intuitive knowledge? What are they? How do we recognize them? The self's existence and the existence of things are the only intuitive *and immediately certain* knowledge discovered by the transcendental philosopher's scientific skepticism. But there are, potentially, other instances which are not indubitable – God, for instance. Chapters XII and XIII define the objective features that characterize knowledge that is intuitive rather than sensuous in origin. Principal among these, of course, is the relation of part to whole variously called 'polar unity' or 'organic unity'.[15] For the literary critic, an important index of the intuitive (or imaginative) origin of a work will be the unanimously favorable judgment of qualified readers over time, and the consistent effect on any sensitive reader. The critic's intuitive knowledge of artistic greatness is not indubitable or fundamental to all human minds, but it is real or genuine knowledge. For the *Biographia* as a whole, the importance of Thesis VII is this grounding – or sketch for a grounding – of the consistent judgment of good critics on which Coleridge relies so heavily as a literary theorist.

One question about Thesis VII still remains: how can reason or the spirit maintain the unity of knowing and being *as a unity* while yet knowing being *per se*? It can do so because it is an act, not a thing.

. . . a spirit is that, which is its own object, yet not originally an object, but an absolute subject for which all, itself included, may become an object. It must therefore be an ACT . . . the spirit (originally the identity of object and subject) must in some sense dissolve this identity, in order to be conscious of it: fit alter et idem. But this implies an act, and it follows therefore that intelligence or self-consciousness is impossible, except by and in a will. The self-conscious spirit therefore is a will. . . . (I, 184–5)

A notebook draft for chapter XII supplies a helpful explanation:

. . . to be known, this Identity must be dissolved – and yet it cannot be dissolved. For its Essence consists in this Identity. This Contradiction can be solved no otherwise, than by an Act. (*CN*, III, 4265 f. 11)

In 'the act of constructing itself objectively to itself', the spirit knows being directly. The spirit is the continual simultaneous dissolving and recreating of the unity of being and knowing: it 'dissolves, diffuses, dissipates, in order to recreate' (I, 202). As the organ of philosophy, spirit (or self-consciousness via the philosophic [secondary] imagination) operates spontaneously.[16] It cannot be compelled. It is the free act of the will that testifies to and grounds the essential difference between persons and things.

Theses VIII, IX and X draw conclusions from the principles stated in VI and VII. Thesis VIII, on immortality, in part reveals chapter XII's origins as part of a draft for the Logosophia (*CN*, III, 4265 n). It also justifies the speaker's earlier claim that 'all the organs of sense are framed for a corresponding world of sense; and we have it. All the organs of spirit are framed for a correspondent world of spirit: though the latter organs are not developed in all alike. But they exist in all . . .' (I, 167). Thesis IX, clarifying VII, asserts that the unity *per se* of being and knowing is will. Knowing as such is reason; *spirit* is the more comprehensive term for knowing and being as an identity. And this unity or identity is sustained through imagination. Chapter XII defines the will relative to knowing as an act, the act of imagination, just as chapter 10 defines will relative to being as faith. Thesis IX also distinguishes among natural, transcendental and total philosophy to insist that the 'equatorial point' or absolute unity of being and knowing is God.[17] Such a division of inquiry is crucial for Coleridge's endeavors in chapter XII, because it allows transcendental philosophy to be a complete system *sui generis*, a complete part of the whole of human knowledge.

Thesis X addresses misunderstandings that would reduce transcendental philosophy's first principle into a relative or mediate one. First, it repeats the distinctions among inquiries defined in Thesis IX: transcendental philosophy does not seek the ultimate ground of knowing in the absolute unity of knowing and being. Self-consciousness is not itself absolute, but only absolute for our knowing. Secondly, it argues that the knowing of knowing does not generate an infinite regress: even one who could know the knowing of knowing still comprehends nothing beyond knowing itself. Self-consciousness is not a higher form of being, antecedent to a still higher form. It is knowledge of the operations of our own minds.[18]

The concluding paragraph of Thesis X sketches the 'interrupted' intent of chapter XIII: to abstract from self-consciousness a single power generating two polar forces, and from their interactions to evolve 'the fulness of *human* intelligence' (I, 188). We may rightly ask what relation this one force has to the God of the Scholium to VI. The answer would be that transcendental philosophy treats God as absolute knowing, not as a person, and not as a deity; natural philosophy, correspondingly, treats God as absolute being. Only the total philosophy (in which philosophy passes into religion) deals with God as a person, as a 'moral creator, and governor' (I, 133).

That is a good and adequate answer, strictly speaking. But *Biographia Literaria* as a whole is not strictly transcendental philosophy. Coleridge veers repeatedly into the total philosophy, particularly in his arguments about moral responsibility in chapters V to IX, and in his discovery of the common ground of the personal God and things in themselves in chapter X. The actual gap in this book is between Thesis VI and its Scholium, between the one force or single ground and the personal triune God. Philosophical resolution of that gap is repeatedly deferred to the Logosophia. Autobiographical resolution takes its place 'temporarily': the speaker knows that the orthodox Christian God underlies his coherent experience of both an independent material reality and his own moral freedom. He urges orthodox values and perspectives at every turn. That strategy sharply limits – or attempts to limit – the range of implication and inference from transcendental philosophy that the reader will perceive as valid. Despite the logical appearance of pantheism in chapter XII, the dramatic autobiographical form of the whole work is to preclude our taking that appearance literally. The problem, as I noted with regard to chapter VIII, is that the reader's logical powers have been fully engaged by chapter XII's arguments. The speaker's orthodoxy lacks the rhetorical potence necessary to preclude the pantheist interpretations. Coleridge's deficient sense of audience becomes startlingly apparent – or, perhaps, his vulnerable openness in asking us to trust the orthodoxy of his morals and the powers of his mind. On such issues as these, the man and the speaker can be only theoretically distinct.

IV

Chapter XII's concluding transition is unusually complete. The speaker presents some new terms and repeats chapter X's defense of technical language as if to suggest that we have arrived at a major internal division in his analysis of being and knowing. His repeated lament about 'popular' philosophy echoes the chapter's opening, reinforces the impression of major internal division, and ironically prepares us both for more technical argument and for the 'deletion' of that argument in the next chapter.

The chapter also concludes with a glance toward chapter XIV. The speaker explains that in rereading Wordsworth's 1815 preface he has discovered that he disagrees with Wordsworth's account of the 'poetic fruitage' of the interaction between fancy and imagination (see I, 64).[19] Had Wordsworth's account been acceptable, of course, then much of what Coleridge argues in chapters XIV to XXII would have been precluded. At most, Coleridge's commentary on the controversy about diction could have been formulated as a deduction from Wordsworth's *accurate* definition of the poetic aspects of the two powers. But, rather than undertake such a reconciliation of the transcendental root with the Wordsworthian 'poetic fruitage', the speaker attributes most of the controversy to inaccuracies and imprecisions in the 1800 Preface. In short, Wordsworth assumes a role analogous to that assigned Aristotle or Kant or Schelling: he formulates ideas that Coleridge finds it convenient to adapt and to argue against as a way of structuring his own presentation. As we shall see later, Coleridge misrepresents parts of the Preface to his own ends.

The infamous chapter XIII offers little more than a selection of previously defined ideas as the basis for a rigorous 'construction' in transcendental philosophy. The lines from Milton affirm God's creativity and creation's order, yet in Coleridge's context, and given Coleridge's syncretism, no precise philosophic significance can be assigned. As Lovejoy argues, the great chain of being created by emanation from One Almighty is an ancient idea rich with its own complexities:[20] the range of interpretations here must stretch far beyond *Paradise Lost*. Yet this much is clear: Milton's lines begin from mind and arrive at matter. Leibnitz's direction, in the succeeding passage, is just the opposite: 'all the truth about corporeal things cannot be collected from logistic and geometric axioms along'.[21] In examining matter, one discovers mind: 'even as natural philosophers we must arrive at the same principle from which as transcendental philosophers we set out; that is, in a self-consciousness' (I, 187). The final citation, from Synesius, affirms again that the 'equatorial' unity of being and knowing is an act:

> I worship the hidden order of intellectual things;
> The Mean dances and is not still.[22]

The portion preceding the 'letter' repeats and expands chapter XII's explanation of polarity (cf. I, 188). The transcendental philosopher contends that the universe can be rendered 'intelligible' by postulating a single power that generates two forces, 'one of which tends to expand infinitely, while the other strives to apprehend or *find* itself in this infinity'

(I, 196). The equipoise of these forces is not stasis, but 'finite generation': a real physical world, growing, reproducing, renewing – the 'process and mystery of production and life' (I, 185).[23]

At this point the speaker 'interrupts' himself to cite a 'letter from a friend' that, as he said later, he composed without interruption as a part of the chapter.[24] From one perspective at least, the letter is 'a philosophical route, a mad dash from an untenable position'.[25] There are two major problems with the philosophic position delineated in chapters IX to XII. For the argument to succeed, being and knowing must be identical. Yet they must also be distinct – actually distinct, not just verbally so. Thesis VII reveals this paradox most fully, and hints at its potential resolution with the Trinitarian's formula, 'fit alter et idem'. Secondly, if being and knowing are identical, and we have immediate knowledge of independently real objects, then objective reality as portrayed by transcendental philosophy will be identical with reality as portrayed by natural philosophy, and these together will reveal God: the total philosophy will be implicit in the conclusion of either of its subsidiary branches. Coleridge cannot rigorously pursue his transcendental construction of the 'intelligible' world without engaging the whole range of unsolved metaphysical problems – an error soon recognized (*CL*, IV, 874).

The two parts of chapter XIII – the initial philosophy, and the letter – try to avoid the consequences of leaving us philosophically in mid-air by assimilating the missing construction to an ancient philosophic tradition, and by asserting that the metaphysical problems have been solved but withheld from publication. The lines from Milton and Synesius and the explanation of the productive union of polar opposites assert that the deferred philosophic argument will be nothing new and ingenius but, rather, the 'purification' of what the speaker calls the 'Dynamic System . . . begun by Bruno' but boasting such ancestors as scholastic theologians, Plato, Plotinus, Ficino, Proclus and Gemistius Pletho (see I, 94; 98, xxxiii; 103–4). Either this system is pantheism, or it rests on the mystery of the one and the many – a mystery that literally or logically breaks down into pantheism. Both the unity of being and knowing and the mystery of the one and the many contradict the fundamental principle of discursive logic: A cannot be *not-A*. Or, as the speaker explains in chapter IX, 'An IDEA, in the *highest* sense of that word, cannot be conveyed but by a *symbol*; and, except in geometry, all symbols of necessity involve an apparent contradiction' (I, 100). All other symbols depend for their intelligibility upon the complex cognitive power of faith and conscience. As the many references to the Logosophia indicate, for Coleridge the Logos is the central or organizing symbol for all inquiry. By locating his philosophy in the historical past, Coleridge seeks to bolster his claim that it is sound and valid: it is a truth neglected by those entranced by popular philosophy. Coleridge firmly and literally believed this was so: the rhetorical strategy here is no mere convenience of the moment.

The letter seeks in a different way to support the validity of Coleridge's philosophy. The 'friend' is a sympathetic dunderhead, a kindly member of the Lockean 'populace' whose miscomprehensions have been predicted all along. His letter justifies these predictions; the strategy seeks to persuade us that Coleridge should not demonstrate the transcendental construction of the intelligible world in this generally nontechnical book. In reading chapter XIII, the friend feels as if he is standing on his head. That is how readers of the Preface felt: it signals an inability to reconcile thoughts with feelings, and thus a feeble imagination (I, 51–2). Lest we fail to recognize this parallel, Coleridge includes a page-number reference. In a more subtle echo, the images of light and darkness in the friend's analogy match those in the speaker's earlier explanations that those who lack philosophic imagination will find transcendental philosophy baffling and disorienting. The friend reports finding himself "*Now in glimmer, and now in gloom;*" *often in palpable darkness not without a chilly sensation of terror; then suddenly emerging into broad yet visionary lights with coloured shadows of fantastic shapes*' (I, 199). As the speaker had explained in chapter XII:

> The first range of hills, that encircles the scanty vale of human life, is the horizon for the majority of its inhabitants. . . . By the many, even this range . . . is but imperfectly known. Its higher ascents are too often hidden by mists and clouds from uncultivated swamps. . . . To the multitude below these vapours appear, now as the dark haunts of terrific agents, on which none may intrude with impunity; and now all *a-glow*, with colours not their own. . . . (I, 164–6)

Or, slightly later:

> A system, the first principle of which it is to render the mind intuitive of the *spiritual* in man (i.e. of that which lies *on the other side* of our natural consciousness) must needs have a greater obscurity for those, who have never disciplined and strengthened this ulterior consciousness. It must in truth be a land of darkness, a perfect *Anti-Goshen*, for men to whom the noblest treasures of their own being are reported only through the imperfect translation of lifeless and sightless *notions*. (I, 168)

All three passages describe the sensation of confusion as frightening darkness broken only by an equally disconcerting light. Those who achieve only partial intuition of the spiritual will be as frightened as the boy Wordsworth by the apparently external source of the power that 'suddenly shines upon us' (I, 167). To those even less disposed toward philosophy than the letter's 'author', of course, Coleridge remains entirely 'obscure'.

The friend's account of the cathedral's statuary reflects the speaker's judgment of poets and philosophers. Such upending of the popular hierarchy follows necessarily, the speaker has warned, from a true understanding of imagination (I, 11–16, 52 and n). The contrast to

Mackintosh has further emphasized the speaker's 'unusual' view of history. The friend's complaint about substances and shadows mirrors the speaker's inversion of Mackintosh's charges about nonempirical meta-physics: Hartley's 'oscillations' are proved shadows; suprasensuous knowledge is proved solid, not vaporous.

The friend argues against publication by claiming that chapter XIII is not suited to a literary life and opinions, ignoring the speaker's claims that he wishes to offer deductions from established principles (I, 64–5), and that some readers will have trouble understanding him, but some will not (I, 65, 74, 105–7, 149, 160–7, 188–92). The friend's suggestion that there may be too much metaphysics already formulates a complaint of all but one contemporary review, and of a good many readers since then as well.[26] The friend's derogatory comparison of *Biographia Literaria* to Berkeley's *Siris* provides a useful clue to the *Biographia*'s form and its tradition.

The friend's final paragraph refers to familiar features in the speaker's character: his chronic inability to consider his reputation and financial needs (I, 31–2, 110, 119, 145), and his diligent study (I, 14, 60–5, 93–5, 104–5, 112, 137–41, 148–51). When the speaker defers to the judgment of his friend, it is only worse imprudence. Yet the reader is to be convinced by the letter, and by the consistency or predictability of the speaker's response, that at least part of the Logosophia has been completed. The letter thus completes a pattern of references whereby the Logosophia's status as a work-in-progress has been gradually enhanced. What is at first 'a work, which I have many years been preparing', becomes a manuscript whose transcription for the press has been abruptly curtailed (I, 91–2, 102, 179–80). It has become more real as the relation between being and knowing has been more closely specified.

From another perspective, then, this 'mad dash' is no dash at all, no spur-of-the-moment tactic. However severely one might judge Coleridge's strategies or his motives in chapter XIII, it is not accurate to say that he has suddenly broken off his disquisition in horrified recognition of the spectre of pantheism, or in frustration at the intractability of Schelling's text, or in confusion about his own argument. The letter is not the abrupt thing it appears, but the completion of a pattern painstakingly established. Yet to say as much solves little. If we cannot write this off as error, panic or exhaustion, where does that leave us? There are two primary sources of explanation: the text itself, and the man.

Let us look first to the text. Although the speaker asserts that a sense of self is present in inverse proportion to the imaginative power, and although his stories show him unconcerned with the niceties of social status, he is outraged at what has been said about him in print, and claims that such defamation has caused him 'serious injury' (I, 150). Because truly imaginative works derive from 'our nobler being', one gifted with such power exists under some moral obligation to defend his works from scurrilous attacks (I, 32), such as those by critics 'who have taken so much

pains to render me ridiculous for a perversion of taste, and have supported
the charge by attributing strange notions to me on no other authority than
their own conjectures' (I, 65). Such comments are scattered throughout the
first four chapters' commentary on anonymous criticism. The climax of
such short moments of self-defense is chapter X, which records years of
study and writing coming to little because of the influence of fanatics, who
have then accused him 'of having dreamed away [his] life to no purpose' (I,
150). One cannot but sympathize with the wish that

> the criterion of a scholar's utility were the number and moral value of the
> truths, which he has been the means of throwing into the general
> circulation; or the number and value of the minds, whom by his conver
> sation or letters he has excited into activity, and supplied with the germs
> of their after-growth! A distinguished rank might not indeed, even then
> be awarded to my exertions; but I should dare look forward with
> confidence to an honorable acquittal. . . . By what I *have* effected, am I to
> be judged by my fellow men; what I *could* have done, is a question for my
> own conscience. (I, 149–51)

Such a person, with this reputation and this sensitivity to it, has in an
autobiographical work asserted that a major undertaking has been accom
plished.

The assertion will not help his reputation – it is past redemption, as the
friend's miscomprehensions indicate – but a strong if counter-productive
claim has been made: I have not wasted my life. The speaker has been
portrayed all along as one who says what must be said, regardless of
consequences. His (in effect) refusal here to mask his motive for deleting
the construction, to rewrite so as to avoid insulting the noncomprehending
populace, is a coherent and integral act. Imprudent, certainly – but he is
imprudent and noted for bad judgment in such situations. However
frustrated we feel, we are to recognize him as more frustrated yet – as once
again stymied by the very people who damn him as a dreamer. Coleridge
counts on that sympathetic understanding to sustain his authority with us,
the 'good' readers. Our anger at him is to be deflected into anger at the very
dangerous influence of popular philosophy.

I suspect that Coleridge underestimated how vividly interested readers
would become in his analysis of consciousness. Granting that he was in
some ways seriously depressed, that he often felt abandoned by friends and
tormented by an inability to share more widely the fruits of his
monumental study, granting all this, I think it possible that he could not,
in 1815, strongly and consistently enough imagine the good reader he
hopefully addresses now and then. In the works written after 1815, we find
these same thorny metaphysical problems handled with grace and clarity.
Aids to Reflection, the *Biographia*'s closest of kin, perhaps, after 'Appendix
C' of the *Statesman's Manual*, offers a bolder and far more difficult form of

he same basic design found in *Biographia Literaria*; yet it has always njoyed a better reputation as a coherent and integral piece of writing.

But 1825 was not 1815. In 1815, Coleridge was emerging from a long eriod of study, illness, addiction, family problems, problems with friends nd, above all, of limited *public* productivity. The need to assert his ntellectual worth may have been strong. The ability to imagine his proper eaders may also have demanded a higher level of psychic energy and self-onfidence than he could sustain. Thus the *Biographia* emerged as written or sympathetic members of the populace, for what Haven calls 'Wedding 3uests', with copious illustration of relatively simple points. He brackets he abstract and difficult parts, saying (in effect) 'you may not follow this; ut maybe someone else will be interested'. The fiction of a contemporary :nglish audience for transcendental philosophy complements the fiction of he completed Logosophia. The poignant moments of self-defense suggest hat, were the first real, the second might have been. Chapters XII and <III might have proceeded with Milton and Synesius and an English 'true nd original realism' rather than a pseudo-Schellingeanism. Coleridge's ater writings on such topics are both lucid and graceful because he never gain ventured into numbered propositions and exclusively abstract rguments.

From the letter's clear relation to what has preceded, and its compre-ensible (albeit peculiar) rhetorical purposes, one may conclude that – bjectively regarded – it does no damage to the integrity or completeness f the work as a whole. Regarded subjectively, however, the letter poses a 1ore difficult challenge, because it marks and symbolizes a highly roblematic aspect of Coleridge's theory of the mind's functions. The 1eory is formally incomplete. But from this fact one cannot directly onclude that *Biographia Literaria* itself is incomplete, because the haracter of this problematic part must be taken into account. Most of the rst fourteen pages of chapter XII explain that the major principles of ranscendental philosophy cannot be demonstrated. The mysteries of eing and knowing, or the one and the many, would not have been onverted to logically demonstrable propositions by the missing onstruction. Does this comprise an intolerable break in the book's 1ematic or ideational unity? Critical or scholarly consensus here rincipally exerts a rhetorical and moral force: the mystery is not made less 1ysterious by winning broad support.

This then is the distinction of moral philosophy – not that I begin with one or more assumptions; for this is common to all science; but – that I assume a something, the proof of which no man can give to another, yet every man may find himself. . . . *Omnia exeunt in mysterium*, says a schoolman: that is, There is nothing, the absolute ground of which is not a mystery. The contrary were indeed a contradiction in terms: for how can that, which is to explain all things, be susceptible of an explanation?

It would be to suppose the same thing first and second at the same tim
(*AR*, 154-6)

In its most fundamental terms, the issue here is whether or not one agree
that '*Omnia exeunt in mysterium*'. Those who absolutely agree live in
world fundamentally different from those who absolutely disagre
separated by a gulf across which arguments may carry, but to no usef
purpose. But most of us, I suspect, float about somewhat eclecticall
uneasy with this mysterious assumption that we know and can discours
about a real and coherent world, yet repulsed and unconvinced by th
alternatives. Ultimately, one cannot absolutely and logically prove whethe
or not the abstract formal integrity of *Biographia Literaria* is matched by
theoretical or ideational unity. But we conduct our lives in accord wit
many beliefs that we cannot absolutely establish. In reading and writing a
in living, most of us rely on persuasive probabilities, and common sens
and on those graces of explanation and argument that make more easi
accessible what 'every man may find for *himself*'. One who would reac
beyond the currently fashionable nihilisms can only rely on some versio
of the *Biographia*'s idea that discourse is an essentially creative act designe
for a free agent who consciously chooses to accept some version of the tru
and original realism.

The famous definitions at the end of the chapter add very little that i
new, but they draw together parts of a complex and difficult argument.
We knew in chapter VII that imagination exists in levels, some commo
and others more rare. These are now given titles: the primary imaginatio
is the ordinary agent of perception and consciousness; the secondary – th
knowing of knowing – is the direct or self-conscious knowledge of th
operations of the primary. It is the 'organ' of philosophy, the poetic 'visio
and the faculty divine', that arises spontaneously, or 'suddenly shines upo
us' (I, 173, 166, 167).

A summary of this argument may make the significance of the definition
more easily apparent. In common consciousness, for the ordinary perso
ordinarily, the identity of being and knowing is unknown. This unity i
discovered by the scientific skepticism of the transcendental philosophe
Because the unity is unknown, its two 'products' – common consciousnes
and the perceived world – usually appear as givens, *and as unrelated*. In th
cosmos known by primary imagination, 'I' and 'it' have no fundament
and necessary connection. 'It' is simply there – impassive, inanimat
morally remote. Material association remains on this level, but two flaw
reveal its inadequacies. The first is the failure of the mechanism to explai
the psychic phenomena at hand. The second is that even ordinary peop
sometimes experience the world not as inanimate and remote, but a
beautiful, alive, and translucent with meaning and value. And everyone i
basic psychic health experiences both personal agency and mor
responsibility – further evidence of the higher intellectual powers.

Some people can penetrate to the origin of such experiences: our fundamental unity with the world around us, the common spiritual ground of human being and the world's being. They do so by or through philosophic self-consciousness: they know not simply things, and the self as a thing among things, but the activities that are the self *per se.* This ability is a heightened power to know; it is a further development of the primary imagination, although identical with it in kind. Secondary imagination 'dissolves, diffuses, dissipates' the unity of being and knowing 'so as to recreate' this unity consciously, in full possession of both the common moral ground of being, and the uniquely human power of self-knowing (with its origins and consequences). Even when such resynthesis is impossible, the secondary imagination 'struggles to idealize and to unify' – to heighten the experience of beauty, animation, and translucent meaning by focussing attention on those aspects that embody or reflect these qualities most clearly. When secondary imagination cannot literally transform, it reorganizes so as to make the implicit spiritual form more evident even if not fully realized. The productions of imagination – whether philosophy or art or science – help confirm and encourage the occasional insights of the less self-conscious ordinary person.

The difficult question about imagination is not what the power is, or how it works, but rather how these operations account for the qualities we find in imaginative works. How does rendering the primary unity conscious generate the explicit form of spiritual values and realities through the physical world? *Biographia Literaria* offers Coleridge's fullest statement on this point, through its poetics and practical criticism. As we shall see, this literary criticism depends upon a theory of language as intimately involved with the Logos as the analysis of consciousness, although somewhat less explicitly so. For now, however, let us turn back to Theses VI and VII to see what light they shed.

And let us grant the *fit alter et idem* identity of being and knowing, for without such assent (at least conditionally) most of the *Biographia* remains incomprehensible. Since the self is not a thing but the dynamic union of knowing and being, self-knowing (the spirit) knows the dynamic union both as its parts and as a whole. *In doing so, the spirit directly intuits knowing as such, and being as such.* Knowing as such is God, the creative One Almighty. Being as such (not beings) is the spiritual essence of all reality – God, man, world, interrelated and thus knowable by man, yet distinct. As a result, secondary imagination presents the spiritual in and as the natural. It bridges the gap yet retains the distinction between the human spirit and the physical world by creating symbols. Because language (a system of symbols) is the medium of least resistance to the spirit, and a poem is the most exact use of words, in a poem we are entitled to expect not just physical detail and profound insight, but an integral unity of these two:

> It was not however [Wordsworth's] freedom from false taste . . . which
> made so unusual an impression on my feelings immediately, and sub-
> sequently on my judgement. It was the union of deep feeling with
> profound thought; the fine balance of truth in observing, with the
> imaginative faculty in modifying the objects observed; and above all the
> original gift of spreading the tone, the *atmosphere*, and with it the depth
> and height of the ideal world around forms, incidents, and situations, of
> which, for the common view, custom had bedimmed all the lustre, had
> dried up the sparkle and the dew drops. . . . In poems, equally as in
> philosophic disquisitions, genius produces the strongest impressions of
> novelty, while it rescues the most admitted truths from the impotence
> caused by the very circumstance of their universal admission. (I, 59–60)

The genial unity of thought and feeling, or universal and particular, both
depend on secondary imagination's synthesis of the powers that penetrate
to pure knowing and pure being, and to their absolute union in the triune
God.

The cognitive range achieved through imagination reflects the fact that
'the self-conscious spirit . . . is a will' (I, 185) and 'the evidence of
[religion's] doctrines could not, like the truths of abstract science, be
wholly independent of the will' (I, 135). Imagination is the spontaneous
level of will, intermediate between the will's absolute activity in knowing,
and its relative passivity in being (cf. I, 65–6; I, 85–6; I, 174; I, 182–3).
Imagination, or self-consciousness, draws the full range of our spiritual
knowledge into relation with the full range of our sensory knowledge.
Because it synthesizes the animated world, imagination is truly a
'repetition in the finite mind of the eternal act of creation in the infinite I
AM' (I, 202).[28] But this fact would remain beyond our ken if we could not
know imagination's operation directly, that is, know the parts as parts (and
thus purely), and yet as the whole, as the rich, endlessly fascinating
panorama acknowledged by 'the child's sense of wonder and novelty' but
too often 'bedimmed' by custom and familiarity (I, 59).

The integrative function of imagination is analogous to that of conscience – imagination for our being in the world, and conscience for our
being in God. Because our knowledge of these two aspects of our humanity
is one act, the same knowledge, Coleridge appeals to conscience to
illuminate evidence of imagination. His first argument for the true and
original realism appeals to conscience (I, 133–6), and the second to
imagination (Thesis VII), and yet they are the same argument. In
Biographia Literaria Coleridge argues for the moral depth of art; in *Aids to
Reflection* for the imaginative power of religion. It is easy enough to argue
that he advocates pantheism with a veneer of Christian piety – the most
likely collapse of mystery into mechanism. It is more difficult, but more
accurate, to recognize how precisely he defines *and limits* the supralogical
so as to emerge with a solid base for contending that poetry is not lies, nor
mere entertainment nor simply egoist self-expression, but yet not 'the

truths of abstract science' either. The character of Coleridge's philosophy is not determined by the fact 'that [he] begin[s] with one or more assumptions; for this is common to all science' (*AR*, 154), but by the fact that his assumptions are essentially religious.

Yet poetry is not religion (although great poetry is moral). One need not accept Christianity to make good use of his theory of imagination. The true and original realism makes possible a definition of imagination's poetic workings that is strongly empirical in its appeal to observation, and to critical and poetic tradition. The ultimate basis of this poetics is philosophical and thus religious; but the immediate basis is textual. Coleridge's criticism is rooted in the immediate reactions of the reader to particular linguistic features. One would never reach Coleridge's poetics through the empiricist's modes of inquiry; but, having otherwise attained them, one can explicate and defend on empirical grounds. The true and original realism guarantees and insists on no less.

One point remains. What does chapter XIII add to our understanding of fancy? Very little. By distinguishing the levels of imagination as he does, Coleridge clarifies what chapters V to VIII suggest: fancy is controlled both from above and from below. It gathers and sorts (according to the law of association) the percepts generated by primary imagination; the quality of the work performed by these two powers inevitably influences the level of synthesis or transformation that secondary imagination can achieve. Yet the influence is reciprocal: one who consciously intuits the spiritual realities animating experience will more adeptly perceive their physical signs or correlatives. Because 'the will itself by confining and intensifying the attention may arbitrarily give vividness or distinctness to any object whatsoever', fancy can collect animated perceptions with the same mechanical efficiency with which it collects any other kind of perception. It can provide associations that are trivially witty, or it can provide associations that place the object into a net of relations that illumine a profound significance. In the first, a flea is still just an insect, albeit a more interesting one; in the second, the flea assumes symbolic potence. The difference between the two depends partly on the poet's original insight into the symbolic potential of the flea, and partly on the reader's appropriate synthesis of the associative details into a whole more significant than these parts. For both reader and poet, then, the role of fancy depends on the power of imagination.

6 Poetry

As a fruit-tree is more valuable than any one of its fruits singly, or even than all its fruits of a single season, so the noblest object of reflection is the mind itself, by which we reflect:

And as the blossoms, the green, and the ripe, fruit of an orange-tree are more beautiful to behold when on the tree and seen as one with it, than the same growth detached and seen successively, after their importation into another country and different clime; so it is with the manifold objects of reflection, when they are considered principally in reference to the reflective power, and as part and parcel of the same. No object, of whatever value our passions may represent it, but becomes foreign to us as soon as it is altogether unconnected with our intellectual, moral, and spiritual life. To be ours, it must be referred to the mind, either as motive or consequence, or symptom.

Aids to Reflection, Introductory Aphorism V

'The office of philosophical *disquisition*', Coleridge explains, 'consists in just *distinction*; while it is the privilege of the philosopher to preserve himself constantly aware, that distinction is not division. In order to obtain adequate notions of any truth, we must intellectually separate its distinguishable parts; and this is the technical *process* of philosophy. But having so done, we must then restore them in our conceptions to the unity in which they actually co-exist; and this is the *result* of philosophy' (II, 8) Chapters XIV to XVI restore the distinctions between fancy and imagination, thought and feeling, being and knowing, subject and object to their original unity: the integrity of the human mind as evident in literary language.

A poem reveals the complex unity of the mind because a word names not a physical thing, nor an idea in the mind of the speaker, but the relation between speaker and reality.[1] Words exist *within* the unity of being and knowing, world and mind; and thus a precise use of words (by philosopher or by poet) renders that unity distinctly accessible to the conscious mind. And a poem is our most precise use of language: 'it would be scarcely more difficult to push a stone out from the pyramids with the bare hand, than to alter a word, or the position of a word, in Milton or Shakespeare, (in their most important works at least,) without making the author say something else, or something worse, than he does say' (I, 15); or 'Poetry . . . ha[s] a logic of its own, as severe as that of science; and more difficult, because more subtle, more complex, and dependent on more, and more fugitive causes. In the truly great poets . . . there is a reason assignable, not only for every word, but for the position of every word' (I, 4). A poem reveals both the mind of the poet, and the reality he knows; in examining our reaction to the text, we discover our relation both to the powers of mind and to the aspects of reality. Granting Coleridge's original realism, we see that words precisely used make true statements. The cultural and moral value of poetry depend on this link between precision and truth.

R. H. Fogle said chapter XIV offers 'a microcosm of Coleridge's entire critical system', and so it does – both in what it says, and in how it delineates the complexities that a poem represents.[2] Nowhere does he more frequently shift from objective to subjective perspectives and back again. Objectively, the poem is a use of language, a 'species of composition' (II, 10). As such, it exists in relation to the universe (it makes true or false statements). Yet it also exists in two sets of subjective relations, to the reader and to the poet. To the reader, a poem is both a thing (a text, a 'species of composition') and a psychic experience, an act of reading. In parallel ways, to the poet a poem both expresses what he *knows*, and who he *is*, through the medium of words. The definitions of 'poem', 'legitimate poem', 'poetry' and 'poet' explain these relations. Chapter XV translates this theoretical complex into something useful for the practical critic by explaining how a poem's features both arise from the poet's skills, and elicit the reader's reaction. The subjective orientation of chapter XV is balanced by the objective orientation of chapter XVI which argues that language does more than reveal skills or engender response. It shapes our relation to reality. Coleridge alternates orientations so often because he is trying to define how language incarnates the essentially spiritual relation between being and knowing.[3]

Attending closely to Coleridge's statements about language reveals that his poetics has deep and intricate roots in the first volume, although the bulk of these are not in chapters XII and XIII. Throughout the first volume, Coleridge asserts a connection between precise language and truth. The original realism is denied only by 'philosophers of the schools . . . who live and move in a crowd of phrases and notions from which human nature has long ago vanished' (I, 179). Edmund Burke's power as a '*scientific* statesman; and therefore a *seer*' arises from his habitual precision of expression (I, 125). The vagueness and inconsequence of anonymous critics and decadent modern poets reflect their confused understanding (I, 25–9 and n; I, 15). By contrast, the speaker was rigorously trained in verbal precision even at Christ's Hospital. As he is more fully portrayed as a genius, his care with words is more clearly stressed, as part of the larger argument that any apparent obscurity in a genius's work reveals the difficulty of the topic, or the deficiency of the reader, rather than authorial failing (I, 4–5, 64, 108–10, 146). The link between good poetic diction and truth is often asserted, but especially in the first major paean to Wordsworth, which shifts effortlessly from the praise of his pure diction to a celebration of the truth that his genius properly animates (I, 58–60). In chapters XIV to XVI, Coleridge begins to justify this link by exploring the relations between poet and text, and between text and reader. In doing so, he develops the definitions of imagination and fancy; he does not simply apply them to literary questions.

Critics and scholars have long argued about whether or not the theory of literature presented in these chapters grows coherently from the metaphysics and epistemology in the first volume. Those who would describe Coleridge as the father of the New Criticism tend to disregard these metaphysical roots, and to focus on such famous doctrines as 'poetic faith' or the opposition between poems and science.[4] Those who take these roots seriously encounter a variety of complex and perplexing problems. One who emphasizes imagination's synthesis of being and knowing within a metaphysics of polarity can account quite well for much that is both valuable and influential in Coleridge's literary criticism.[5] But, taken in isolation from the rest of Coleridge's philosophic thinking, these doctrines lead directly, abruptly into pantheism. That makes it difficult to justify the centrality of Coleridge's belief in the moral value of art: the belief appears either extraneous, or inconsistent, or both.[6] Those who try to resolve the conflicts are more or less stymied by the fact that after *Biographia Literaria* Coleridge said and wrote very little about imagination, fancy and poetry.[7]

But he did continue to write about language itself, and the relation between metaphysics and poetics is to be found primarily in what the *Biographia* says about language. This idea of language, like the idea of will, permeates Coleridge's works; but it is fully explicated in no one place. Pausing now to define this idea will establish a locus from which the continuity and balance of first and second volumes can be more easily described.[8] Language integrates subjects with objects, or knowing with being, because words reveal both the real world and the person who uses them. 'I include in the *meaning* of a *word*', Coleridge explains, 'not only its correspondent object, but likewise all the associations which it recalls. For language is framed to convey not the object alone, but likewise the character, mood and intentions of the person who is representing it' (II, 115–16). In the *Biographia* he does not explain how, referring instead to 'some future occasion' on which he will 'attempt to prove the close connection between veracity and habits of mental accuracy; the beneficial after-effects of verbal precision in the preclusion of fanaticism . . . and to display the advantages which language . . . presents to the instructor' (II, 116–17).

Aids to Reflection explains what *Biographia Literaria* somewhat cryptically asserts. Words signify neither things, nor ideas, but rather the mind's activity in perception, reflection and meditation. Words reveal the creative, active mind as it distinguishes between real things and mere artifacts of sensory receptors:

> Now when a person speaking to us of any particular object or appearance refers it by means of some common character to a known class (which he does in giving it a name), we say, that we understand him; that is, we understand his words. The name of a thing, in the original sense of the word name (*nomen, νούμενον, τὸ intelligible, id quod intelligitur*) expresses that which is *understood* in an appearance, that which we place (or make to *stand*) *under* it, as the condition of its real existence, and in proof that it is not an accident of the senses, or *affection* of the individual, not a phantom or apparition, that is, an appearance which is *only* an appearance. (*AR*, 220–1)

The act of naming asserts that the thing named exists in a reality shared by speaker and auditor. Coleridge calls naming 'the condition of real existence' because the speaker effectively distinguishes between real and chimerical when he gives something a name: language does not supply names for entities beyond our imagination. Language expresses and records our knowledge through words, which signify not ideas, nor things, but the relation between an idea and its object.

I can sharpen our focus on Coleridge's definition of 'word' by sketching its context. His assertion of the mind's active role in establishing the meanings of words contrasts sharply with the dominant Lockean tradition in linguistics. Throughout the third book, 'Of words', in his *An Essay concerning Human Understanding* (first edition, 1690), Locke maintains that words signify ideas. Since ideas arise from experience of things (or reflections on such experience), words refer to objects only indirectly. In this contention, Locke himself differs sharply from the dominant linguistic tradition in his own day. The contrast can be simplified as follows: for Locke, words signify ideas (of objects); for John Wilkins and other seventeenth-century linguists, words signify (ideas of) objects. In his *An Essay Toward a Real Character, and a Philosophical Language* (1668), Wilkins undertakes a monumental task: 'the great foundation of the thing here designed [is] a regular *enumeration* and *description* of all those things and notions, to which marks or names ought to be assigned according to their respective natures' (p. 1). Wilkins hopes to remedy the confusion of tongues and advance the cause of the Royal Society by inventing a language (his 'real character') in which there is a completely unequivocal one-to-one correspondence between signs and signifieds. (Despite losing his manuscript in the Great Fire, Wilkins completed this enumeration, and invented a language based on Hebrew.) Coleridge's definition of 'word' as the relation between idea and object places him intermediate between the positions represented by Locke and Wilkins, and in a line that Ernst Cassirer traces through Heraclitus, Plato, Berkeley, Herder and von Humboldt.[9]

Coleridge's definition of 'word' represents language as participating intimately in the complex relation between mind and world: the process of naming and the process of knowing are represented as a single process. As the paragraph cited above continues, Coleridge develops the definition in two directions. First, as 'evidence', he cites the frequent identity in the Bible of *nomen* (name) and *numen* ('invisible power and presence'). His claim here has obvious affinities with such 'Platonic' theories as that of James Harris. Yet Harris contends that words refer not to 'external particulars, nor yet . . . particular ideas' but, rather, to 'general ideas'. These are 'a kind of superior objects; a new race of perceptions . . . each one of which may be found entire and whole in the separate individuals of an infinite and fleeting multitude, without departing from the unity and permanence of its own nature'.[10] For Coleridge, the significance of language depends not on how words name objects (or universals) but, rather, on how words reveal the mind's activity.

Secondly, he supports the definition of 'word' by explaining that the objects of understanding are strictly linguistic:

> Thus, in all instances, it is words, names, or, if images, yet images used as words or names, that are the only and exclusive subjects of under-standing. In no instance do we understand a thing in itself; but only the name to which it is referred. . . . No one would say he understands red or blue. He *sees* the colour, and had seen it before in a vast number and variety of objects; and he understands the *word* red, as referring his fancy or memory to this his collective experience. (*AR*, 222)

Sensation is predominantly a physical act; understanding is predominantly an intellectual one. We do not *know* things in themselves: we feel or smell or touch them. In a characteristically adept use of Kant, Coleridge presents language as the principal vehicle for the interaction of knowing mind and concrete being:

> If this be so, and so it most assuredly is – if the proper functions of the understanding be that of generalizing the notices received from the senses in order to the construction of names: of referring particular notices (that is, impressions or sensations) to their proper names; and, *vice versa*, names to their correspondent class or kind of notices – then it follows of necessity, that the understanding is truly and accurately defined in the words of Leighton and Kant, a faculty judging according to sense. (*AR*, 222)

In studying language, we see how the free spirit or will can engage an intractably stable physical reality without losing its own freedom. When imagination dissolves and recreates the mind's relation to this world, words record the change. Language is framed to reveal the insights that philosophic self-consciousness attains, to express an intuitive penetration to the relation between God and man.

Language is not only the medium of least resistance to the spirit, but also a powerful objective force in its own right. As political language so clearly reveals, those who manipulate the words that name our relations to events can very effectively shape our moral responses to the events themselves. For Coleridge, linguistic accuracy is at heart a moral issue, because precisely written texts are a moral resource. And that is the principal issue uniting the *Biographia*'s transcendental philosophy with its literary criticism.

Let me explain the relation between language and truth in more detail, because it provides a major key to the philosophic origins of Coleridge's criticism. Because words reveal the mind's activity, one can say that language expresses the contents and activity of consciousness. In the manuscript 'Logic' Coleridge explains more fully an idea of grammar and logic that he barely sketches in the *Biographia* (I, 14; II, 63–8, 116–17). Grammar, he explains, 'reflects the forms of the human Mind, and gradually familiarizes the half-conscious boy with the frame and constitution of his own Intellect'. This 'frame and constitution' is logic: 'it is plain that Logic[,] in as much as it presents the universal and necessary rules of the Understanding, must in these rules present likewise the criterion of truth, that is, of formal truth, or truth relative to the constitution or constituent forms, laws and rules of the thinking faculty'.[11] In the 'Opus Maximum' manuscript, Coleridge clarifies his special interpretation of the common eighteenth-century equation between logic and grammar: 'In fact the science of grammar is but logic in its first exemplification or rather in its first product . . . i.e., *thoughts in connexion or connected language*' (my italics).[12] Logic defines both the rules of correct understanding and the rules of correct word-use; as formalized in grammar, logic is the power of language to express relations. Although language itself does not constitute reality, it expresses the constituent forms of the understanding: the power to make relations.

As I explained in the first chapter, the most fundamental relation is that between ideas and the laws governing both physical and spiritual or psychological realities.[13] Language can incarnate the relation between ideas and physical laws because it distinguishes perceptions from illusions. Language can incarnate the relation between ideas and spiritual laws because the logical, grammatical, relational features of language itself reveal the psychological laws of thinking for which the correlative idea is the Logos, the Word of God, whom we know through the fullest concurrent action of will, reason and faith.[14] Because of these complementary capacities, language in its total complexity reveals and enacts the laws of the universe. Language embodies a dynamic and vital metaphysics sharply opposed to the fixity of materialism. In the *Philosophical Lectures* Coleridge explores this idea of language at length, attributing it to Pythagoras and his heirs. Pythagoras was the first to recognize, Coleridge explains, that 'the very powers which in men reflect and contemplate, are in their essence the same as those powers which in nature produce the objects contemplated' (*PhL*, 114). These powers were 'by the Pythagoreans and Anaxagoras called the *Nous*, (the *Logos* or the *Word* of Philo and St. John)' (*PhL*, 175). The *Philosophical Lectures* develop this insight through analyses of such figures as Aristotle and Bacon, who study these powers as manifest in the natural world, and those such as Plato, who study them as manifest in the mind.[15]

Language is one of these manifestations in the mind. Plato 'direct[s] his inquiries chiefly to those objective truths that exist in and for the intellect alone, the images and representatives of which we construct for ourselves by figure, number, and word' (*F*, I, 492). Mathematics had long been taken as a model for absolute certitude; the apparently dramatic correspondence between the pure mathematical system and the observable world had always had metaphysical significance. Coleridge echoes the claim that words, like figures and numbers, are part of a perfect system which none the less reflects the form of an imperfect and changeable world.[16] It is in its capacity to represent a (logical, grammatical) system of relations that language is analogous to mathematics.

Words are to consciousness what geometrical figures are to space, or numbers to time (*F*, I, 440 n). Language symbolically represents both the relations of mind to world (the correlation of ideas and laws), and the relation of human knowledge to divine knowledge (logic and the *Logos*). Language differs from geometry in part because language changes and develops, while geometry does not (or would not have seemed to, for Coleridge). But this difference is minor. Although language is always changing, it is at any given point a perfect system, because it perfectly accords with consciousness itself, which is always changing. Had Coleridge recognized that the properties of space are still developing (in his sense), then he would have seen that geometry must develop apace.

Because accurate language reliably guides us to truth, and because unrecognized truths are apt to require astute linguistic distinctions for their intelligibility, many of Coleridge's arguments appeal to etymology, and to grammar and usage. Throughout his career, he urges desynonymizing as a route to clear understanding. It is, he says, 'the progress of language' (*PhL*, 368–9; see also 200–1). He bases arguments on the exact meanings of words, and cites or invents etymologies to make his point.[17] He frequently structures arguments as inquiries into the precise meaning of a word, or the correct distinction between related words. These pervasive strategies are more than convenient rhetorical habits: they reflect deeply held convictions about the nature of language itself. Read against German transcendentalism, or certain strains in modern literary theory,

Coleridge's view of the interactivity of language and consciousness appears to incorporate a high level of indeterminacy; but this is only an appearance. As the *Aids to Reflection* unequivocally demonstrates, Coleridge firmly believed in the stability and universality of what used to be called 'human nature'. Eliminate this stability, or the theism underlying it, and the ideas which remain change character so radically that they should not be attributed to Coleridge.

Coleridge's idea of language underlies both the textual specificity of his best criticism, and its moral concerns.[18] Poetry guides us to truth not by what it says – not by sermonizing – but by how its language reveals the fundamental relations animating consciousness and the world as humanly experienced. This idea also underlies his willingness to make value-judgments, because the distinction between intellectual knowing and physical sensing guarantees that we can judge the adequacy of verbal formulations by comparing actual experience and linguistic represen-tation. Coleridge would take quick issue with the notion that words refer only to other words, and not to realities. He would say, I suspect, that dissolving either the connection or the distinction between word and signified is the same school-error as dissolving the connection or the distinction between sensation and object sensed: it breeds chimerical problems that only the original realism can escape.

In chapter XIV, Coleridge begins to present a theory of poetry that ties aesthetic pleasure to linguistic qualities that guarantee the moral value of art, yet without subordinating the poet's craftsmanship to a moral censor. Such a theory allows him to explain how philosophic imagination can generate both the pure diction and the moral insight that he recognized in Wordsworth's early poems (I, 56–60). It also allows close and sustained attention to diction *per se*, and to the crucial role fancy plays in the effective presentation of imaginative insight. As the theory unfolds, one begins to see that the complementary functions of fancy and imagination in many ways reflect the complementarity of being and knowing, or faithful representation and self-conscious transformation. Poetics and metaphysics come into their fullest, richest balance in the critique of Wordsworth's theory and practice: Coleridge argues that Wordsworth's mistaken idea of language reflects a mistaken epistemology, and generates defective poems. Analyzing his errors, as Coleridge earlier analyzes the errors of 'the excellent and pious Hartley', reveals how the cooperative energies of fancy and imagination create a poetic cosmos in which mind and world are perfectly balanced and fully integrated.

Chapter XIV's account of the 'plan' for *Lyrical Ballads* introduces an objectively oriented definition of poetry as a 'species of composition'. But as the chapter develops, Coleridge shifts the objective orientation into its opposite, primarily by changing from poem as text, to poem as reading, to poem as expression. He maintains the unity of this progression partly by anchoring himself in the poem as language, and partly by incorporating images that signal imagination's activity into his objective descriptions. The most striking such image is the reference to light in the account of *Lyrical Ballads.* The image is repeated from chapter XII and, more directly, from the description of Wordsworth's genius in chapter IV (I, 164–7; I, 59–60).[19]

> . . . our conversations turned frequently on the two cardinal points of poetry, the power of exciting the sympathy of the reader by a faithful adherence to the truth of nature, and the power of giving the interest of novelty by the modifying colours of imagination. The sudden charm which accidents of light and shade, which moon-light or sun-set diffused over a known and familiar landscape, appeared to represent the practicability of combining both. These are the poetry of nature. (II, 5)

Light affects not only how well we see, but also what we see. It both creates and reveals. The poet's rhetorical task is to modulate imagination's light so as to engage the reader's sympathy, and to avoid the disorientation reported by the 'friend' in chapter XIII. One who succeeds in this task opens new worlds to the reader, whether the purely fictional world of 'The Ancient Mariner', or the realistic but too often unknown world to which Wordsworth restores us (cf. I, 60; II, 6).[20]

In defining *poem* as 'a species of composition', Coleridge explains how the poet achieves these ends through poetic form. A poem is distinct from other uses of language by its use of rhyme, or metre, or both (II, 8), and by its immediate purpose or intent: pleasure for the reader (II, 9). This pleasure principle – the opposition between poems and 'works of science' – indirectly but no less certainly ensures that the great poem will fully embody an imaginative access into profound and fundamental truths. Because 'nothing can permanently please, which does not contain in itself the reason why it is so, and not otherwise', the features of poetic form must justify and require each other. These justifications and requirements can be for the reader's sake, or the poet's, or both; and so the argument begins to shift toward the subjective.

Before following, let us look more closely at the quality of pleasure poems afford, and its relation to truth. We delight primarily in what one may generally call the 'aptness' of a poem's expression, the reflexivity of 'form' and 'content', rather than the 'content' *per se.*[21] But the nature of words and the nature of grammar guarantee that the utterly apt expression will truly reveal some aspect of the relations among God, man and a shared, immediately accessible reality. Lear was not a real king, perhaps; but to discredit or to ignore the play's truth on that ground is akin to discrediting Mendel's conclusions because his peas are not all peas. It is to mistake, profoundly, the character of the human activity in question. One attains truth about the laws governing physical reality by directly testing one's ideas. One attains truth about the laws governing intellectual or spiritual realities indirectly, by aiming at precise expression, by relying on the Logos. Only through primary, immediate attention to the delights of accurate and beautiful language does the poet reach poetry's 'proper ultimate end'. The ultimate truth of *King Lear* is not Lear's fate, nor even the sum of propositions extractable from major speeches, but, rather, what the play reveals about human minds. The critic's task is to discover and to represent that truth in relation to its medium – as Coleridge himself does, for instance, in his famous study of *Hamlet*'s opening scene.[22] This highly psychological (or epistemological) approach to literature has considerable value for much of the literature written since 1800, but it is not necessarily the most fruitful approach to Wordsworth's experiments with descriptive poetry. Coleridge sharply criticizes his attempts at a rigorous but enlightened objectivity.[23]

Whether or not truth is compatible with aesthetic pleasure from the utterly apt or self-justifying poetic form will depend upon the 'state of society' and the 'character of the author' – not the genre of the work (II, 9). Given what we have seen about contemporary society, and the authors who pander to it, this distinction between immediate and ultimate purpose resonates deeply with the controversy over *Lyrical Ballads*. Coleridge's account of the controversy often involves this distinction. When Wordsworth confuses the two ends, he sermonizes or bogs down in excessive detail. When he distinguishes and manages them properly, his diction improves; but he ensures the hostility of anonymous critics who either cannot or will not respond to genuinely imaginative works. The flaws of Wordsworth's theory make the flaccid diction of the immediately moral poems seem deliberate, and provide anonymous critics with excuses for ignoring the ultimate truth and immediate beauty of the imaginative poems.

Coleridge links proper aesthetic pleasure to the reader's imagination when he defines a *'legitimate'* or excellent poem. Any poem must provide 'such delight from the *whole*, as is compatible with a distinct gratification from each component *part*' (II, 10). But the great poem has more than such balance: it has unity in diversity. '. . . the parts . . . mutually support and explain each other; all in their proportion harmonizing with, and supporting the purpose and known influences of metrical arrangement', i.e. 'perpetual and distinct attention to each part' (II, 10). Metre enforces attention to parts, which reciprocally enforce attention to the whole. It leads the sensitive reader to the imaginative synthesis of an organic unity. Poetic language and poetic form together arouse the reader's imagination, and thereby generate aesthetic pleasure. Coleridge's account of this pleasure echoes both the first critical aphorism (I, 14) and the water-insect passage (I, 85–6):

> The reader should be carried forward, not merely or chiefly by the mech-
> anical impulse of curiosity, or by a restless desire to arrive at the final
> solution; but by the pleasureable activity of mind excited by the attrac-
> tions of the journey itself. Like the motion of a serpent, which the

Egyptians made the emblem of intellectual power; or like the path of sound through the air; at every step he pauses and half recedes, and from the retrogressive movement collects the force which again carries him onward. (II, 11)

Because the quintessential aesthetic pleasure arises from the act of reading, not – strictly speaking – from the content of what is read, one can reread, and reread again, with no diminution of pleasure. Novelty is not the point, although it is the principal attraction of the works written and praised by anonymous critics (I, 27 n). The identity of parts yet their unity in the whole reflects the identity of being and knowing yet their unity in consciousness. A poem can so intimately reveal or enact the nature of consciousness because language symbolizes the unity of being and knowing. Thus, the imaginative synthesis responsible for self-consciousness, and for truth, is also responsible for aesthetic pleasure.

From this it follows that aesthetic pleasure can be generated by a work whose immediate purpose is truth, not pleasure – if the author is most powerfully imaginative (II, 11). In theory even metre is not crucial; it is principally an aid to modulating attention and thus increasing the pleasure most fully appropriate to poems. A poem differs from such poetry as Plato offers by using metre to accommodate the whole most completely to the intensely imaginative parts; it is crucial to the highest degree of such accommodation, whether from the poet's or the reader's standpoint. By using the word 'poetry' to refer to that which generates aesthetic pleasure generally, Coleridge affirms that the objective features of a poem (such as metre or poetic diction generally) exist to enhance, facilitate and sustain the reader's imaginative response. It is obvious that truth – the unity of being and knowing – cannot be the logical opposite of aesthetic pleasure. Although pleasure and truth will not be compatible for all readers, or for all poets, at all times, the highest aesthetic pleasure and the greatest truths will most probably and most often be found together.

In describing a poem's imaginative qualities, Coleridge has worked his way back to the imaginative qualities of great poets: 'What is poetry? is so nearly the same question with, what is a poet? that the answer to the one is involved in the solution of the other' (II, 12). The synthetic power of great poems can only arise from the synthetic power of great poets; the linguistically embodied relation between knowing mind and real world presumes an author for whom that relation is lucid and self-conscious. The famous portrait of the 'poet, described in *ideal* perfection', translates the familiar features of imaginative activity generally into terms useful for describing the literary products of that activity. Imagination, we are told once again, functions within a complex of powers that must be balanced and coordinated properly. It is spontaneous, not relatively passive, nor chosen in complete independence, but retained under the 'gentle and unnoticed control' of the will and understanding (the relatively active and passive poles that it synthesizes). These familiar ideas are repeated here because they will play a major role in Coleridge's theory of metre, and his use of that theory as a basis for criticizing Wordsworth's theory and his poems. The description ends with a long catalogue of the relatively active and relatively passive qualities that imagination '*fuses*, each into each'. Coleridge breaks this catalogue into subordinate groups by changing whether the initial member of each group is objective or subjective:

same	different
general	concrete
idea	image
representative	individual
old and familiar objects	novelty and freshness
order	emotion
judgment	enthusiasm and feeling
artificial	natural
art	nature
manner	matter
admiration for the poet	sympathy with the poem

This catalogue has obvious affinities to the table of distinctions concerning will, and to the distinctions between relatively active and relatively passive in chapter IX (I, 66, 108–9). It also accords with chapter XVI's distinctions 'between the Poets of the present age and those of the 15th and 16th centuries' (II, 20). It represents again 'the two cardinal points of poetry': sympathy with the familiar, concrete, particular world; and interests in the novelty supplied by intellectual and artistic transformations. Because Wordsworth is quite nearly this ideal poet, these oppositions appear time and again in the commentary on his work. Coleridge's successful emphasis on this description helps make evident that Wordsworth's poetry – like all great poetry – synthesizes the powers of spirit with the animated world the spirit knows.

The catalogue serves thematic unity as well. Beginning here, the opposition between knowing and being shifts back into its earlier, more vivid and more useful forms: head and heart, judgment and passion, the centrifugal and centripetal forces of exactness and liveliness. So, too, the lines from Davies (as amended by Coleridge) translate the metaphysics of original realism into something less abstract and more useful for criticism: the insistence that imagination's powers must '"Steal access through our senses to our mind"' (II, 13), that imagination's powers can and must be concretely manifest in the experience of living and the experience of literature. This insistence strikes me as the quintessentially English side of

Coleridge's theory, and simultaneously as the most fundamental appeal his theory makes to that soul within us who must 'awake and start up' at the annunciation of a genuine idea. A poem synthesizes intellectual, moral and emotional powers, not *by* its words or their paraphrases, but *through* its words, through the words' simultaneous relations to consciousness and to reality in all the complexities of both. A poem symbolizes the integrity of the human spirit in the fullness of its relation to all that is 'other'.

And yet this unity is fully susceptible of analysis, because words are not the only medium of relation to the other. We have hands and eyes and ears to tell us whether a line successfully arouses an imaginative revision of the world we have known. In chapter XV, on 'The specific symptoms of poetic power', Coleridge examines the roles played by four major components of a poem – versification, topic, imagery and ideas – to anchor the activity of imagination in particular features of the text. The chapter's design sets a pattern that later chapters often follow. On the one hand, the chapter offers numbered judgments on a single issue: the objective signs of poetic genius. On the other, the justifications for these judgments maintain an independent progression that gradually illuminates a major principle: the role of imagination in reading and writing. The numbered sequence engenders a sense of orderly momentum that is somewhat rare for Coleridge's prose, while the justifications hover in more characteristic fashion over a single but very complex idea. The strategy may be a carry-over from the conveniences of Schelling's numbered theses. Although helpful to the reader in a mechanical way, its artificiality – so rare a flaw in Coleridge – tends to obscure the center about which he circles.

The first section, on versification, defines how the poem's language sustains the poet's intimate relation with his reader. The poet's musical delight moves through the text to a reciprocal delight *in the reader*. The poet reduces the plenitude of his materials to unity of effect *on the reader*. One legitimate measure of a poem's quality, then, is the reader's response – a measure that underlies several crucial rhetorical patterns later on. These ideas come into much sharper focus when Coleridge examines Wordsworth's versification: his feeble prosody fails to move the reader; and the prosody is feeble because he himself lacks the passion or the materials that arouse musical prowess.

The second section, on the choice of subjects, explains that the poem's beauty (its imaginative fusion of universal and particular) derives from contemplation not observation – from secondary imagination, not primary. The comic tale of the indifferent statue with the divine legs enforces what is by now a familiar point in Coleridge's favorite way. The sexual passion of Venus or Adonis is even more easily distinguished from Shakespeare's creative passion (although, as with the goddess, distinction is not division: opposites meet). Once again, the poet's imaginative powers shape the reader's experience through the medium of the poem.

['Venus and Adonis'] is throughout as if a superior spirit more intuitive, more intimately conscious . . . of the flux and reflux of the mind in all its subtlest thoughts and feelings, were placing the whole before our view; himself meanwhile unparticipating in the passions, and actuated only by that pleasurable excitement, which had resulted from the energetic fervor of his own spirit in so vividly exhibiting what it had so accurately and profoundly contemplated. . . . You seem to be told nothing, but to see and hear everything. Hence . . . the perpetual activity of attention required on the part of the reader; from the rapid flow, the quick change, and the playful nature of the thoughts and images; and above all from the alienation, and . . . the utter *aloofness* of the poet's own feelings, from those of which is he at once the painter and the analyst. (II, 15–16)

The reader repeats the poet's dissolving and recreating through his distinct attention both to the parts as such and to the whole. The reader engages the artwork, not the sexual passion; he responds to contemplation's product, not its immediate subject. Coleridge further develops this point when he links Wordsworth's emphasis on observation and literal experience to the poems he regards as inexcusably dull.

The third section explains that the poem's images enact the transforming power of imagination. In a legitimate poem, images are shaped by the poet's creative or contemplative passion. Regarded objectively, images transcend space, time, and fragmented particularity by 'reducing multitude to unity, or succession to an instant' (II, 16). When engaged in the text, poet and reader dwell together and apart, not in 'that inanimate cold world allowed/To the poor loveless ever-anxious crowd' but in 'A new Earth and new Heaven,/Undreamt of by the sensual and the proud'. How? Images define relations, not just things. Pines like women with their backs to the wind are not just trees, but trees as seen by a human observer. The poet's power to observe himself observing, and his access to the spirit with all that involves, is most evident in the poem's imagistic language. By attending to the imagery, the reader sees the world as the poet sees it: the reader knows the poet's knowing. Coleridge later argues that Wordsworth's dramatic poems often fail because they delete this mediating consciousness: one sees *what* the poet sees, not *how*.

The fourth section is the second of Coleridge's three general descriptions of poetic genius (II, 12, 19–20, 122–4). The first defines the polar oppositions that the poet reconciles in his works. This second one defines the oppositions reconciled in the consciousness of the poet *qua* poet: the unity and identity in imagination of creative originality and fidelity to nature. Familiar images reappear to stress that this specifically poetic union develops gradually from the primary psychic unity of self-consciousness.

In Shakespeare's *poems* the creative power and the intellectual energy wrestle as in a war embrace. Each in its excess of strength seems to threaten the extinction of the other. At length in the DRAMA they were reconciled, and fought each with its shield before the breast of the other. Or like two rapid streams, that, at their first meeting within narrow and rocky banks, mutually strive to repel each other and intermix reluctantly and in tumult; but soon finding a wider channel and more yielding shores blend, and dilate, and flow on in one current and with one voice. (II, 19)

The tumult that permanently characterizes the fanatic is also a stage of development for the genius; hence the speaker does not mind 'a certain degree of disputatiousness in a young man . . . provided I find him always arguing on one side of the question' (I, 13). For the genius, the will or true self soon fuses or reconciles opposing tendencies into a single, stronger power. Even in Shakespeare's early poems, however, we find his imagination clearly at work, and his 'dominion, often domination, over the whole world of language' (II, 19).

And it is to the nature of language, particularly the poetic language of rhythm and image, that Coleridge turns in chapter XVI. Wordsworth's centrality in this poetics reflects his place in Coleridge's pantheon of great English poets. Shakespeare 'passes into all the forms of human character and passion'; Milton 'attracts all forms and things to himself, into the unity of his own IDEAL' (II, 20). There must be an intermediate kind of poetic genius, neither absorbed in nor absorbing the material world – just as a word names neither idea nor thing, but their relation. And this is the genius of Wordsworth, who is capable of writing the 'FIRST GENUINE PHILOSOPHIC POEM' (II, 129).

Like chapter II, on 'the supposed irritability of men of Genius', chapter XVI at first glance seems digressive. Italian poets of the fifteenth and sixteenth centuries do not seem to have much relevance either to Wordsworth, or to the analysis of poetry and poetic genius. That is because the predominant transition or relation between chapter XVI and the two preceding rests not on poetic theory, but on the chronological narrative of the speaker's 'literary life and opinions'. The continuity of that narrative relies primarily on renewing patterns and themes established in the first four chapters. Looking back at how chapter XIV echoes these early themes will show not only how chapter XVI fits in, but also how the genius–fanatic contrast provides a crucial context for the analysis of Wordsworth.

The most important contrast renewed in chapter XIV is that between anonymous and philosophical criticism. The speaker claims that Wordsworth and he have been victims of a literary inquisition in which acrimony replaces analysis.

From the conjunction of perceived power with supposed heresy I explain the inveteracy and in some instances, I grieve to say, the acrimonious passions, with which the controversy has been conducted by the assailants[.] . . . the intellectual energy of the author, which was more or less consciously felt, where it was outwardly and even boisterously denied, meeting with sentiments of aversion to his opinions, and of alarm at their consequences, produced an eddy of criticism, which would of itself have borne up the poems by the violence, with which it whirled them round and round. (II, 7)

These reviewers are not critics, but 'assailants' who 'boisterously' deny their own intuitive apprehensions. The tornado-like 'eddy' that would of itself have borne the poems to prominence repeats the rising circular image of swarming bees from the first definition of the fanatic (I, 19). Whatever the equivocations of the Preface, such irresponsible and frantic criticism reveals more about the critic than it does about the poet.

The speaker wishes to extricate himself from this situation by declaring his differences from Wordsworth, and to extricate Wordsworth by explaining what he 'really meant'. The painstaking definitions of poem, legitimate poem, poetry and poet reinforce the speaker's status as a precise thinker. The visual, aural and semantic similarities of these terms may unnecessarily confuse and delay the reader, but they enhance the appearance of extreme precision. In much the same way, chapter XV reminds us that the speaker is a learned man who knows relevant history thoroughly. Its numbering enforces the same sense of clarity and precision: nothing 'boisterous' here.

In this context, chapter XVI's account of Italian poets further enforces the speaker's scholarly responsibility. These poets may lack novelty or particularity, but the speaker certainly prefers their work to the utter confusion reigning in the diction of his contemporaries, whether poets or prose writers: '. . . the composition of our novels, magazines, public harangues, &c., is commonly as trivial in thought, and yet enigmatic in expression, as if ECHO and SPHINX had laid their heads together to construct it' – in pointed contrast to his own style in the preceding two chapters (II, 21–2).

Reading the chapter this way leads us easily enough to its role in the *Biographia* generally: the qualities of fanatics always reverse those of geniuses; the discussion of fanaticism often introduces an explanation of the ground of the difference. The genius–fanatic contrast here points in two directions at once. First, it asserts that the poet must 'fuse, each into each', the interesting surprises of novelty and the utter predictability of a mannerist style. An excess of the first generates a work that gratifies curiosity alone; an excess of the second mutes attention to particular parts, and thus the pleasure of reading as an activity. Neither work will be reread as often as truly genial works are.

Secondly, the denunciation of decadent modern style introduces Coleridge's major statement of the relation between truth and precision, or knowing mind and knowledgeable expression. The Italian side of a lost balance between the novel and the predictable is better than the fanatic side, because the Italians retain precise diction. They may be dull at times, but they are exact. In a manner characteristic of the *Biographia*, this fullest statement of a crucial unproven point is a quotation – acknowledged properly, but not translated.[24] The passage defending the Italians' style summarizes and reemphasizes the links among imagination, truth and pure diction that first appear in chapters I to IV.

> Nay, even of those who have most rescued themselves from this contagion [by the style of magazines and harangues], I should plead inwardly guilty to the charge of duplicity or cowardice if I withheld my conviction that few have guarded the purity of their native tongue with that jealous care which the sublime Dante, in his tract 'De la nobile volgare eloquenza,' declares to be the first duty of a poet. For language is the armoury of the human mind; and at once contains the trophies of its past, and the weapons of its future conquests. 'See how easily men fall from the wrong use of words into errors about things themselves!' [Hobbes]. 'There are certainly plenty of things in this short life and dark world which are worth time to study, so that we need not spend time in trying to understand confused and many-sided discussions. Alas, cloudy words are so many failures, they say so much that they say nothing – clouds, rather, from which hurricanes burst, both in church and state! What Plato has said in the Gorgias is indeed true: "Anyone who knows words will know things too"; and as Epictetus says, "the study of words is the beginning of education"; and Galen wrote most wisely, "Confusion in our knowledge of words makes confusion in our knowledge of things." J. C. Scaliger has indeed said excellently, in book I of his *Plants*: "A wise man's first duty (he says) is to think well so that he can live for himself; the next is to speak well so that he can live for his country."' (II, 22)

The references to church and state, to public duties, and to hurricanes focus the basic threat posed by anonymous critics: they corrupt the language. Bad judgment follows from bad writing, and bad writing from bad thinking; the popularity of their bad judgments impedes the healing and proper influence of genius – as both the speaker's and Wordsworth's careers demonstrate. Only the precise use of words will lead us to the truth about 'things themselves'. The original realism and the nature of language guarantee that any method which leads to the astute and exact knowledge of the physical world will simultaneously lead to knowledge of the spirit, because the transcendental analysis of consciousness shows that these proceed apace.

Chapter XVI ends with a transparent reference to Wordsworth: 'A lasting and enviable reputation awaits that man of genius, who should attempt and realize a union' (II, 24). One who achieves the syntheses characteristic of the ideal poet will be hailed as a genius – or ought to be. When Coleridge describes Wordsworth's poetry as achieving these qualities, we are to see Wordsworth as wrongly deprived of the laurels that are his. As the portrait of genial Wordsworth gains detail, so does the condemnation of his critics (chapter XXI), and the speaker's (chapter XXIV). We are left with the idea of a choice between genial imaginative Christianity and fanatical materialist atheism, a choice that we are to see as influencing every human activity and every aspect of our own experience. Wordsworth, and to a lesser extent the speaker himself, are to stand as symbols for the great traditional values both in literature and in life.

7 Wordsworth and Poetic Diction

> Poets (especially if philosophizers too) are apt to represent the effect made on themselves as general – the Geese of Phoebus are all Swans, & Wordsworth's Shepherds & Estatesmen all Wordsworths, even (as in old Michael) in the *un*poetic traits of character. Whether mountains have any particular effect on the native inhabitants, by virtue of being mountains exclusively, & what that effect is, would be a difficult problem. . . . – But this subject I have discussed, & (if I do not flatter myself) satisfactorily in the Literary Life, & I will not conceal from *you*, that this inferred dependency of the human soul on accidents of Birth-place & Abode together with the vague misty, rather than mystic, Confusion of God with the World & the accompanying Nature-worship, of which the asserted dependence form a part, is the Trait in Wordsworth's poetic Works that I most dislike, as unhealthful, & denounce as contagious. . . .
>
> Letter to Thomas Allsop, 8 August 1820
> (*Collected Letters*, V, 94–5)

In his arguments about diction, Coleridge builds upon the classical rhetoricians' belief that language can both express and evoke emotion. According to Coleridge, however, poetic language expresses and evokes not feelings but imaginative activity itself. This dual capacity arises from and requires the essential interdependence of imagery, metre, subject-matter and thought. As Abrams has so lucidly explained, Coleridge's subsequent influence on literary criticism has followed in large measure from his successfully accommodating rhetorical tools of analysis with a philosophically grounded idea of the creative imagination.[1] In chapters XVII and XVIII, Coleridge explains at length how effective poetic diction simultaneously derives from and arouses imagination, an explanation that proceeds step by step with his critical commentary on Wordsworth's Preface to *Lyrical Ballads*.

To meet the needs of his own exposition, Coleridge 'adapts' the Preface, just as he adapts the works and the theories of Kant, Aristotle and

Schelling. But in each case, and most clearly with Wordsworth, the adaptation is probably also intended to illuminate more clearly a fundamental truth – or a fundamental error – that the author himself represents only partially. Coleridge follows a principle of interpretation that he enunciates most clearly in the *Philosophical Lectures*: 'the individual is . . . subordinated to the history of philosophy' (*PhL*, 205). In Wordsworth's case, the fundamental error is trying to describe imaginative works in associationist terms that ultimately attribute to the landscape a spirit and moral purpose that belong only to God and to man. According to Coleridge, Wordsworth's befuddled theory and its consequences combine the worst errors of both English mechanism and Continental pantheism, because he does not sufficiently emphasize the mind's priority over matter. In reading the Preface and the poems, Coleridge seizes the points where Wordsworth does not assert this logical and moral priority so as to develop at length the aesthetic inadequacies of an associationist theory of poetry and poetic diction.

Coleridge's criticism of Wordsworth's theory depends in part on his conflating Preface and Appendix, and in part on his ignoring how the Appendix qualifies and clarifies several major ideas. Wordsworth has been ably defended on several fronts; only a few points need to be repeated here.[2] The most important of these concerns what Wordsworth means by contrasting the 'real language of men' with 'poetic diction'. In the opening paragraphs of the Appendix, Wordsworth contrasts 'real language' with the 'distorted language' known as 'poetic diction' – the special stock of words and images regarded as poetic because they are remote from ordinary speech and utilitarian prose.[3] This poetic diction, Wordsworth explains, is characterized by 'various degrees of wanton deviation from good sense and nature', whereas real language maintains a 'natural connection' with 'feelings and thoughts'. The real language of men has two subclasses: 'ordinary language' and the 'genuine language of passion', which is 'daring, and figurative'. So-called poetic diction falsely imitates 'the original figurative language of passion' through the 'mechanical adoption of these figures of speech . . . applied . . . to feelings and thoughts with which they ha[ve] no natural connection whatsoever'. In time, 'by the influence of books upon men', the distortions and inanities of poetic diction become to some extent the conventional diction of all writers of verse.[4] In proposing 'to adopt the very language of men', consequently, Wordsworth asserts his fidelity to 'good sense and nature', and to the 'daring, and figurative' language of genuine passion.

He is not proposing to wander about with a notebook, as Coleridge suggests; but he is judging poetic diction primarily by the quality of the words' relations to realities they name. Wordsworth's account of poetic diction probably reflects Hartley, Don Bialostosky explains, for whom a 'real language' is one in which words refer to sensations and feelings rather than to other words, as in a 'nominal language'.[5] To Coleridge, this entire view of language is profoundly mistaken: words name the complex activity of the mind in knowing and reacting, not just the things known or the consequent emotions. Coleridge ignores the qualifying contexts of Wordsworth's statements about 'the real language of men' so as to focus more sharply on this mistakenly empiricist idea of language.

Similar motives underlie Coleridge's reading of the statement, '*There neither is or can be any essential difference between the language of prose and metrical composition*' (II, 45).[6] Wordsworth makes this equation to deduce the applicability of 'good sense and natural feeling' as criteria for poetic imagery. If these criteria apply, then the distortions of poetic diction lose validity. Furthermore, the prose works he has in mind are not scientific treatises, but 'works of *imagination and sentiment*'.[7] Coleridge ignores Wordsworth's context so as to make this statement into an appropriate opposition for his own argument that metre, imagery and passion are essentially interdependent. Once again, however, a genuine disagreement underlies Coleridge's questionable reading. As I will explain in more detail later, Wordsworth attributes a balancing power to metre that Coleridge attributes to imagination itself.

Coleridge seldom demonstrates much scholarly responsibility in his use of others' texts, and his handling of the Preface is no exception to this fault. But in this case, at least, some of his motives remain quite near to the surface, especially if one compares the 1800 and 1802 editions of the Preface. In 1802 and subsequent editions, Wordsworth's expanded explanation of 'real language' discredits Coleridge's account of an unduly literal observation and selection, but Wordsworth does insist that the poet cannot hope to replicate the 'liveliness and truth' of the language of actually impassioned men.[8] Nature remains greater than art. Coleridge disagrees: 'In poetry, in which every line, every phrase, may pass the ordeal of deliberation and deliberate choice, it is possible, and barely possible, to attain that ultimatum which I have ventured to propose as the infallible test of a blameless style; its *untranslatableness* in words of the same language without injury to the meaning' (II, 115). Deliberation and revision, not immediate passion, underlie the most lively, exact and potent expression. As Wimsatt and Brooks explain, reformers of poetic diction can usually be classified in two ways: those who appeal to 'the directly passionate, the naturally spoken word', and those who appeal to the 'educated spoken word', as models of clarity and vitality.[9] This division is, perhaps, the poetic equivalent of the division into Aristotelians and Platonists; Wordsworth is in one group, and Coleridge in the other. Each argues that meditation and observation must be finely balanced, but each portrays the balance from the perspectives supplied by his own experience and character.

The design of chapters XVII and XVIII is at once pellucid and extra-ordinarily difficult to describe. As I said before, Coleridge argues the necessary interdependence of subject-matter, metre, imagery and thought in producing the highest aesthetic effects. But this whole argument is closely interwoven with his evaluation of Wordsworth, and its central point unfolds as slowly as a flower's opening. Because all of Coleridge's transitions orient us to Wordsworth, the integrity and coherence of his counter-argument appear only retrospectively; yet this counter-argument supplies the single perspective that unifies Coleridge's analysis of Wordsworth's theories and his poems. As a result, the narrative account of Wordsworth and the philosophical account of poetry and imagination are so closely interwoven that neither makes much sense without the other.

Let me sketch this main point as briefly and plainly as I can. The interdependence of parts, or the 'organic' unity of a poem, derives from the poet's imagination. Poetic skill depends on contemplation, on imaginative self-consciousness, not on observation of things or imitations of traditions, because it is a verbal art. Words exist within the relation between mind and all that it knows; words embody consciousness itself. It follows that one who is most fully self-conscious will use words most precisely, and thereby reveal most reliably both the exquisite physical sensibility and the moral insight that comprise imaginative genius. Words can carry such a burden only when organized into metre (which embodies, evokes and sustains passion) and images (which characterize realities *as known by* a human consciousness). The reality that poems 'imitate', then, is not the objective world as such but, rather, the consciousness of the poet himself *in his encounters with* the objective world. Poets must rely not on primary imagination's rendering of the objective physical world, but on secondary imagination's rendering of man's intimate relation to that world. Only through the secondary power of 'wedding Nature' do we find in poems pine-trees like women with their backs to the wind. Only thereby do we find in poems not a world of fixed and morally remote objects but, rather, a world animated by value and meaning. It follows from this that the poet's only genuine subject-matter is himself, and the only ideas he presents will be ideas about the activity of consciousness in the world around it. Wordsworth's theories err and his poems fail when he attributes to objects – to metres, to landscapes, to garrulous seamen – imaginative qualities and aesthetic powers that properly belong only to himself. This is truly a fault of which none but the genius is capable, and so Coleridge's criticisms are a backhanded praise slowly verging into full celebration of the great philosophic poet.

Coleridge's adaptation of Wordsworth's theory begins with the speaker's opening summary of their agreements. The speaker praises Wordsworth's call for 'a reformation in our poetic diction', but without acknowledging Wordsworth's predominant concern with how convention and tradition can shape the reader's expectations and thus his judgment (II, 28). Wordsworth's interest in what he calls the 'contract' between reader and poet locates the question about diction in pragmatic contexts sometimes remote from Coleridge's philosophical and theoretical concerns. The speaker's opening criticism of Wordsworth's rule that proper diction for poetry 'consists altogether in a language taken, with due exceptions, from the mouths of men in real life' also fails to supply the context that makes the rule intelligible (II, 29).

These deficiencies permit Coleridge to open his own account of poetic diction by shifting Wordsworth's issue from qualities of imagery to qualities of style generally: the less declamatory kinds of poetry will use sentence structures and vocabulary not profoundly different from those found in ordinary prose or in educated speech:

> My objection is, first, that in *any* sense this rule is applicable only to *certain* classes of poetry; secondly, that even to these classes it is not applicable, except in such a sense, as hath never by any one (as far as I know or have read) been denied or doubted; and lastly, that as far as, and in that degree in which it is *practicable*, yet as a *rule* it is useless, if not injurious, and therefore either need not, or ought not to be practised. (II, 29–30)

Coleridge was certainly familiar with the criticism that both denied and doubted the propriety of the less stylized diction Wordsworth advocates, and his readers would have been just as familiar.[10] The speaker's paradoxical statement directs emphasis to what will prove to be Coleridge's major point. If by imitating the real language of men Wordsworth means no more than following the conventions of pure, distinct English, why is the rule 'as a rule . . . injurious'?

Any rule that directs the poet toward observation at the expense of meditation threatens or weakens imaginative self-consciousness. The poet does not imitate; he contemplates himself observing. Even grammar is but 'the laws of universal logic, applied to psychological materials' (II, 38).[11] The *Philosophical Lectures* provide a useful gloss here: the wise man realizes, Coleridge explains, that both observation and meditation are crucial. But which is primary? For Coleridge, as we have seen, meditation is primary. The hazard posed by the Preface is in its according primacy to observation – whether of real men or of beautiful landscapes.

The speaker's initial evaluation of rustic diction turns in part on a demographic quibble: those Wordsworth imitates – shepherds like Michael – are not '*low* and rustic'. Wordsworth mistakenly attributes to rural residence what he ought to attribute to the economic status and educational level of the self-employed working class. The speaker's argument seems to suggest that Coleridge would have been satisfied if Wordsworth had imitated educated and prosperous rustics because they are usually free from the affectations and ambitions of the rising urban middle class. But the speaker's further critique of rural life itself begins to reveal the basic issue: Wordsworth confuses the essentially rural character with the essentially self-conscious character. Setting is ultimately

:relevant to the self-conscious mind: Wordsworth's idea of low and rustic fe attributes to environment a power it does not have.

The speaker's defense of his position unfolds the aesthetic principles that ught to guide the poet's choice of characters. Properly imagined haracters must synthesize an idea with its image in the natural world:

> I adopt with full faith the principle of Aristotle, that poetry as poetry is essentially ideal . . . the *persons* of poetry must be clothed with *generic* attributes, with the *common* attributes of the class: not with such as one gifted individual might possibly possess, but such as from his situation it is most *probable* before-hand that he *would* possess. (II, 33–4)

Vordsworth's emphasis on the rural particularity of his essentially self-onscious characters is inappropriate because these particulars are not *ecessarily* related to the universal he is portraying. A long footnote escribes this error as both an aesthetic flaw and a failure to meet art's ltimate end:

> One of the essential properties of Geometry is not less essential to dramatic excellence; and Aristotle has accordingly required of the poet an involution of the universal in the individual. The chief differences are, that in Geometry it is the universal truth, which is uppermost in the consciousness; in poetry the individual form, in which the truth is clothed. (II, 33 n)

he poem's involution of ideal and individual transforms the reader's onsciousness in the same way that the unity and identity of parts does. he symbolic union of particular and universal leads to the 'temporary olivion' of the literal self because it is that change in the form (i.e. the tivity) of the reader's consciousness called 'aesthetic pleasure'. oleridge's argument shifts, from a critique of 'low and rustic' characters a critique of any character particularized by what is not essential. Only rough an essential and necessary relation between particular and aiversal does a character achieve the symbolic potence and moral value pected in literature. Only through such characters can a poet 'transport e mind to a sense of its possible greatness . . . suspending our individual collections and lulling them to sleep amid the music of nobler thoughts' I, 33 n).

The speaker's analysis of Wordsworth's poems about rustics suggests at the essentially self-conscious character is the poet himself. 'ordsworth's willingness to de-emphasize the observing eye – to look eadily at the object *qua* object – leads too often to a mere objectivity in nich the reader encounters nothing he might not have seen for himself.[12] he reader's vision is neither clarified nor purified by such poems, which .l to achieve the synthesis that first drew Coleridge to Wordsworth's rse (see I, 59–60). In the quoted passage from 'Michael' we watch

116 *The Design of* Biographia Literaria

Wordsworth describing, judging and explaining. We observe h observing. But in 'The Thorn' we see *what* the poet observes, not *how* Garrulous old seamen and their tales can be charming, if one is in th proper frame of mind to be charmed – but the charm is absent from th poem itself because the observing and transforming mind is relativel absent. Wordsworth in effect demands that his readers possess imaginativ powers equal to his own, as if he need only supply such materials as prove congenial to his own genius. In Coleridge's eyes, such methods reveal failure to understand the origins of aesthetic pleasure. In 'The Thorn' 'th parts . . . which might as well or still better have proceeded from the poet own imagination, and have been spoken in his own character, are tho which have given, and which will continue to give, universal delight' (I 36). In 'The Thorn', and even more clearly in 'The Mad Mother Wordsworth's excessively objective portraits have limited aesthetic powe because the muting of imagination allows the reader's fancy to have its ow way, to supply associations that do not belong to the created whole (I 35).[13]

Wordsworth's defense of rustic language *per se*, the speaker suggest reflects the same mistaken and excessive objectivity as his choice of rust characters. The 'best part of language' derives not from the best objec ('the beautiful and permanent forms of nature'[14]) but from the most pote imaginations. The best part of language is relational and philosophic; distinctly refers to the activities of the mind, not to the material world *p se*:

> . . . the educated man chiefly seeks to discover and express tho *connections* of things, or those relative *bearings* of fact to fact, from whic some more or less general law is deducible. For *facts* are valuable to wise man, chiefly as they lead to the discovery of the indwelling *la* which is the true *being* of things, the sole solution of their modes existence, and in the knowledge of which consists our dignity and o power. . . . The best part of human language, properly so called, derived from reflection on the acts of the mind itself. It is formed by voluntary appropriation of fixed symbols to internal acts, to process and results of imagination, the greater part of which have no place in t consciousness of uneducated man. . . . (II, 39–40)

The 'internal acts' that are the 'processes and results of imagination' are, course, perception and self-consciousness. Because a word refe simultaneously to the consciousness of its speaker and to the extern world, language is ideally suited for the discovery and communication relations – and hence principles (cf. I, 124–5, 146–7).[15] In a poet's hand language can generate the identity and unity of pleasure and trut particular and universal, part and whole that underlie aesthetic pleasur because the dual reference of words (a duality most evident in a goo image) reveals self-consciousness directly. The usage Wordswor advocates, the speaker explains, is not essentially rustic but essentially imaginative, and therefore the possession of no one social or economic class. The diction ideally suited for poetry is the poet's own.

It is worth pausing here to recall I. A. Richards's often-criticized argument that the difference between imaginative and fanciful verse derives from the number and quality of relations among 'parts or units of meaning'.[16] Grant the importance of *relation* in Coleridge's thought and in his idea of imaginative aesthetic response, and Richards's argument does not necessarily reduce the difference between fancy and imagination to a difference merely of degree. The superior intimacy of relation of imaginative verse, as Richards so brilliantly describes it, can only derive from the fact that each 'unit' relates to the others not as object to object, but in and through the ways in which each 'unit' relates to the expressive human consciousness. The more fully the self-conscious imagination synthesizes the moral spirit with the world it knows, the more coherently and beautifully will that world be represented in words. The quality of relation that the best part of language expresses underlies both poetry's aesthetic power and its moral value.

Chapter XVII's concluding remarks on 'in a state of excitement' draws a necessary distinction. Not any language used by the imaginative poet is thereby a poem. However deep Coleridge's interest in 'expressive' theories of poetry, his original realism in its literary bearings locates aesthetic value in textual features. These features are defined in chapter XVIII, but first, here in the concluding lines of chapter XVII, the speaker establishes the necessary link between textual features and the poet's consciousness. Passion, he argues, translates ability into performance, arousing the fullest possible exertion of faculties subordinated to each other:

For the nature of a man's words, where he is strongly affected by joy, grief, or anger, must necessarily depend on the number and quality of the general truths, conceptions and images, and of the words expressing them, with which his mind had been previously stored. For the property of passion is not to *create*; but to set in increased activity. (II, 42)

But neither is any impassioned speech thereby poetry. If it were, of course, then Wordsworth would be right: it is probable that actually passionate men would use a more vivid and poetic language than poets writing silently at their desks. Chapter XVIII, on metre, takes up this problem.

The transition from chapter XVII to chapter XVIII, over which I suspect most readers barely pause, deserves a moment of consideration. The transition is designed to be hurried past: chapter XVIII begins 'I conclude' and its opening paragraph closes the analysis of Wordsworth's idea of rustic language by arguing that he who can select and purify must possess principles that obviate the need to imitate at all. This style of connecting suggests that we are to see the chapters as distinct, but hardly separate. Why? Why not assemble chapters XVII and XVIII into one whole the size of chapter X or XII? The symmetries thereby established would have been elegant indeed, and utterly Coleridgean in their complexity.

But other Coleridgean subtleties are at work here. Coleridge often closes off one chapter or essay or section at the point where an underlying problem impedes progress, so that the next part can address that problem directly. One not alert to the growing impediment may feel that Coleridge has veered off into a tangent, when in fact he has delved under his main argument. These subterranean pursuits are most evident in the shifts into chapter II, on the irritability of men of genius, or chapter VIII, on idealism and materialism, or chapter IX, on mystics and German philosophers. Coleridge's habits in this regard suggest that the prudent reader must reflect carefully on chapters that end at unexpected points, and on chapters that engage unexpected issues. But the question remains – why the failure to orient us with conventional transitions? Why not tell us where he is going, and why? Coleridgean carelessness again? More inconsiderate haste? In part, perhaps; but in part also for reasons near to the heart of Coleridge's thought.

These impeding problems are commonly metaphysical ones and, as such, usually ask questions for which, Coleridge argued, no irrefutable logical answer is possible. To write a highly visible, sharply focussed transition, he would have to engage these difficult technical problems in all their original complexity. But on that technical level his own solutions are themselves lengthy and elaborate. He chooses instead – and most prudently – to engage only the practical consequences of the metaphysical problem, and furthermore to engage only those consequences immediately crucial for the problem at hand. (Given the sophistication of Coleridge's thinking, that sometimes excludes only a little of the technicalities; but in general I have observed notable restraint at various points throughout his prose works.) Readers are apt to lose themselves none the less because Coleridge's prudent decisions require transitions that are exquisitely sensitive to the needs and perceptions of the audience. Coleridge seldom demonstrates such tact. The reader perplexed by chapter divisions often has few options but rereading, searching diligently for the relations between one chapter and the next. It is an annoying task, because Coleridge has bungled a rudimentary aspect of his craft; but one who persists will always be rewarded.

The unformulated technical problem here, as I have suggested, concerns the relation between passion and language, or the distinction between the genial poet's ordinary use of language and his poetry. One might argue that any impassioned statements by an imaginative person ought to be imaginative, and thereby to possess interior relations that stir the attentive reader or auditor to imaginative aesthetic response. Common sense objects that the notion is nonsense, but chapter XVII does not preclude the error.

So far as I know, chapter XVIII's definition of the relation proceeds in the only style Coleridge ever uses on the problem: practical discussions of poems and of reading. These discussions appeal to the ear and to the mind of an experienced literary critic. They argue not about linguistics, but about prosody and figures.

Before considering this argument, let me summarize the position Coleridge has advanced in opposition to Wordsworth's. A poem's best speaker or its best character must be ideal, or a fully representative instance of the universal that the poem reveals. The best language for a poem is relational or philosophic. It follows from all this that the best model for the poet, or the best diction for poetry, is the language of the impassioned philosopher – the poet himself: 'No man was ever yet a great poet, without being at the same time a profound *philosopher*' (II, 19). This idea underlies Coleridge's disapproval of Wordsworth's dramatic poems (II, 36, 53, 55, 109), and his suggestion that Wordsworth's theory is not what it appears to be (II, 29, 69, 77, 95).

Chapter XVIII begins and ends by asserting that the interrelation of parts in poetry depends upon imagination. The genuinely educated (i.e. imaginative[17]) man can 'subordinate and arrange the different parts according to their relative importance, [so] as to convey [his meaning] at once and as an organized whole' (II, 44), whereas in 'pseudo-poesy' one finds only 'compulsory juxtaposition' (II, 65, 68). The highest degree of this accommodating of parts to the whole, we were told in chapter XIV, requires metre (II, 11). In chapter XVIII, Coleridge argues that metre is essential (II, 49–57), that the quality of metre and the quality of diction are interdependent (II, 57–63), and that both depend on the potence and facility of the poet's imagination. Accommodating Wordsworth to this argument requires interpreting his 'essential difference' as a matter of style – what Coleridge calls 'the formal construction, or architecture, of the words and phrases' (II, 48). Wordsworth's account of the relation between prose and poetry is not entirely clear, I grant; but Coleridge's interpretation of his meaning seems beyond defense. Coleridge's painstaking analysis of the word 'essential' serves primarily to rule out Wordsworth's most probable meaning: the neoclassic (or pseudo-neoclassic) stock of images and figures, now reduced to blurred clichés, are not absolutely requisite for poetry. Coleridge's motive is again out of sight, but not entirely out of reach. The error signaled by the equation, although not embedded in it, is the idea that expressive authenticity is an adequate measure of poetic diction if the expression reflects a pure and proper relation to the landscape. But the poet must look steadily at both his subject and his audience.[18] Wordsworth's ultimate error, in Coleridge's eyes, is his somewhat naïve faith that the unbiased reader will respond to the poet's 'subject' in the ways that the poet did.

Chapter XVIII is quintessentially Coleridgean in the style of its argument. Coleridge's theory of poetic diction, like his theory of mind, depends on intuition. Such a theory can be both accurate and rigorously conceived because all knowledge ultimately depends upon 'the IMMEDIATE, which dwells in every man, and on the original intuition or absolute affirmation of it' (I, 168). The critic, like the transcendental philosopher, cannot achieve 'objective' verification because the phenomenon he studies is not an object, but a self-conscious experience. The quality of a poem does not reside in the text as a thing in itself, but in the poem as read, in the poem's power to evoke a particular kind of response from the sensitive and experienced reader called the 'philosophic critic'. And yet the 'original realism' guarantees that the text as read and the text as a thing in itself are the same, so that it is possible to define and to argue about how specific features of the text *per se* affect the reader's response. The experience of reading is the foundation of all critical analysis. In many ways, the whole logical structure of chapter XVIII is designed to focus our detailed and self-conscious attention on the fact that reading poetry *feels* differently from reading prose. When this feeling is not evoked by a versified text, we are disappointed, we feel cheated of a pleasure that is our due – even if the bad lines offer interesting ideas or true statements.

The arguments on the origin and effects of metre define metre's significance both for the poet and for the reader. For the poet, metre expresses the balance of passion with order: the imagination spontaneously seeks to reassert the symmetry of passion and thought that an excess of passion threatens. This high-energy synthesis can be deliberately maintained, and its expression will be 'organized into *metre* . . . by a supervening act of the will and judgement, consciously and for the foreseen purpose of pleasure' (II, 50). The psychic and linguistic processes that require metre require imagery as well:

> this union [of '*spontaneous* impulse and of *voluntary* purpose'] can be manifested only in a frequency of forms and figures of speech (originally the offspring of passion, but now the adopted children of power) greater than would be desired or endured, where the emotion is not voluntarily encouraged and kept up for the sake of that pleasure, which such emotion, so tempered and mastered by the will, is found capable of communicating. (II, 50)

The poet's fancy and his imagination must co-operate both in the deliberate sustaining of the imagination's synthesis, and in the deliberately metrical and figurative expression of this synthesis. Voluntary and spontaneous powers of mind must interpenetrate.

The decision to write in metre is, after all, a deliberate choice. Metre *per se*, the assembling of iambic pentameter lines, is a mechanical (albeit skilled) task. The poem will succeed, however, only to the extent that the mechanical regularity of metre can be transformed into rhythm – only to the extent that metrical regularity is enlightened by variations and substitutions that reveal the passion in all its vitality. The poem's success also depends on the propriety of the forms and figures the poet chooses: it is 'the prerogative of poetic genius to distinguish by parental instinct its proper offspring from the changelings, which the gnomes of vanity or the fairies of fashion may have laid in its cradle' (II, 64–5). When imagination fails to vitalize the composing process itself, the poem's images degenerate into 'mere creatures of an arbitrary purpose, cold technical artifices of ornament or connection' (II, 64). In short, the cooperative agency of fancy and imagination in poetic diction ultimately depends upon the continued governing power of imagination itself.

Metre not only expresses the poet's sustained, modulated passion, but also arouses the reader's faculties. For the reader, metre 'tends to increase the vivacity and susceptibility both of the general feelings and of the attention'; it functions 'as a medicated atmosphere, or as wine during animated conversation' (II, 51). The speaker offers no proof of this point, just as he presumes the equally traditional link between the poet's passion and metrical expression. And once again he uses the connection as grounds for insisting on highly figurative diction:

> Where, therefore, correspondent food and appropriate matter are not provided for the attention and feelings thus aroused, there must needs be a disappointment felt; like that of leaping in the dark from the last step of a stair-case, when we had prepared our muscles for a leap of three or four. (II, 51)

The intimate relations among the poet's passion, prosody and diction and the reader's pleasure supply the grounds for Coleridge's particular judgments about the diction of individual poems: undistinguished or prosaic diction and flaccid prosody will vary together (see II, 53–4).

The speaker pauses here to refute the Preface in more detail, because Coleridge's argument to this point resembles Wordsworth's in several regards. Both poets assert the commonplace connection between metre and pleasurable excitement in both poet and reader. But for Wordsworth metre modulates the poet's impassioned expression, elevating or damping its effects as necessary to maximize the reader's pleasure.[19] For Wordsworth, metre and diction are complementary opposites; for Coleridge, they are the coinherent expressions of a prior balance within the poet's consciousness. Coleridge makes so much of this point because Wordsworth's error apparently underlies his inferior poems (II, 53). Metres do not modulate passion to create an integral aesthetic effect: the synthetic imagination does. The poems to which the speaker refers resemble each other principally in the disproportionate bulk of physical details that are not immediately requisite to the poet's impassioned response to the event depicted in the poem. Once again, Coleridge complains that Wordsworth attributes to things themselves – to metres *per se*, or to the edematous ankles of old huntsmen – a power that resides not in the thing but in imagination.

'Notwithstanding the beauties which are to be found in each of them where the poet interposes the music of his own thoughts', the speaker remarks, these poems would have been 'more delightful to me in prose . . . in a moral essay or pedestrian tour' (II, 53). Where Wordsworth's diction fails to provide appropriate matter for the reader's awakened feelings and attention, 'the metre itself must often become feeble' (II, 54). The speaker paradoxically attributes this excessive objectivity and prosodical flatness not to a lack of passion, as his theory would predict, but, rather, to 'the susceptibility of [Wordsworth's] own genius' (II, 54). As we shall see in much more detail later on, Coleridge deflects this potentially crucial failure into a criticism not of Wordsworth's impassioned imagination but, rather, of his fancy. Wordsworth must attend more carefully to the general state of association if he is to communicate his imaginative vision intelligibly (II, 105). When he fails to accommodate his own exquisite 'susceptibility' to the needs of blunter minds, his prosody and diction are apt not to communicate his passion. They are apt to be prosaic. And such prosaicism, like his theoretical errors, is the fault of none but a genius. Coleridge himself makes a characteristic mistake at this point: the paradox presented here gives rise to most of chapter XXII, but there is little that communicates this link to even the most sympathetic reader.

The speaker's third argument for metre defines the relation between passion and metre in more generally applicable terms. Lyrics are not the only poetic kind, after all; and even lyrics are not unrelentingly emotional. The speaker begins with references back to chapter XIV: metre is essential to poetry because it excites the distinct attention to parts that underlies aesthetic pleasure. But not all parts of a poem are essentially poetic – not all parts are the immediate expression of imaginative vision (II, 10–11, 55–6). There must be a mordaunt – a chemical fixative – to integrate these relatively unpoetic parts within the whole. This mordaunt is the poet's excitement in the act of composing. Such excitement is not an emotion *per se*, but it is none the less a passion in the philosophic sense. As a passion, it, too, will require and involve metrical, figurative expression. The speaker's fourth argument restates this point more simply: poetry requires metre because metre underlies both the integral relation of distinguishable parts and the aesthetic pleasure of imaginative reading. The fifth argument appeals to literary tradition – a weighty argument for a conservative like Coleridge, but, as time has shown, his least reliable. Literary history no longer so unequivocally supports the necessity of metre.

In the last part of chapter XVIII the speaker apparently moves from abstract theorizing to practical examination of lines from Gray, Spenser and Daniel. But Coleridge is very seldom 'redundant' in this way. Although never losing hold of metre as the contested issue, Coleridge shifts his predominant argument to qualities of imagery and then, more generally, to diction in the comprehensive sense. He can shift emphasis gracefully because animated prosody and adeptly figurative expression are the coinherent manifestations of imaginatively sustained passion. From the proper perspective he seems not to shift at all, but to make the implicit explicit.

Wordsworth's use of Gray, and Coleridge's use of Wordsworth's use, can be read as subsuming many of the complex delicate shifts in literary sensibility in the late eighteenth century. Ransom has argued that Gray himself in this sonnet criticizes the inadequacies of the inherited 'poetic diction'.[20] Coleridge uses the lines to present the guiding principles of his own idea of diction. First, the essentially poetic diction may have qualities in common with prose, but it will also possess qualities unique to itself and not suitable for prose (II, 57–8; see also II, 50). This argument allows the speaker to accede to Wordsworth's account of poetry's kinship with prose without 'agreeing' that they are identical twins.[21]

Secondly, the speaker asserts 'GOOD SENSE' – not equality with prose – as the only proper measure of poetic imagery. Gray's use of 'Phoebus' differs from Spenser's because Gray's line 'conveys incongruous images, [and] because it confounds the cause and the effect, the real *thing* with the personified *representative* of the thing' (II, 58). As the speaker has already argued at length, this pseudo-poetic modern imagery reflects both blunt sensibility and enfeebled imagination. One need not equate poetry and prose to demonstrate its fraudulence. As the contrasting lines from Spenser demonstrate, quality depends not on the image *per se*, but on its place and function in the whole. Neither rustics' diction nor pseudo-classical diction can supply the lack of imagination.

But 'GOOD SENSE' alone is not a sufficient measure. Daniel's lines are full of good sense. Daniel's diction fails not because it is incoherent, but because it lacks the 'more frequent employment of picturesque and vivifying language' that ought to distinguish poetry from prose (II, 50). One can obliterate Daniel's metre by transcribing his verse without its proper lineation. Given Coleridge's idea of the essential interdependence of diction and metre, the failure of one testifies to the other's failure. Daniel's commonplace images – disorder as disease, society as a fabric – do not catalyze the reader's imagination into activity. There is here no 'union of deep feeling with profound thought', nor do the lines awaken any 'freshness of sensation' or 'new feeling' concerning English history (I, 59–60). We remain firmly planted on the Cis-Alpine side of consciousness, in the day-to-day world of inanimate objects. Yet notice that the speaker does not develop this indictment as fully as I have developed it. For Coleridge, enough has been said when he demonstrates (or invites the reader to discover) the limpness of Daniel's prosody. He relies on the reader's concurrent judgment, as he has done before when invoking the original realism. In his criticism, no less than in his metaphysics, Coleridge requires an extraordinarily active, thoughtful reader.

Having finished with Gray, Coleridge draws another statement from the Preface so as to argue that good sense and aesthetic potence apply to metre as fully as they apply to imagery. Wordsworth errs, the speaker contends, in claiming that 'the distinction of rhyme and metre is voluntary and uniform': prosody varies in quality just as imagery does. In neither case is the reader 'at the mercy of the poet', because the reader has – or ought to have – relevant criteria for judgment.

And this point unfolds into chapter XVIII's concluding issue: literary value-judgments. The end of criticism, the speaker argues, is to establish the principles of writing, not the principles of judgment. And the first principle of writing is that the poet must be guided by a meditative and fully self-conscious imagination:

> But if it be asked, by what principles the poet is to regulate his own style . . . I reply; by principles, the ignorance or neglect of which would convict him of being no *poet*, but a silly or presumptuous usurper of the name! By the principles of grammar, logic, psychology! . . . by such a knowledge of the facts, material and spiritual, that most appertain to his art, as, if it have been governed and applied by *good sense*, and rendered instinctive by habit, becomes the representative and reward of our past conscious reasonings, insights, and conclusions, and acquires the name of Taste[.] . . . by the power of imagination proceeding upon the *all in each* of human nature[.] By *meditation*, rather than *observation*[.] And by the latter in consequence only of the former[.] . . . Could a rule be given from *without*, poetry would cease to be poetry, and sink into a mechanical art. It would be [a fashioning] not [a creation]. The *rules* of the IMAGINATION are themselves the very powers of growth and production. (II, 63–5; phrases in brackets translated from the Greek)

The speaker immediately insists that such criticism none the less supplies an adequate basis for value-judgments. Such a critic has no difficulty distinguishing Donne's apostrophes from Cowley's Pindaric Odes, or 'poetic fervor self-impassioned' from 'the startling *hysteric* of weakness over-exerting itself' (II, 65–7).

Adequate judgments flow from distinguishing the origins of such verse in the powers and quality of the poet's mind – provided, of course, that one has a fully developed theory of such origins, and their relations to aesthetic power and to literary form. (A theory, of course, that Wordsworth had no intention of elaborating in his Preface.) Pseudo-poesy derives neither from fancy nor from imagination, but from the mere wit (or degraded fancy). Its juxtapositions of incompatible things are not even unified by a coherent associational flow, much less by imagination's unifying vision. In asserting his grounds for value-judgment, Coleridge alludes again to the coherent development of the speaker's idea of literature, because the speaker in his youth had judged the merits of a poem by faculties to which it appealed (I, 14). Wordsworth's poems had appealed quite powerfully to the speaker's imagination, yet Wordsworth's theory (as interpreted here) neatly reverses almost every detail of an imaginative theory of composition. 'There is not', the speaker none the less affirms, '. . . a man now living, who has, from his own inward experience, a clearer intuition, than Mr. Wordsworth himself . . . [of] the true sources of *genial* discrimination' (II, 64).

8 Wordsworth and the Imaginative Particular

> . . . a man's principles, on which he grounds his Hope
> and his Faith, are the life of his life. We live by Faith,
> says the philosophic Apostle; and faith without prin-
> ciples is but a flattering phrase for wilful positiveness,
> or fanatical bodily sensation. Well, and of good right
> therefore, do we maintain with more zeal, than we
> should defend body or estate, a deep and inward con-
> viction, which is as the moon to us; and like the moon
> with all its massy shadows and deceptive gleams, it
> yet lights us on our way, poor travellers as we are, and
> benighted pilgrims.
>
> *The Friend*, I, 97

Having argued against Wordsworth's views on rustic language and poetic diction, the speaker claims that Wordsworth does not in fact believe the theory that the speaker has been systematically demolishing for forty pages. Fortunately so: by definition the self-conscious genius knows what he is about. Despite his own 'inward experience', Wordsworth 'suffered himself to express, in terms at once too large and too exclusive, his predilection for a style the most remote possible from the false and showy splendor which he wished to explode' (II, 64, 70). Chapter XIX defines the neutral style Wordsworth 'meant' to defend, and illustrates it with excerpts from Chaucer and Herbert. Yet even this is not what Wordsworth *really* meant, because the style of his own poems is both specifically poetic and highly individual. Chapter XX illustrates this imaginative individuality. Chapter XXI analyzes the critical methods of those who have condemned Wordsworth; they have misunderstood Wordsworth's individuality, and mismanaged their own. Chapter XXII provides what such critics do not: a 'fair and philosophical' examination of Wordsworth's poems on their own merits.

Once again the analysis of Wordsworth also serves as an exogenous skeleton for Coleridge's arguments about other things. Chapters XX and XXI assert the need for particularity in poetry and in criticism. Chapter XXI explains the quality of particular which is essential to philosophic criticism. Chapter XXII does the same for poetry: Wordsworth's defects illustrate the proper role of fancy in providing appropriate particulars; his beauties define the synthesis of universal and particular that imagination and fancy together achieve. Through self-conscious imagination, the poet knows the interpenetration of particular and universal. The symbolic character of language expresses this interpenetration; the associative power of fancy renders the expression effective. It follows that one can work backward from objective features of texts to their origins in the relative activity of fancy and imagination. Chapter XXII thus complements chapters VII and XII, demonstrating the concrete manifestations of powers defined abstractly. The concluding chapter not only laments the disproportion between public abuse and actual deserving that has been the fate of both men; it also draws us back to the foundation of 'original realism': the unity of being and knowing in imaginative self-consciousness.

Throughout these chapters Coleridge explains how imagination governs fancy. This is a major question, as Lowes demonstrates in *The Road to Xanadu*. Lowes's understatement has lost none of its force in the half-century and more since he wrote: 'imagination must have materials on which to work'. And, as both his book and Baker's *The Sacred River* fully demonstrate, association supplies imagination with the material it needs.[1] Yet not all materials are suitable: the thoroughness of an energetic fancy virtually ensures that much of what wells up will be inferior, or at least unworkable. The sources Lowes cites are remarkable more for their dross than for their gold.

Fancy's role may be compared to an architect's shipments of bricks and beams. Everything depends upon what he does with his materials, but without them he can do nothing at all. He cannot embody his prior vision. The architect's creative process stretches out over time what probably happens almost instantaneously for a poet. Fancy is a mode of memory emancipated from time and space; its associative power collects from the artist's past those words and images and rhythms generally suitable to his present purpose. Yet these remain disparate heaps of things until imagination begins to work with and within what it has 'sent' fancy to gather. In imagination's final product, the diverse materials are fragments no longer, but parts of a whole which places each within a network of relations. These relations are so many and so intimate that each part is rendered integral both to the other parts and to the whole as such. Or, to put this matter another way, fancy's function is merely instrumental, but it is none the less a crucial instrument.

Coleridge's analysis of Wordsworth's faults proceeds apace with his explanation of the principles by which one selects from the plethora fancy provides. In the most general of terms, Coleridge praises Wordsworth's vivid particularity and his highly individual voice, but criticizes the welter of meaningless detail and foggy moralizing that intrudes when Wordsworth loses control over his vision and his voice. These judgments strike me as apt, although in my judgment Coleridge exaggerates

Wordsworth's faults to facilitate his own account of fancy. His acknow-ledging how seldom Wordsworth errs does not adequately counter-balance the detail to which these faults are examined, nor the tones in which they are condemned. Coleridge's tone and manner, especially concerning Wordsworth's apparently pantheist empiricism, perhaps make more sense if one keeps the 1805 *Prelude* in mind, and the still-vital plans for the great philosophic poem. These chapters are probably relevant to much more than the poems they particularly examine. Wordsworth's faults are explicated first because fancy's role is clearest when most inappropriate. When genially empowered judgment properly manages fancy, its contri-bution is dissolved, diffused, transmogrified. '"As we our food into our nature change"' (II, 12). Celebrating Wordsworth's beauties last allows Coleridge to end his critical essay both with resounding praise for the philosophic poet, and with his last, most resonant account of imagination's power.

Coleridge's account of Wordsworth's genial powers is matched by renewed emphasis on the speaker's own philosophic genius. Chapter XIX's references to German literature and to the history of English pronunciation enforce again the speaker's scholarship; the passage from Chaucer, like the earlier one from Spenser (II, 59), pinpoints the issue in question most precisely. By its brevity and simplicity, the chapter qualifies as what Coleridge elsewhere calls a 'landing-place': a pause in a sustained and difficult argument, often an illustration of a practical or amusing aspect of the matter at hand. Herbert's poems illustrate both the neutral style, and the tendency for poets of his day to convey 'in the most fantastic language . . . the most trivial thoughts' (II, 73) or to sacrifice 'the passion and passionate flow of poetry, to the subtleties of intellect, and to the starts of wit' (I, 15). The chapter offers two short 'burlesque' passages from Drayton and from Herbert, and then three reasonably characteristic seventeenth-century religious poems. The first two of these poems represent disorder of intellect; the last two, moral disorder; the central one, the relation between physical and moral loss. Yet the poems do more than illustrate the range and power of the neutral style. On the one hand, it is clear that the three religious poems display the translucency of the spiritual within the natural. 'The Bosom Sin' reappears in *Aids to Reflection* as an illustrative commentary on the reluctance of many to know themselves – a reluctance evident in anonymous critics (*AR*, 75 n–76). But, on the other hand, this whole set of poems seems inescapably comic. The 'ludicrous tone of feeling' remains. What is going on here?

The speaker playfully and indirectly suggests an analogy between his own 'obscurity' and that of metaphysical poets. Drayton's reader wonders why he must 'wrest invention'; Coleridge has abundantly explained the arresting new vision that the genius supplies. The poet's or philosopher's 'lunacy' is literal only for the unperceptive. Both 'unravel' ordinary perceptions in order to reweave, restoring our consciousness of the transcendental in part by heightening our sensitivity to words. For both, clarity and unity depend upon the reader's ability to discern the relation between verbal play and substantial idea. The speaker laughs at his reputation, and recognizes its necessity: the neutral style includes both Herbert's poems and his own prose. The earlier bitterness concerning his reputation is softened here, and the speaker as a distinct personality appears more clearly at this point than he has for several chapters. Yet Coleridge's failure to close chapter XIX leaves us up in the air. Chapter XX – '*The former subject continued*' – picks up the main argument without reference to these poems. I suggest that Coleridge's fancy was caught by the analogy I have sketched, but that he could not see how to subordinate it to his account of Wordsworth's style. Rather than revise, he picks up where he left off, with a somewhat apologetic chapter headnote.

Chapter XX explains that the neutral style is not Wordsworth's, nor is the rustic style (II, 77, 83). It is, the speaker wryly notes, 'a singular and noticeable fact' that Wordsworth's theory advocates a diction quite different from his own (II, 77). Wordsworth's imaginative individuality is stylistically evident in 'modes of connections . . . [and] breaks and transitions' as well as in 'grammatical connections' – in those means whereby an author depicts not just things, but relations (II, 83–4). In these qualities his style is as remote as possible from actual rustics' styles, and near instead to Milton and Shakespeare. At his best, which the speaker amply illustrates, Wordsworth brings physical objects 'before the mind, as the actions of a living and acting power' (II, 84). He awakens in others a 'meditative mood' (II, 85). His poetry is both aesthetically powerful and capable of showing that the being of all things, both windswept trees and human minds, is ultimately an act. This account of Wordsworth's successful fusion of individual expression and universal truth stands between Coleridge's balanced accounts of the excessive concreteness and philosophical errors marring both Wordsworth's theory and some of his poems. It prepares us for chapter XXII's more detailed account of how his very best poetry combines vivid particularity with stunning imaginative insight.

Anonymous criticism has failed to acknowledge the character of Wordsworth's individuality, condemning him for trivial characters and ludicrous or exaggerated responses, because it cannot (or will not) properly manage its own particulars. Chapter XXI analyzes the misplaced concreteness that vitiates anonymous criticism. 'Fair and philosophic' criticism requires a balance and blending of universal principles and particulars from the text to be judged. Arguments conducted in this way result in conclusions that the reader accepts 'in the light of judgement and in the independence of free-agency' (II, 85). They appeal to the activity of will, not the passivity of sensation; they engage the judgment, not the emotions. Such philosophical debate underlies popular government, just as demagoguery underlies tyranny (I, 121–32). Thus, the speaker would respect as nobility any group of critics following 'fair and philosophical' procedures: they are natural leaders (see I, 124–5, 155–6). Unlike the violent hurricanes of fanaticism and anonymous criticism, philosophic criticism is a windmill grinding grain: 'All the two and thirty winds alike are its friends. Of the whole wide atmosphere it does not desire a single finger-breadth more than what is necessary for its sails to turn round in' (II, 88).

The announced plan for the *Edinburgh Review* promised such philosophic criticism, but the magazine has not remained faithful to its plan. The speaker condemns not the 'asperity of the damnatory style' (which he does not hesitate to use himself), but the inappropriate particularity (II, 86). The particulars on which anonymous critics dwell reveal that their principles derive from politics and personality, not 'the essence of human nature' (II, 58; cf. I, 44). When they do not draw particulars from irrelevant details of the poet's private life, these critics offer either no particulars at all, or particulars that fail to illustrate the fault they would condemn. The speaker cites one such condemned passage as evidence that behind such criticism one finds a diseased moral feeling (II, 92–4): what the critic condemned other readers have found consonant with 'an intuitive certainty in their own inward experience' (II, 91). Minds crippled by illogic and a degraded fancy cannot respond properly to poetry. In a quick sketch of what will preoccupy chapter XXII the speaker explains that a poem's 'sense' must be 'consonant with all the best convictions of my understanding' and its 'imagery and diction [must collect] round these convictions my noblest as well as my most delightful feelings' (II, 91). Only imagination can so completely fuse both the understanding's knowledge of the true and the false with all a man's passions, and in doing so imagination relies on the drawing power of an enlightened fancy.

Like Wordsworth's 'Essay Supplementary to the Preface' of 1815, this chapter's denunciation in effect gives up any hope of winning the approval of these powerful critics and their readers. It is the high point of the condemnation to which Coleridge had been urged by friends.[2] *Biographia Literaria* naturally provoked vitriolic reviews. However unfortunate for the subsequent reputation of the book, this reaction could not have been a surprise. In some ways, Coleridge traps the reviewers quite handily: when they denounce him for diseased egotism, rather than engage the complex philosophic problems he engages, they cast themselves as fanatics.

Before considering chapter XXII, let us look back a moment over the preceding three chapters, and then forward to chapter XXIV. Chapters XIX, XX and XXI are swifter afoot, and far less dense, than any passage of comparable length since chapter X. And, like chapter X, they serve as a prelude to a long, slow, technical argument. Just as chapter X contrasts the speaker's genial quest for principles with the political and philosophic fanaticism of his day, so these chapters contrast Wordsworth's genial reform of poetic diction with the literary fanaticism of his day. They do so in part by locating his style within the English tradition, and in part by evaluating the kinds of reviews his work has had. The speaker assimilates the apparent plainness of Wordsworth's style – its lack of high rhetorical ornament – to the 'neutrality' of poets from Chaucer to Herbert. The assimilation suggests that Wordsworth's plainness is ancient and pure, not primitivist or 'democratic' or empiricist. Although the speaker hastens to add that this poetry is not Wordsworth's best, nor his most characteristic, the chapter none the less suggests that Coleridge recognized and understood Wordsworth's aesthetic purposes rather more fully than chapters XVII and XVIII alone might suggest.

And it is significant that this recognition comes so closely interwoven with the familiar indictments of anonymous critics. Because their imaginations are feeble, their sensibility is blunt. Their relation to reality – textual or physical – is vague and foggy. These are the very last readers from whom one ought to expect the acuity, the sensitivity or the subtlety that Wordsworth's plain and 'objective' descriptions can demand. But in *Biographia Literaria* the phrase 'anonymous criticism' stands more for the taste and sensibility of the age than it does for the works of men like Hazlitt and Jeffrey. From this perspective, then, Coleridge censures Wordsworth not only for writing bad poetry, but also for failing to adapt his style to his actual readers. The complaint applies to Coleridge's own work, I have argued; and this elaborate, somewhat indirect reflexivity often characterized Coleridge's advice to his friends. In chapter XXII, when Coleridge contends that Wordsworth's lack of rhetorical finesse does result in bad poetry, he seeks more to explain fancy's role in aesthetically effective poetry than to account for Wordsworth's contemporary status.

Chapter XXI's account of anonymous criticism also connects chapters II and X with chapter XXIV, so as to integrate the 'anonymous criticism' theme with the seminal philosophic issue of causality. As we saw, in chapters V to IX the speaker complains that materialist associationism cannot account for causality, and thereby denies both personal agency and moral responsibility. He builds his alternative account of cognition upon the testimony of conscience that we are indeed responsible for our acts and our motives: the properly formed conscience requires imagination's self-consciousness, or the distinct knowledge of the acts and forms of one's own will. And, as we have seen in chapters I to IV and XII, imagination also provides distinct knowledge of the particular physical world: the genius is blessed with exquisite sensibility. The philosophic critic, no less than the poet, needs imagination, because argument no less than poetry requires not only the distinct knowledge of both causality and particulars, but also a delicate, astute apprehension of how the two are related. Anonymous critics cannot support their argument with particulars because their dislike is caused by politics not by the poems, and because their response to particulars is warped by anger and envy. The quality of their criticism reveals not just aesthetic failure, or bad taste, but a deeply grounded moral failure as well. As the speaker later explains, they write and act in bad conscience (II, 129–30).

The *Biographia*'s enormously complex arguments about causality and particularity lie submerged beneath the lucidity of chapter XXII. As I have suggested, from one perspective Wordsworth's misplaced causality and his excessive particularity suggest the undue influence of Locke and Hartley. But there are other perspectives; the issue is not as simple as this. Coleridge's original realism guarantees that the animated nature Wordsworth describes is 'really there'. Is the poet, then, required – as the philosopher surely is – to maintain, distinctly and explicitly, and at all times, that the animation is 'reflected' not 'bestowed'? Must good poetry first of all be good epistemology? No. Obviously not: 'a poem is that species of composition, which is opposed to works of science, by proposing for its *immediate* object pleasure, not truth' (II, 10). Even though the ultimate object of poetry is truth, and even though the greatest works of art will be found to achieve that ultimate end, the critic can demand neither doctrinal nor philosophic orthodoxy as a measure of artistic success. All he can rightly demand is good sense and fidelity to nature, and the proper interdependence of parts. These alone directly affect the reader's aesthetic, imaginative response.

But these are sufficient measures to discredit what Coleridge calls Wordsworth's 'vague, misty . . . Confusion of God with the World', because his excessive particularity and empiricism reflect a school philosophy that *does* contradict the common sense of every man (I, 77, 82–3, 178–9).[3] But these measures require some subtlety: too literally applied, they would devastate Wordsworth's attempts to explore the psyche, attempts surely beyond the ken of the actual common sense of most of his contemporaries. All of which is perhaps only to say that no one's critical principles – and especially not those of one like Coleridge – can be applied without regard for judgment and taste. Coleridge's application, although profoundly rhetorical, also attends closely to the interior relations of the work itself, because these relations most firmly govern the reader's response. His balancing subjective response with objective textual features presupposes his whole idea of language. Poems can most fully express *and most fully communicate* what imagination reveals because words – regarded broadly, as language itself – express the consciousness common to their users. But words also express the particular consciousness of their individual speaker. The consciousness common to the group, and the special imaginative consciousness of the poet, are intelligibly related through the poem by means of the real world to which words also refer. In seeing not just *what* but also *how* the poet sees, as well as his impassioned response, we gain access to the moral unity of what it is to be a human being, and what it is to be a conscious thinker. The greatest poems render concretely accessible Coleridge's whole transcendental analysis of consciousness.

And that is why Coleridge so sharply condemns Wordsworth's pantheism, and his faith in the aesthetic and moral power of a keenly described scene or situation. These must be flaws, *demonstrable* flaws in his art, or what is to be the clear, concrete enactment of Coleridge's orthodox Christian transcendentalism turns instead into the ghost of Spinoza. Coleridge wants Schelling's view of art, but St John's idea of Man, God and Logos. Wordsworth's best poetry does enact this synthesis, the speaker has been saying all along; but Wordsworth's theory and at least some of his poems show all too clearly the weak side, the dark side of Coleridge's own vision. Thus it is that chapter XXII's account of the defects and the beauties of Wordsworth's verse recapitulates many of the distinctions between empiricist associationism and Coleridge's original realism. In the *Biographia*'s first volume, this distinction is focused subjectively: the two philosophies are evaluated as rival accounts of mental experience and cognition. The focus here is objective: literally faithful observation *versus* the imaginative association of properly managed fancy as rival origins of vividly particular, aesthetically potent verse. Wordsworth's most authentic, most characteristic poems, like the speaker's most authentic, most characteristic philosophy, accommodate fully the rival claims of imagination's transforming power and the green world's serene stability.

The duality of Coleridge's design attains a culminating richness in chapter XXII, where the critique of Wordsworth's poems proceeds simultaneously with a detailed explanation of the correlative operation of fancy and imagination. Wordsworth's defects and excellences are closely related to one another (II, 115), as one would expect in the writings of genius (I, 43). His usual balance between thought and sensibility sometimes deviates into prolixity and bombast. His proper fidelity to nature sometimes degenerates into excessive detail. His pure and individual diction sometimes lapses into undistinguished, unimpassioned prosaicism. His usual balance of thought and image with subject-matter allows him to write truly philosophic and imaginative poems, but the loss of this proportion mires him in a confused variety of materialism and pantheism. Both his flaws and his beauties demonstrate that the fullest aesthetic pleasure requires appropriate particulars (i.e. properly managed fancy), because the poet reaches the reader's imagination only through his detailed representations of the reality known by both. Yet, to have their wonted effect, these representations must form parts of an aesthetic whole, one in which parts are interdependent. Wordsworth's defects are consistently described as comprising the organic unity of his poems, and thus their aesthetic power.

The first defect, occasional prosaicism, draws on the necessary relation between passion and imagery to explain that full aesthetic power requires *sustained* imagery. The reader does not maintain the pleasurable excitement through his own imaginative power, but through the images:

Even in real life, the difference is great and evident between words used
as the *arbitrary marks* of thought, our smooth market-coin of
intercourse, with the image and superscription worn out by currency;
and those which convey pictures either borrowed from *one* outward
object to enliven and particularize some *other*; or used allegorically to
body forth the inward state of the person speaking[.] . . . excitement
aris[es] from concentered attention[.] . . . in the perusal of works of
literary *art*, we *prepare* ourselves for such language; and the business of
the writer . . . is so to raise the lower and neutral tints . . . to produce the
effect of a *whole*. Where this is not achieved in a poem, the metre merely
reminds the reader of his claims in order to disappoint them. (II, 98)

Images concenter attention by conveying relations which transcend space
and time (II, 16) and obliterate the sense of self (II, 33 n) by changing the
form of activity of consciousness. But for the poet to sustain imagery
effectively, for the images to contribute to unity and identity of parts in the
whole, he must adapt each image not simply to the relation it is to convey,
but also to the other images, to the whole system of relations to which it
belongs.

But not any images, and not any concrete descriptive details, will suffice.
As the account of the second defect explains, particulars should reveal
universals: the historian records particulars *per se*, but the poet offers '*truth
operative, and by effects continually alive*' (II, 102). The poem's visual
descriptions should generate simultaneous wholes, not geometrical
constructions nor topographical surveys (II, 102–3; cf. II, 16–18). The
imaginative whole is intuited, not assembled from parts; it consists in
relations conveyed by images. The most effective image, consequently, is a
symbol that 'partakes of the Reality which it renders intelligible' (*LS*, 30).
The poem's particulars reveal a living truth only when they succeed in
creating an imaginative whole.

But what interrelation of particulars generates an imaginative whole?
The poet must forge unity from the reader's conventional associations with
the poem's particulars. This associative activity unfolds to define an
imaginative center that only the poet sees beforehand, and this is the only
way in which rare imaginative vision becomes intelligible generally.[4] For
the poet to shape the reader's associations, the reader in turn must accept
all the poem's parts and interrelations of parts. He must not discard or
ignore some. Poet and reader thus co-operate: the reader must be willing to
'believe for his own sake', to 'permit the images presented to work by their
own force, without either denial or affirmation of their real existence by the
judgement' (II, 101, 107). The poet in turn must not provoke probability-
judgments, or contrast poetic faith with real faith by too closely
juxtaposing poetic fiction and real fact (II, 107). The poet must work from
within his best estimates of the reader's literary habits and his conventional
associations.

Yet the Preface suggests Wordsworth's distrust of such expectations.

And he refuses at times to appeal to the general state of association because he wants to 'attack and subdue' its pernicious associations with economic and social status (II, 104). The speaker responds that truth and aesthetic pleasure may differ only because of the fallen state of men, yet this is the reality with which the poet must cope.

> Now till the blessed time shall come, when truth itself shall be pleasure, and both shall be so united, as to be distinguishable in words only, not in feeling, it will remain the poet's office to proceed upon that state of association, which actually exists as *general*; instead of attempting first to *make* it what it ought to be, and then to let the pleasure follow. . . . For the communication of pleasure is the introductory means by which alone the poet must expect to moralize his readers. (II, 104–5)

By aiming directly at truth, not pleasure, Wordsworth arouses neither aesthetic response nor moral conviction. Such works are neither good poems nor good sermons, because the particulars embody neither universals nor principles (II, 104–5). The speaker echoes his earlier appeal to Aristotle, and calls down the authority of Horace: the poetic particular must not perplex or contradict the reader's feeling if the poem is to achieve the ideal unity and universality proper for art.[5] Decorum remains a useful principle because the poet cannot hope to control the reader's associations. He can only try to elicit those associations most useful for his own ends.

Decorum also helps supply the quality of unity essential for aesthetic imaginative activity in the reader, and its role reveals more fully what an imaginative fancy contributes to aesthetic power. For Coleridge, the universal and permanent exist within the particular and transitory if one has grasped the relation between the being of the particular and the being of the universal. One must, then, scrutinize a single tulip, or the fleeting impression of a beggar or a bed of daffodils, to clarify not the sensations of things, but the consciousness of the self's perceiving. But, for an image to lead the reader to an imaginative apprehension of the underlying relations (whether in reality itself, or in the poem), the image must seem an appropriate object for the poet's meditation. Images will not 'work by their own force' on a reader who judges the poet's meditative energy misspent. An imaginative fancy seeks images that will both provide an adequate vehicle for the poet's meditative passion, and appeal to the ordinary reader. Without the poet's imagination, there is no unity; without the reader's correlative response, the unity is not perceived.

Concern for the reader's expectations, feelings and associations is equally evident in the speaker's account of the third defect: Wordsworth's 'undue predilection for the *dramatic* form' (II, 109; cf. II, 36, 53, 55). Such poems are either good plays, and thus disconcerting for the reader of poems; or they are bad plays, and thus not convincing. Coleridge's enforcing generic distinctions, like his enforcing decorum, provides grounds in post-Kantean psychology for ancient and valuable critical principles. Wordsworth's errors matter not because he fails to imitate properly a given form, which in turn imitates a given aspect of reality, but because he confuses his readers. Conventional associations with dramatic dialogue generate stylistic expectations that Wordsworth disappoints.[6]

In citing the last two defects, the speaker explains that effective images and particulars – an effective style – must be suitable not only for the audience, but also for the poem's essential balance between thought and feeling (II, 109; cf. II, 19, 49–51). When the feelings are disproportionate to the objects described, the thought cannot progress. The relations among parts are befuddled. When thoughts and images are disproportionate to the originating situation, the poet's impassioned response seems ridiculous. Several illustrations reveal that this error arises when Wordsworth fails to distinguish between associations appropriate to his ideas, and those accidentally linked with it in his mind from the situation in which the idea originated (II, 109–10). These inappropriate associations are worse than merely ineffective associations, because they are illogical uses of words:

> If the words are taken in the common sense, they convey an absurdity; and if, in contempt of dictionaries and custom, they are so interpreted as to avoid the absurdity, the meaning dwindles into some bald truism. Thus you must at once understand the words *contrary* to their common import, in order to arrive at any *sense*; and *according* to their common import, if you are to receive from them any feeling of *sublimity* or *admiration*. (II, 114)

Wordsworth's lapses into this pseudo-sublime lead him into an incoherent pantheism that the speaker criticizes most sharply.

To set this famous critique of the 'Intimations' ode in its full context, however, we must pause for a summary that will transform the speaker's proscriptions into prescriptions. Properly literary language, he has said, conveys pictures either to enliven and particularize objects or to embody the inward state of the speaker. These properly literary descriptions and characterizations must convey '"*truth operative, and by effects continually alive*"' through the pleasure they arouse (II, 102). They must, therefore, remain generally conventional or representative or decorous, lest the reader be confused or distracted, and thus not pleased, and thus not instructed. Yet they must also remain consistent and congruous with their dramatic speaker, whose emotional and intellectual responses to the objects and characters he encounters must therefore be both authentic and believable. In sum, a genially directed fancy maintains properly literary (i.e. aesthetically potent) relations between the poetic voice and the reader by gathering vivid particulars whose associative range covers the intersection between fully imaginative sensibility and the common sensibility. Only by manipulating the ordinary reader's ordinary responses can the poet transform the reader's consciousness into an imaginative echo of his own. That is why Coleridge so consistently describes critical taste as itself an imaginative power: the best reader, the truly philosophic critic, will most fully share the poet's imaginative sensibility. When Wordsworth misgoverns his fancy, when he presumes that his readers will – or ought to – associate exactly as he associates *even when his associations are random or arbitrary*, then he becomes dull, prosaic, confusing and fragmentary.

So would any poet. Little to this point in chapter XXII specifically characterizes Wordsworth himself, rather than Wordsworth the *Biographia*'s ideal poet. Little, that is, except the critique of 'Intimations', which defines the error sometimes visible in Wordsworth's own associations with objects. When Wordsworth attributes to things what he ought to attribute to imaginative relations among perceiver and things, then he recapitulates the error of pious Hartley: he attributes moral animation to the unconscious object *per se*. He derives from objects themselves what he ought to derive from self-conscious activity of mind. In the pantheist tendencies of Wordsworth's associations with objects, he fails to meet not only art's ultimate end, but also its immediate purpose, because he misuses words and thereby disorients his reader.

The speaker's account of this false tendency begins with 'I wandered lonely' and 'Gipsies', where Wordsworth makes no more serious error than exaggeration. But the third instance, 'Intimations', demonstrates the moral danger and the abuse of language inherent in Wordsworth's associations with the material world.

> In what sense can the magnificent attributes . . . be appropriated to a *child*, which would not make them equally suitable to a *bee*, or a *dog*, or a *field of corn*: or even to a ship, or to the wind and waves that propel it? The omnipresent Spirit works equally in them, as in the child; and the child is equally unconscious of it as they. (II, 113)

Coleridge himself verges into polemical exaggeration here, and Wordsworth has not lacked defenders.[7] Coleridge objects to Wordsworth's attributing such a rich philosophic wisdom to a yet-unconscious child. The unconscious child cannot discover moral values by meditating with full philosophic rigor on the activity of his mind. Whatever he may know for himself of those 'truths . . ./Which we are toiling all our lives to find', he can only know through observation. If such a child is the 'best philosopher', then the best philosophy must be pantheism. In short, Wordsworth's vision of the child reveals the dangerous moral and philosophic tendencies of his own naïve faith in beautiful landscapes and unsophisticated characters.

Wordsworth seldom makes this mistake, the speaker acknowledges; but defends his own tone by asserting that Wordsworth sets a dangerous example for others. That seems to me a lame excuse, another attempt to gloss over the places where the real Wordsworth's ideas and values differ from those predicated of the utterly self-conscious, fully imaginative ideal poet. The account of Wordsworth's defects as a poet is replete with

qualifications: his style lapses in less than one hundred lines; his pseudo-
sublimity is 'a fault of which none but a man of genius is capable' (II, 109).
He mismanages fancy only by subordinating it directly instead of
mediately to his moral sense. Such flaws, although significant at times,
dwindle even further when contrasted to his imaginative achievement.
Wordsworth's beauties reveal all that a truly philosophic imagination and
an imaginative fancy together can achieve. The account of Wordsworth's
virtues as a poet provides Coleridge's most complete and by far his most
accessible definition of imagination's powers.

Pre-eminent among these powers, of course, is dominion over language.
Wordsworth's 'perfect appropriateness of the words to the meaning'
guarantees more than truth about things (see II, 22), because the speaker
'include[s] in the *meaning* of a word not only its correspondent object, but
likewise all the associations which it recalls. For language is framed to
convey not only the object alone, but likewise the character, mood and
intentions of the person who is representing it' (II, 115–16). An
imaginatively directed fancy makes possible a portrait of the active mind
itself, because it is through imagination's modulating of connotations that
the poem reveals the knowing of knowing. Such precision is 'good for the
understanding', because self-consciousness provides our most exact
knowledge of the world around us; it is also an 'antidote' for an age of
'corrupt eloquence' because a precise use of words fosters the development
of self-consciousness in the reader. The speaker's appeal to 'the beneficial
after-effects of verbal precision in the preclusion of fanaticism' (II, 116–17)
echoes his account of Christ's Hospital, and the very different 'improved
pedagogy' that produces anonymous critics (I, 4–8). This idea of language
so exactly reflects his original realism that the speaker pauses here to
promise a full-scale treatise on the topic.[8] One begins to recognize that all
of his 'incomplete' or 'promised' works are one work, a discourse on the
relations among mind, world and God – with applications to a multitude
of practical matters.

The explanation of Wordsworth's second beauty develops the same
point further. At his best, he exactly balances intellectual and emotional
responses, both of which originate in his 'meditative observation' – i.e. in
his imaginative response to the world around him. Although such poems
have all the clarity and good sense of Samuel Daniel at his best, his most
imaginative ones so directly reveal imagination itself that they are
accessible only to the philosophic reader. Despite his earlier criticism of
parts of 'Intimations', the speaker lavishes praise on the ode's account of
the *poet's* consciousness. Wordsworth's meditative observations of his own
mind are

drawn up from depths which few in any age are privileged to visit, into
which few in any age have courage or inclination to descend. . . . A poem
is not necessarily obscure, because it does not aim to be popular. . . . the

['Intimations'] ode was intended for such readers only as had been accustomed to watch the flux and reflux of their inmost nature, to venture at times into the twilight realms of consciousness, and to feel a deep interest in modes of inmost being, to which they know that the attributes of time and space are inapplicable and alien, but which yet can not be conveyed save in symbols of time and space. (II, 120; cf. II, 15)

In such poems, Wordsworth so coherently relates the being of the particular with the being of the universal that his figurative, impassioned style forges symbols of imagination's activity (cf. *AR*, 110, 236). It does not just vividly describe objects he has known, and his reactions to them.

Anonymous critics' complaints about the 'Platonism' of such poems merely display their own inadequacies. The lines from Pindar that the speaker cites in response echo both the lines from Plotinus cited earlier in reference to his own discourse (I, 80), and chapter II's account of the genesis of an anonymous critic (I, 27–9):

'I have many a swift arrow in the quiver beneath my arm to sing for those with understanding. But the masses need interpreters. The true poet is he who knows much by the light of nature, but those who have only learnt verse as a craft and are violent and immoderate in their speech waste their breath in screeching like crows against the divine bird of Zeus.' (II, 121)[9]

Coleridge brings the whole force of his philosophic inquiry to bear here not only to illuminate Wordsworth's accomplishment, but also to transvalue the reviews of *Poems in Two Volumes*. The tones and judgments of such reviews are to become direct evidence for Wordsworth's genius and the incompetence of his magazine critics.

The third beauty, the 'sinewy strength and originality of single lines and paragraphs', was illustrated at length in chapter XX (II, 121). Like Shakespeare and Milton, Wordsworth achieves art's greatest universality in a highly individual way. His precision and objective truth arise from within his own deeply imaginative personality, and remain true to their origin. That fidelity guarantees universality because it proceeds from the '*all in each*' of human nature' (II, 64): the common ground of human being in the absolute, infinite 'I Am'. The quality of his poetic diction, and his 'real poetic character' come at last to the same thing: imagination's power in and through language.

The account of the fourth and fifth beauties extends the domain of Wordsworth's accuracy. He is precise not only in his use of words and in his portrait of imaginative activity, but also in his descriptions of the natural world. These reveal 'a long and genial intimacy with the very spirit which gives the physiognomic expression to all the works of nature' (II, 121). As the speaker recognized even in Wordsworth's early poems, his works rescue truths otherwise neglected on the 'dusty high road of custom'

(II, 121; cf. I, 59-60). His poems also reveal the richness of his sympathetic knowledge of human nature in general, 'the sympathy indeed of a contemplator, rather than a fellow-sufferer or co-mate, (spectator, haud particeps) but of a contemplator, from whose view no difference of rank conceals the sameness of the nature' (II, 122-3). Imagination and imaginative observation – not observation alone, nor mere obedience to 'rules' for poetry – provide both the pleasure and the truth that the very best art attains.

When the speaker says at last that 'in imaginative power, [Wordsworth] stands nearest of all modern writers to Shakespeare and Milton', he repeats a claim and a conclusion that have been variously evident all along. Wordsworth's power to '"add the gleam,/The light that never was"' confirms his mastery of 'the cardinal points of poetry': exciting the reader's sympathy with worlds beyond his usual ken (II, 124-5). Although his fancy is 'not always graceful, and sometimes *recondite*', sometimes subordinated to powers other than imagination, at least it never operates randomly. There is nothing in Wordsworth of *mere* wit. The landscape analogy for Wordsworth's genius makes the same point more vividly: his mind is no flowery sod over a hollow, nor an egg-shell, but a towering forest rich with granite outcroppings (II, 128-9; cf. I, 25, 26, 42). By standing midway between Shakespeare's absorption into the object, and Milton's absorption of all objects into himself, Wordsworth is most capable of portraying imagination's mediation directly in 'the FIRST GENUINE PHILOSOPHIC POEM' (II, 129; cf. II, 20).

This analysis of Wordsworth's poetry ends abruptly with a single-sentence paragraph reorienting us to the anonymous criticism of both men:

> The preceding criticism will not, I am aware, avail to overcome the prejudices of those, who have made it a business to attack and ridicule Mr. Wordsworth's compositions. (II, 129)

No rational argument will dissuade 'a gossip, backbiter and pasquillant', because his motives are personal, not rational (II, 87). The speaker claims that these reviewers are not so insensitive to imagination as their reviews suggest: one must not confuse the critic and the man. They are not insensitive louts, but liars and opportunists whose degraded 'personal' style helps to sell copies of their magazines (II, 129-30). They are not, as Wordsworth says, 'too petulant to be passive to a true poet, and too feeble to grapple with him' (II, 129). They are really much worse: they encourage fanaticism in the hope of financial return (see I, 130-1). The speaker then turns to Wordsworth's sentimental admirers. They will not be persuaded, either. Yet their indiscriminate and mawkish admiration is even more disgusting than the critics' malice. At least the critics perceive Wordsworth's genius – in private. The speaker thus finds himself once again intermediate between two equally erroneous extremes because he bases his inquiry on principles.

Because his Bristol printer mistakenly paginated for two volumes, Coleridge padded out the second volume by inserting here three of his letters from Germany (previously published in *The Friend*) and a long critique of the play *Bertram*.[10] In spirit and in content, these belong in chapter X. The lively and amusing *Letters* complement the *Watchman* anecdotes in displaying the speaker's delight in observation, and his self-ironic humor. The critique of *Bertram*, like the earlier commentary on Jacobinism, asserts the dangers and the depravity of political fanaticism. But, in their present place, these interpolations mask chapter XXIV's origins in the conclusion of chapter XXII. The critics who 'have made it a business to ridicule Mr. Wordsworth's compositions' have done the same to the speaker.

Chapter XXII's analysis of Wordsworth's poetry reveals how fully he achieves both art's immediate end and its ultimate purpose. His poetic portraits of the mind's activity can exert a profoundly moral influence because the delights of his diction successfully carry his truths alive into the hearts of his readers. In chapter XXIV the speaker explains that his rigorous philosophic inquiries into imagination's activity have generated the same abusive reviews as Wordsworth's poems. Even 'Christabel' was 'assailed with a malignity and a spirit of personal hatred that ought to have injured only the work in which such a tirade appeared' (II, 211). *The Statesman's Manual* was reviewed 'with a malignity so avowedly and exclusively personal, as is, I believe, unprecedented even in the present contempt of all common humanity that disgraces and endangers the liberty of the press' (II, 214). As a consequence, 'the innuendo of my "potential infidelity" . . . has been received and propagated with a degree of *credence*' entirely disproportionate to the intellectual merits of the review (II, 214).

Such a lack of proportion confuses and disorients, and thus sends one seeking after some ground of order and coherence. As we have seen, the speaker's philosophy is the quest for such ground; here, he explains his theory of faith by comparing the intuition of God to the intuition of causality:

The sense of Before and After becomes both intelligible and intellectual when, and *only* when, we contemplate the succession in the relations of Cause and Effect, which, like the two poles of the magnet manifest the being and unity of the one power by relative opposites, and give, as it were, a substratum of permanence, of identity, and therefore of reality, to the shadowy flux of Time. It is Eternity revealing itself in the phenomena of Time: and the perception and acknowledgement of the proportionality and appropriateness of the Present to the Past, prove to the afflicted Soul, that it has not yet been deprived of the sight of God, that it can still recognise the effective presence of a Father, though through a darkened glass and a turbid atmosphere, though of a Father that is chastising it. And for this cause, doubtless, are we so framed in mind, and even so organized in brain and nerve, that all confusion is painful. (II, 207–8)

Causality – and, presumably, all of the Kantean categories – is one mode of God's presence to us. Although the intelligibility of all experience rests immediately on the synthetic power of imagination, it rests ultimately on the knowledge of God, on faith and reason. The speaker refutes the charge of infidelity by asserting that only his faith in God comforts him in the face of such unmerited and unreasonable abuse.

Hume had argued that causality cannot be empirically demonstrated; *The Statesman's Manual* argues that miracles are not empirical proof of God. All suprasensuous knowledge, whether of God or the Kantean categories, must be self-grounded: 'REASON AND RELIGION ARE THEIR OWN EVIDENCE' (II, 215). The three branches of inquiry – natural philosophy, transcendental philosophy, and religion – come together at this point: all certainty is grounded in self-consciousness. We should not attempt 'to master by the reflex acts of the Understanding what we can only *know* by the act of *becoming*. . . . [I believe, because I understand,] appears to me the dictate equally of Philosophy and Religion' (II, 216; sentence in brackets translated from the Latin).

An analysis of causality structures the speaker's very first argument that the mind is active, and that the will is a morally free and responsible agent.[11] This argument develops into the theory of imagination, and here Coleridge works his way back again to the fundamental moral issue. He explains the true nature of faith by repeating the chain image from the scholium to thesis II. Let us look at the scholium before going on.

A chain without a staple, from which all the links derive their stability, or a series without a first, has been not inaptly allegorized, as a string of blind men, each holding the skirt of the man before him, reaching far out of sight, but all moving without the least deviation in one strait line. (I, 180)

As the following theses explain, the staple or guide of this series is the activity of will. Will relative to knowledge is faith, which supplies a certainty one can never attain through empirical methods alone:

. . . the Scheme of Christianity . . . though not discoverable by human Reason, is yet in accordance with it . . . link follows link by necessary consequence . . . Religion passes out of the ken of Reason only where the eye of Reason has reached its own Horizon; and . . . Faith is then but its continuation; even as the Day softens away into the sweet Twilight, and Twilight, hushed and breathless, steals into the Darkness. (II, 218; cf. I, 134–6)

This definition of faith anchors both the autobiographical self-defense that reaches its zenith in this chapter and the philosophic inquiry that has been the speaker's lifework. His 'settlement of the long-continued controversy concerning . . . poetic diction . . . [and] the real *poetic* character of the poet' depends upon our accepting this definition of faith as the valid but intuitive ground of all knowledge beyond immediate sense data.

By concluding *Biographia Literaria* as he does, Coleridge asserts again the unity of being and knowing. Who Wordsworth *is* – the genuine poet – cannot be separated from what he *knows* about words, about nature and about humanity itself. The attacks on Wordsworth's poems are then scarcely distinguishable from attacks on the man himself, and they are rendered even less distinguishable by the critics' degraded personal style. Similarly, what the speaker knows and who he is are so intimately united that one book can tell both tales. The unity of being and knowing cannot be physically demonstrated, as one might demonstrate a steam engine; it must be intuited and therefore its ultimate validity rests on an act of faith. But Coleridge trusts that the coherence of his being and knowing, and Wordsworth's being and knowing, will persuade those who apprehend it, because such unity elegantly and truly resolves a painful confusion. All critics, finally, can do little more than appeal to the persuasive force of a reasonable order.

9 Conclusion

In reading Dykes Campbell's book on Coleridge . . . I
was infinitely struck with the suggestiveness of
S.T.C.'s figure – wonderful, admirable figure – for
pictorial treatment. What a subject some particular
cluster of its relations would make for a little story, a
small vivid picture. . . . Would not such a drama
necessarily be the question of the acceptance by someone . . . of the general *responsibility* of rising to the
height of accepting him for what he is, recognizing
his rare, anomalous, magnificent, interesting, curious,
tremendously suggestive character, vices and all, with
all its imperfections on its head, and *not* being guilty
of the pedantry, the stupidity, the want of
imagination, of fighting him, deploring him in the
details – failing to recognize that one *must* pay for
him and that on the whole he is magnificently worth
it.

Henry James, *The Notebooks of Henry James*,
ed. F. O. Matthiessen and Kenneth B. Murdock
(New York: Oxford University Press, 1947), p. 152

The *Biographia*'s dual design solved problems peculiar to this text: the
logical incompleteness and apparent pantheism of the theory of
imagination. The design solved a more general problem as well: it makes
the reader think about fundamental philosophic issues in part by relating
them to a contemporary controversy. As I explained in the first chapter,
making readers think was one of Coleridge's most abiding aims. Duality
characterizes Coleridge's design in part for this reason, and in part for a
more mundane one: the need to publish. There would not, after all, have
been much of an English audience for Coleridge's technical philosophy.
But he could not apply himself to hackwork. Writing about contemporary
problems, not as a hack but as a philosopher, made it possible to publish,
and yet remain true to his own aims and his own values.

Coleridge's numerous plans for works of this sort suggest the ease with
which he could forge such links between the popular and the perennial. As
McFarland observes, Coleridge had 'an organic, coherent, and fully

worked-out viewpoint that could be quickly focused on a given topic because all the larger problems of structure had already been solved'.[1] A look at just one of these projected works will reveal how Coleridge's habits as a writer differ from those of most serious thinkers who engage popular or local problems.

An 1810 notebook entry plans a study of Socinianism. His purpose, Coleridge states, is to undertake

> a full and free Examination of the Credibility of Socinian Christianity, or rather *Jesuism* – Is the historical Evidence fairly weighed sufficient to verify the facts of the O. and N. Testament, and to ascertain their *miraculous* nature – & 2. are these miraculous Facts fit and adequate evidences of the Dogmata of these Books, supposing them to be such and only such as are held by the Unitarians – namely, the renewal of Life after Death by a resurrection of each Man's Body, to happiness or misery according to the preponderance of his good or bad actions in this life. I would proceed in this manner. . . . (*CN*, III, 3817)

There is a fairly straightforward procedure explicit in the statement of purpose. Coleridge might have divided the work in two parts, and set about answering the two questions he asks by applying criteria already available.[2] But Coleridge's procedure runs a full page and a half in Coburn's edition of the notebooks: it describes a full-scale inquiry into the history and the psychology of faith. Coleridge divides this inquiry into three parts: (1) a study of Priestley and Socinian divines to demonstrate (*a*) that materialism and necessity are inevitable deductions from Socinianism and (*b*) that Socinianism has no basis in the Gospels, and (*c*) that its doctrines are neither certain nor comprehensible; (2) a history of Christianity backwards from the Council of Nice to establish criteria for miracles and to provide 'a compleat Canon of Belief, deduced from History & Psychology, in all ages & Religions & Sects of Religion, Philosophy, Medicine, Superstition, &c &c'; and (3) 'an attempt to frame certain criteria of the Authenticity of Books' so as to establish the canon of the Bible.

Through this procedure, Coleridge transforms the local topic of Socinianism into an occasion to advance a major religious and philosophic principle:

> Above all, I would lose no opportunity of enforcing the prodigious difference between the auxiliary evidence required for a religion whose Truth & Necessity is proved a priori, & merely a *condition* of its being received as a Revelation, i.e. Legislator leges suas conscientiae datas nunc solemniter per intuitum sensitivum reconfirmans, and the absolute evidence which is to support a weight solely on itself.

Socinianism seems to fall from view, just as poetic diction disappears as an issue for nine chapters, while Coleridge explores the underlying issues. Unlike more prudent authors, Coleridge refuses to choose between writing a sophisticated but practical analysis of Priestley, and writing a wholly philosophical and theoretical treatise on faith. One might say that Coleridge's books are too ambitious, that they try to do too much. But this same unswerving allegiance to the larger, more difficult issues is the heart of his permanence as a thinker.

The same duality characterizes the designs of such serial works as *The Friend* and the *Philosophical Lectures*. The first volume of *The Friend* moves inexorably to the distinction between reason and understanding in the final two essays, yet progressive unity is sustained by reference to the author's responsibility in publishing such a periodical. An author's primary duty, of course, is to communicate truth: the two strands of argument can be interwoven because one neither knows the truth, nor communicates it properly without distinguishing correctly between reason and understanding.

The second volume continues and develops the reflexivity evident in the first, until the philosophic inquiry into reason and understanding and the discourse on writing intersect in the famous 'Essays on Method' comprising most of the third volume. These derive principles of both inquiry and discourse from the nature of reason and understanding. Coleridge integrates the local political issues of volume two at the beginning of 'Section the second' in volume three. There he renders explicit the moral concerns that have been clear all along, and relates morals, discourse and politics by discussing the Sophists. Throughout all three volumes, the Friend stands between mirrors: he explains how one ought to write and to think about problems in part by writing about his thinking about his own writing.

Coleridge's dual design works well in serial essays: we tolerate a higher level of discontinuity, so he can move from local problem to philosophic issue and back again without disorienting us too badly. General integrity and progressive unity are sustained by long, somewhat clumsy transitions usually at the beginnings of essays. These commonly refer to the Friend's digressiveness, obscurity and prolixity, or to his excessive interest in metaphysics. Yet Coleridge's richly evident irony turn these 'confessions' into a mode of self-defense that orients the reader to his most fundamental moral and metaphysical concerns.

Duality is even more evident in the design of *Philosophical Lectures*. These lectures are organized both chronologically, as a history of philosophy, and conceptually, as a history of the gradual, direct evolution of a proper idea of method. They are the 'Essays on Method' writ large. Teleological histories are common enough, of course. Coleridge differs in the centrality of his desire to explain correct method *per se*: the lineaments of correct method provide the work's major structural elements. Historical chronology, like autobiographical narrative, is used chiefly for unifying.

The *Philosophical Lectures* are not at all polished: their 'digressive' texture is quite pronounced; transition and emphasis are idiosyncratic. But their basic design is none the less reasonably clear and accessible, probably because Coleridge need merely 'exaggerate' the conventions of teleological history.

The aphoristic style of *Aids to Reflection* meets Coleridge's needs even better than the serial essay, by cueing the reader even more clearly to seek interrelations on his own: it is Coleridge's most successful, most sophisticated use of a dual design. James D. Boulger has astutely described both the dual design and the difficulty of this work:

> Unfortunately for *Aids to Reflection*, its two structural principles of organization are intricate without being clear. Coleridge's division into Introductory, Prudential, Moral and Religious, and Spiritual aphorisms, unintentionally belies the importance and number of the religious issues considered; nor does it coordinate the numerous allusions to contemporary religious figures and problems. . . . On the surface this entire structure seems quite arbitrary, external, and rambling. . . . Is there, then, any organization in the baffling arrangement which resulted from the merger of the 'Beauties of Leighton' with the 'Moral Prudential, and Spiritual aphorisms'? If there is, it is certainly not a schematic but an ideational principle, and only corresponds occasionally with the putative structures.[3]

We have seen this 'ideational principle' at work in *Biographia Literaria*: Coleridge's desire to make his readers think about issues in ways that will lead them to accept the necessity of ideas whose corresponding laws cannot be directly demonstrated. *Aids to Reflection* is more difficult reading than *Biographia Literaria* because its issues are more subtle and more complex, but it does not squander the reader's energy as the *Biographia* occasionally does.

Aids to Reflection provides three elaborate sets of spiritual exercises, designed to conduct the meditating reader from the most basic question, 'How shall I behave?' through some of the most intricate and fundamental problems in Christian doctrine. Coleridge argues that self-interested prudence leads the thinker to morality, which in turn leads him to revealed religion, and then to Christianity as the most perfect of religions. But it does so, of course, only for those who can examine the issues rigorously and correctly. Conducting this rigorous examination – with Leighton's help, and others' – allows Coleridge both to explicate his own system of thought and to engage contemporary religious controversies. He manages both tasks so well by writing for a distinct and specialized audience: students of the ministry, who presumably know both the classical and the contemporary arguments about doctrine.

Coleridge had tried defining a limited audience in *The Statesman's Manual*; but philosophical politicians have always been, I suspect, in rather short supply. Furthermore, 'political skill and foresight' usually depend at least as much on pragmatic skills as on philosophical acuity. Consequently, the contemporary, local half of the argument is both strained and feeble.[4] Placing great chunks of the philosophical argument into appendices – an attempt, perhaps, to disguise the radical disproportion of parts – only complicates the reader's attempt to make consecutive sense of the whole. The second of the *Lay Sermons* avoids appendices, but does not improve upon the vaguely defined local argument. The two *Lay Sermons* are brilliant, satisfying books for readers who plunder them boldly, seeking out the intriguing parts; but their designs are clumsy.

Coleridge's other early dual design is not so awkward, nor does it address an utterly fictitious audience: the lectures on Shakespeare speak to one who expects literature both to entertain and to teach. One can read them both as literary criticism and as an explanation of what Peter Hoheisel calls 'the basic moral principles at work in human life and . . . the consequences of those principles'.[5] For Coleridge, Hoheisel explains, it was Shakespeare's genius to have grasped and embodied these principles in his plays; the lectures are organized as simultaneous commentaries on the plays and on the moral principles.

Coleridge's last work, *On the Constitution of the Church and State*, is his most conventional. The contemporary problem of Catholic emancipation, and the philosophical problem of 'church' and 'state', stand so closely together that the plaguing problems of transition and emphasis nearly solve themselves. Coleridge has at last found a contemporary issue well suited to the philosophical problems he wants to address. *Church and State* depends, no less than his other works, on ideas and distinctions that cannot be fully demonstrated; but the difficulty of making us think is not compounded to the same extent with mundane problems of unity and progression. Yet *Church and State* plods a bit, at least to my sensibilities. It is less playful, less exuberant, more labored than his earlier works.

Yet had the *Biographia* such sobriety, it might have infuriated fewer readers. But something vital would be lost if Coleridge returned to edit away the Baroque complexities of *Biographia Literaria*. To wish them away is somewhat like wishing away Milton's endlessly involuted sentences, or Wordsworth's timelessly undulating pentameters. And perhaps this is my last but most important point: one must read Coleridge's prose as if it were poetry. His prose requires that same patiently acquired knowledge of the text, that same minute attention to meanings and etymologies and repetitions of words, that same sensitivity to images. But, in the end, the sad, stubborn fact remains: *Biographia Literaria* is not a poem after all. Coleridge criticized Wordsworth for the obscurities introduced by the intrusion of deliberate philosophy into his poetry; I suspect that the poet's judgment usurps the philosopher's at times in Coleridge's prose. The 'speaker' is an image in whom we are to believe for our own sakes, for the imaginative pleasure and insight we can derive from contemplating an image in full poetic faith. But the accounts of 'his' scholarship are not strongly enough integrated into the autobiography to preclude their provoking the wrong kinds of expectations. And these mistaken or at best confused expectations place inordinate stress on all other unifying devices, most of which are far too delicate to support the extra burden. Like Wordsworth's excessively objective poems, *Biographia Literaria* requires a level of sympathetic imagination that it does not itself elicit and sustain. If one willingly expends the energy Coleridge's poetic prose requires, it is because, in James's words, 'on the whole he is magnificently worth it'.

And because Coleridge is worth it, one tolerates his failings. Yes, the *Biographia* is flawed, but it is also brilliant. Both judgments are accurate, but one must begin by acknowledging what generations of thoughtful readers have affirmed: the book is obscure beyond what its imaginative purposes can justify. I have worked too hard for too many years untangling the snarled threads of Coleridge's discourse to credit any claim to the contrary. And yet, and yet, with equal equanimity do I assert that the book deserves its status as 'masterpiece' no less fully than it deserves various other epithets. When its design is understood, when Coleridge's imaginative purposes are distinguished from his inept execution, then his mistakes become manageable. Nothing can make the *Biographia* graceful, but such knowledge renders it moderately accessible.

'Vices and all, with all its imperfections on its head', *Biographia Literaria* none the less succeeds in illuminating the imaginative powers animating art. Generations of thoughtful, weary readers have also affirmed this. Proposing as his immediate object truth, not pleasure, Coleridge offers a vision of how the greatest poems can reconcile lively delight and moral value. While demanding his reader's unflagging energy, Coleridge illuminates his difficult path with imaginative appeals that assert, over and over again, the intimate relation between literary criticism and life itself. Presenting no rigorous proof, he relies instead on our intuitive assent, on our 'ascertaining vision'. He relies on our imagination.

Notes

Chapter 1

1 *Life of John Sterling*, in *The Works of Thomas Carlyle* (New York: Charles Scribner's Sons, 1897), Vol. XI, p. 56.

2 Among the Victorians, see, for instance: Matthew Arnold, *The Complete Prose Works of Matthew Arnold*, ed. R. H. Super (Ann Arbor: University of Michigan Press, 1960–77), Vol. III, p. 189, and Vol. IX, p. 237; Walter Pater, *Appreciations*, 3rd edn (London: Macmillan, 1901), pp. 65–104; John Ruskin, *Ruskin as Literary Critic*, ed. A. H. R. Ball (London: Cambridge University Press, 1928), pp. 267–8; Leslie Stephen, *Hours in a Library* (1909; reprinted London: John Murray, 1919), Vol. III, pp. 324, 331, and Stephen's entry on C in *The Dictionary of National Biography*, Vol. IV. C's influence on his century was substantial. See Graham Hough, 'Coleridge and the Victorians' in *The English Mind: Studies in the English Moralists presented to Basil Willey*, ed. D. H. Sykes and G. Watson (London: Cambridge University Press, 1964), pp. 175–92; and Philip C. Rule, SJ, 'C's reputation as a religious thinker: 1816–1972', *Harvard Theological Review*, vol. 67 (1974), pp. 289–320. Thomas McFarland analyzes the history of C's reputation in the introduction and first chapter of *C and the Pantheist Tradition* (Oxford: Clarendon Press, 1969).

3 Discussed in Chapters 2 and 5.

4 These plans have been discussed by George Whalley, 'The integrity of *Biographia Literaria*', *Essays and Studies*, n.s., vol. 6 (1953), pp. 87–101; and by Earl Leslie Griggs, *CL*, III, xlvii–lii; and most recently by Kathleen Wheeler, *Sources, Processes and Methods in C's 'Biographia Literaria'* (Cambridge: Cambridge University Press, 1981), pp. 8–28. See also Daniel Mark Fogle, 'A compositional history of the *Biographia Literaria*', *Studies in Bibliography: Papers of the Bibliographical Society of the University of Virginia*, vol. 30 (1977), pp. 219–34. On the original intention to write a preface, see *CL*, IV, 584–5, 578–9.

5 McFarland, *C and the Pantheist Tradition*; Elinor Stoneman Shaffer, 'Studies in C's aesthetics', *Dissertation Abstracts*, 28 (1967), p. 1409, col. A (Columbia University), esp. ch. 2 (pp. 18–70), which reappears in very condensed form as 'The "Postulates in Philosophy" in *Biographia Literaria*', *Comparative Literature Studies*, vol. 7 (1970), pp. 297–313. The issue is a complex one, as McFarland's history shows. Other views on the issue are discussed below, Ch. 5, n. 2.

6 The work referred to is *Lay Sermons*. C continues: 'Before a just tribunal of Criticism I could apply still more triumphantly the same test . . . to two distinct Treatises in the Literary Life, besides the Essay on Authorship as a Trade [Ch. XI].' C would not have written 'in' if he meant 'comprising' or 'constituting'; these two essays are probably chs I to X, and XIV to XXII.

7 This thematic unity has been defined most fully by George Whalley, 'The integrity of *Biographia Literaria*. George Watson extends one aspect of Whalley's argument in his introduction to *Biographia Literaria*, ed. George Watson, Everyman's Library (London: Dent, New York: Dutton, 1965). Very short summaries, less comprehensive than Shawcross's, are numerous. J. R. de J. Jackson defines another aspect of the *Biographia*'s unity: it methodical basis and consistency. See his *Method and Imagination in C's Criticism* (Cambridge, Mass: Harvard University Press, 1969), esp. pp. 63–72. Most

recently, Kathleen Wheeler (*Sources, Processes and Methods*) has argued that C uses a higher or Socratic irony to devise a work whose unity depends upon the reader's imaginative response to certain densely metaphoric passages that ultimately render the *Biographia* almost entirely self-reflexive.

8   Owen Barfield, *What C Thought* (Middletown, Conn.: Wesleyan University Press, 1971), p. 13.

9   Introduction to *Biographia Literaria*, ed. Henry Nelson Coleridge and Sara Coleridge, in Shedd III, p. xxii.

10 See Sara Coleridge (n. 9, above); Henry Nelson Coleridge, preface to *TT*, p. 233; Thomas De Quincey, *De Quincey's Collected Writings*, ed. by David Masson, 2nd edn (Edinburgh: Adam & Charles Black, 1889–90), Vol. II, pp. 152–3; William Wordsworth as reported by Christopher Wordsworth, *Memoirs of William Wordsworth* (London: Edward Moxon, 1851), Vol. II, p. 443; and, more recently, Jackson, *Method and Imagination in C's Criticism* p. 72; or Arthur Symons, introduction to *Biographia Literaria*, ed. Ernest Rhys, Everyman's Library (London: Dent, 1906), pp. ix–x. Traveling provides many conventional images for the process of reading; these uses of the 'travel' metaphor are notable for the clarity and consistency with which the authors use the image to distinguish between the clarity or value of the ideas, and the difficulties of the style or manner.

11 Bishop C. Hunt, Jr, 'C and the endeavor of philosophy', *PMLA*, vol. 91 (1976), pp. 829–39.

12 C's marginalia on Schelling document his response to arguments for rare and radically independent intellectual powers. These marginalia are compiled and annotated by Henri Nidecker, 'Notes marginales de S. T. Coleridge en marge de Schelling', *Revue de littérature comparée*, Vol. 7 (1927), pp. 736–46. For a discussion of the issue, see Shaffer, 'C's aesthetics', pp. 38–40, and below, Ch. 3, n. 12. See also Wheeler's account of the ways in which C avoids solipsistic idealism: *Sources, Processes and Methods*, pp. 34–41.

13 For definitions of idea, see *CCS*, 12; *LS*, 113–14. For the relations between idea and law, see *PhL*, 107–8; *CCS*, 13, 19–20.

14 See *BL*, II, 85–94.

15 Jerome C. Christensen ingeniously seizes this fact to argue that *BL* is radically self-deconstructed: it reveals C's understanding that statements are prisons, or that freedom is possible only within indeterminacy. A deconstructionist no doubt serves major strategic ends by arguing that even *BL* actively undermines its own traditional humanism, but C *never* valued the kind of indeterminacy Christensen describes. None the less, Christensen's description of C's 'marginal' method of composition holds great promise as the basis for a systematic theory of C's use of his own notebooks and others' texts. See 'The genius in the *Biographia Literaria*', *Studies in Romanticism*, vol. 17 (1978), pp. 215–31; and 'C's marginal method in the *Biographia Literaria*', *PMLA*, vol. 92 (1977), pp. 928–40. Lawrence Buell takes much the same approach, contending that C is systematically 'deformalizing' his text: 'The question of form in C's *Biographia Literaria*', *ELH*, vol. 46 (1979), pp. 399–417. On the whole, Wheeler's account of C's facility with the higher or Socratic irony explains far more convincingly why it is that he so persistently represents his works as fragments or fragmentary: *Sources, Processes and Methods*, pp. 59–80.

16 Jackson, *Method and Imagination*, p. 40.

17 'Coleridge', *Tait's Magazine*, n.s., vol. 1 (Aug 1834), p. 514; reprinted in *De Quincey's Collected Writings*, ed. Masson, Vol. II, pp. 152–3.

18 J. A. Appleyard, SJ, *C's Philosophy of Literature: The Development of a Concept of Poetry, 1791–1819* (Cambridge, Mass: Harvard University Press, 1965), reveals even more fully the hazards of such dismissal. He discounts chs II and III (p. 174, n. 10) and chs X and XI (p. 188), because he has chosen to study the *Biographia* as 'Coleridge's own immediate deliberations on his theories' of poetry and imagination, a perspective sharply distinguished from studying it as 'an exposition of a philosophy or even as a biographical sketch of literary opinions' (p. 170, see also p. 176). Such an approach

foreordains his inability to see how the theory of secondary imagination can explain both the spontaneous activity of the mind requisite for poetry, and the unity of being and knowing in perception: 'Coleridge sets up requirements for the imagination that it cannot possibly fulfill in terms of its original [i.e. temporally prior] conception' (p. 183). Appleyard's willingness to discount not only major sections of the text, but also C's explicit intention to provide the philosophy underlying his literary theories, leads necessarily to his conclusion that the *Biographia* is a 'remarkable failure' (p. 169). Appleyard's methods also lead directly to his reading the epistemological function of imagination in unduly Schellingean terms: imagination is not the source and guarantor of truth. As the neglected ch. X explains, God is this source and guarantor.

19   Introduction to *Biographia Literaria*, ed. Watson, p. xv.
20   Documenting and analyzing C's grasp of this equation are among the principal endeavors of McFarland, *C and the Pantheist Tradition*, and Wheeler, *Sources, Processes and Methods*.
21   For a fuller explanation of this view of C's idea of symbol, see J. Robert Barth, SJ, *The Symbolic Imagination: C and the Romantic Tradition* (Princeton, NJ: Princeton University Press, 1977), pp. 3–21. A submerged issue here is quite complex: how can human knowledge generally attain the precision and predictive value characteristic of mathematics? This is one of the major issues Kant addresses in *Prolegomena to Any Future Metaphysics* and, at greater length, in *The Critique of Pure Reason*.
22   Barth, *The Symbolic Imagination*, pp. 14–17.
23   ibid., p. 14.
24   Richard Mallette, 'Narrative technique in the *Biographia Literaria*', *Modern Language Review*, vol. 70 (1975), pp. 32–40.
25   Jackson, *Method and Imagination*, p. 72.
26   Richard Haven, *Patterns of Consciousness: An Essay on Coleridge* (Amherst: University of Massachusetts Press, 1969), p. 12.
27   James Olney, *Metaphors of Self: The Meaning of Autobiography* (Princeton NJ: Princeton University Press, 1972), pp. 3–4. Olney argues for the propriety of autobiography as a vehicle for philosophy. Coleridge's adaptation of his literal life and his enigmatic promise in the last chapter to write a *personal* autobiography suggest a highly developed understanding of the philosophic potential of the genre as Olney has described it.
28   See, for instance, *F*, I, 107–26, 149–53; *LS*, 43–52; *AR*, 167–8, 199–200, 235–8, 276–81. The lengthy summarizing transitions in *The Friend* and the *Lay Sermons* are not literal summaries, but attempts to provide a single perspective from which the reader might integrate what has gone before, and preview terrain ahead. These do not appear in *Biographia Literaria*, perhaps because Coleridge relies instead on the perspectival function of chronology: one who continually tries to relate each part of the *Biographia* to the autobiography does in fact begin to integrate the whole. Transitions become relatively shorter and more effective in *Aids to Reflection*, and quite graceful in *On the Constitution of Church and State*. He also seems to have objected to the 'orienting' transition itself: 'Hotheaded men confuse, your cool-headed Gentry jumble, the man of warm feelings only produces order and true connection – in what a jumble M. & H. write – every third paragraph beginning with – "Let us now return" or "We come now to the consideration of such a thing" – i.e. what I *said* I *would* come to in the Contents prefixed to the Chapter' (*CN*, I, 868). When Coleridge deviates from his own ideal, it is obviously toward hotheadedness.
29   Wheeler, *Sources, Processes and Methods*.
30   Symons, introduction to *Biographia Literaria*, ed. Rhys, pp. ix–x.

Chapter 2

1   Beginning with Ch. 2, citations to the *Biographia* will be identified by volume and page number alone; '*BL*' will not appear.

2 In the 'Essays on Method' in *The Friend*, C calls education 'the most weighty and concerning of all sciences . . . the nisus formativus of social man' (*F*, I, 493–4). His abiding interest in the process of thinking underlies his complementary arguments about education and about method. For further discussion, see Jackson, *Method and Imagination*, ch. 2; and Barfield, *What C Thought*, chs 1 and 2.

3 C's accounts of the intellectual and emotional hazards of heartless philosophy are often misread as indictments of philosophizing generally, especially in commentaries on 'Dejection: An Ode'. Geoffrey Yarlott offers a statement that is exemplary in its failure to distinguish false from genuine philosophy: 'Since experience showed that thought and feeling must go together it followed that to differentiate and isolate them was merely inviting trouble. It led to what he called "the thinking disease", on which "no moral being ever becomes healthy". Though metaphysics provided incidental compensation (it being a salve for his wounded self-esteem that here was a sphere in which he outshone all rivals), because it was basically a neurotic activity it could afford no final anodyne' (*C and the Abyssinian Maid* (London: Methuen, 1967), p. 222). Major portions of C's achievements are waved aside here as 'neurotic', and radically isolated from what Yarlott rightly depicts as the central issue of C's value-system: reconciling ideas and feelings. Yet, in the midst of the years to which Yarlott refers, C writes to Southey, 'Believe me, Southey! a metaphysical Solution, that does not instantly *tell* for something in the Heart, is grievously to be suspected as apocry[p]hal' (*CL*, II, 961). The 'blessed interval' to which C refers at I, 10, is the period before his complex emotional difficulties rendered it distressing to think about his feelings; 'abstruse researches', although technically useful, become morally and intellectually dangerous if they are mistaken for the enterprise of philosophy itself (see I, 98, *F*, I, 523 n, and Haven, *Patterns of Consciousness*). As McFarland argues, C was always a poet and always a philosopher; and he was a philosopher of such erudition that his work poses major methodological problems for its students (*C and the Pantheist Tradition*, pp. 112–16, xxiii–xi).

4 Unless epistemology anchor itself to a real world immediately known, C contends, it sinks into extreme forms of materialism and idealism – extremes that are inimical not only to religion, but also to the most rudimentary forms of moral responsibility. For a further discussion of C's rejection of these extremes, see McFarland, *C and the Pantheist Tradition*. I. A. Richards's analysis of the two extremes remains a model of lucidity and economy (*C on Imagination* (1935; 2nd edn, New York: W. W. Norton & Co., 1950), ch. 3). C's definition of faith as both volitional and cognitive is the key to the solution he sought; for an introduction to the doctrinal controversy, see J. Robert Barth, SJ, *C and Christian Doctrine* (Cambridge, Mass.: Harvard University Press, 1969), ch. II.

5 There are two thorny problems here: Did C complete a system? and, Is it pantheist? McFarland contends that no formally closed philosophic system could encompass all that C wanted to include (*C and the Pantheist Tradition*, p. 192, and ch. 3 passim). Barfield says that one can judge C pantheist only by ignoring his statements about the Trinity (*What C Thought*, pp. 149–50). Although Barfield is not as concerned with formal philosophic criteria as McFarland (ibid., pp. 149–50), he none the less explicates in great detail the consistency of C's thought (see pp. 5, 13). In a review, McFarland contends that the polar metaphysics Barfield explicates is ultimately pantheist, and was later abandoned (*The Wordsworth Circle*, Vol. 4 (1973), pp. 165–70). But McFarland also acknowledges that Barfield's book remains a most valuable guide to C's thinking on many issues, particularly at the stage represented by *Biographia Literaria*. At one point, Barfield describes his whole book as basically a commentary on ch. 12 (p. 63). The major theoretical issues engaged by Barfield and McFarland cannot be addressed thoroughly within the scope of the present study, although I will later note both the ways in which C diverges from Schelling to link his psychology, his poetics and his metaphysics to the orthodox Christian God, and the ways in which this philosophically frail link is strengthened rhetorically.

6 In '*Quisque sui faber*: Coleridge in the *Biographia Literaria*', *Philological Quarterly*, Vol.

50 (1971), pp. 208–29, M. G. Cooke attributes the 'letter' in ch. XIII in part to C's loss of confidence after literally stopping his composition to reread Wordsworth's 1815 preface, but this judgment does not take adequately into account either this distinct reference to the central disagreement with Wordsworth, or the elaborate pattern culminating in the 'letter' (discussed below, Ch. 5). Neither does it fully enough consider the body of evidence testifying to C's much earlier recognition that he and Wordsworth disagree in significant ways (cited and discussed by Whalley, 'The integrity of *Biographia Literaria*'). There is none the less great merit in Cooke's describing the autobiographical self as a self-creative psychological act; Cooke very sensitively evaluates the stylistic and philosophic consequences of C's own recognition that he had not fully and adequately defined his theory of imagination. The rhetorical functions I describe add to the *Biographia*'s complexity as a psychological document: much work remains to be done.

7 Barfield, *What C Thought*, p. 87.

8 Shawcross points out that C exaggerates his revision of his poems in response to early reviews (I, 3; I, 204–5), and shortens his list of publications by omitting *The Watchman, The Friend* and *Conciones ad Populum* (I, 38; I, 218). Yet since the speaker later describes his efforts with *The Watchman* in great detail, and several times quotes or refers to *The Friend*, it is difficult to put a precise interpretation on the misrepresentation (I, 114–21; I, 60; I, 110; I, 119). In general, the character or achievements of the speaker are exaggerated or deflated from those of the real man so as to sharpen the contrast between philosophic and anonymous criticism.

9 Yarlott, *C and the Abyssinian Maid*, ch. I et passim.

10 For a discussion of C's philosophy of history, and the influence of his views, see Robert Preyer, *Bentham, C, and the Science of History*, Beitrage zur englischen Phil., 41. Heft. (Bochum-Langendreer: H. Popinghaus, 1958).

11 C's portrait of anonymous critics at I, 25–9, should be compared to Pope's portrait of the evolution of the inept critic in 'An Essay on Criticism', which of course has origins of its own, as the lines from Pindar at II, 121, suggest. In this context, a footnote in ch. III accuses Jeffrey of maliciously misrepresenting his opinion of C (I, 36 n). Later, C accuses him of lying in the same way about Wordsworth (II, 129). Jeffrey responds in a long footnote to Hazlitt's review in the *Edinburgh Review* (*C: The Critical Heritage*, ed. J. R. de J. Jackson (London: Routledge, 1970), pp. 314 n–318); Hazlitt in turn echoes Dryden's 'MacFlecknoe' (ibid., p. 298). The controversy is picked up in later reviews in *Blackwood's Edinburgh Magazine* (ibid., pp. 344–5) and in *British Critic* (ibid., pp. 366–9). There are still later notes in a letter to the editor in *Blackwood's* (ibid., p. 353), and in Crabb Robinson's diary, published as *Books and Their Writers*, ed. Edith J. Morley (London: Dent, 1938), Vol. I, p. 209. This exchange of views is but a brief indication of the extent to which C's remarks about reviewers provoked lively reaction. For further discussion, see David Erdman and Paul Zall, 'C and Jeffrey in controversy', *Studies in Romanticism*, vol. 14 (1975), pp. 75–83; and Nathaniel Teich, 'C's *Biographia Literaria* and the contemporary controversy about style', *The Wordsworth Circle*, vol. 3 (1972), pp. 61–70. For an account of C's own work as a reviewer, see David Erdmann, 'Coleridge and the review business', *The Wordsworth Circle*, vol. 6 (1975), pp. 3–50. For discussion of C's use of eighteenth-century satirical modes, see Mallette, 'Narrative technique in the *Biographia Literaria*'.

12 For discussion, see David Erdman, 'Coleridge as "Nehemiah Higgenbottom"', *MLN*, vol. 73 (1958), pp. 569–80.

13 The paragraph from *Ecclesiastical Polity* uses metaphors of depth four times to describe first principles. The metaphor of height that C quotes is the only one. See Vol. I, bk 1, sect. 2.

14 The continual insistence that criticism be personally unbiased and properly derived from first principles once found a sympathetic audience among professional academic critics, as did the insistence that poetry has a logic of its own, as severe as that of science but more subtle and more complex. Yet the *British Critic* review disputed the first

claim, asserting that criticism is best served by a literary equivalent of the legal adversary system; Wilson was outraged by the second (Jackson (ed.), *Critical Heritage*, pp. 361–3, 336–7).

15 In *Sources, Processes and Methods in C's 'Biographia Literaria'*, Kathleen Wheeler takes a different position on this issue. She suggests that those who find *BL* obscure are themselves unimaginative, passive or lazyminded (see, e.g., pp. 6, 109, 110, 112, 128). I grant that lazy and unimaginative readers will understand very little of C's argument – and little of Wheeler's, either. But such are not usually taken as representative instances of the 'competent' reader. If one grants Iser's contention that texts do not 'contain' meanings but, rather, provide 'instructions' for the reader's active endeavor to assemble meanings, then some of *BL*'s instructions must be judged inadequate, and many more criticized as excessively idiosyncratic. Wheeler's sweeping indictment fails to take adequately into account the close attention paid to the book by many outstanding scholars, critics and poets both in this century and the last.

16 Southey's role in C's marriage to Sara Fricker casts a shadow of irony over C's statements. In subtle ways, judgment is associated with fancy throughout the *Biographia*; judgment itself is the work of understanding. This link becomes most evident when Wordsworth's disproportions – clearly failures of judgment – are represented as failures to direct fancy appropriately (II, 104–5). One who has exceptionally good judgment, particularly in matters of rhetoric, is one whose fancy is most strongly attuned to 'that state of association, which actually exists as *general*' (I, 105). In coordination with imagination, such attunement is crucially important for poetry; but in isolation from imagination it generates faint praise from C.

17 R. H. Fogle, *The Idea of C's Criticism* (Berkeley: University of California Press, 1962), p. 40.

18 See Barfield, *What C Thought*, pp. 64–7 et passim. McFarland explores at length the consequences of Coleridge's dual allegiance to a creative mind and a real physical world immediately known (*C and the Pantheist Tradition*). In places Wheeler tends to assimilate Coleridge to Kant on this issue (e.g. *Sources, Processes and Methods*, pp. 40–1).

19 Preface to Second Edition, *Critique of Pure Reason*, trans. Norman Kemp Smith (New York: St Martin's Press, Toronto: Macmillan, 1965), pp. 22, 25 n. On Newton, see *TT*, 8 Oct 1830.

Chapter 3

1 For C's explanation of will's centrality, see *AR*, 153–60, 108 n, 246 n. 'I assume a something, the proof of which no man can give to another, yet every man may find for himself' (*AR*, 154).

2 Those seeking a more detailed explication of the relations among will, faith and reason should consult: Barth, *C and Christian Doctrine*, esp. chs II, IV, V; Barfield, *What C Thought*, esp. ch. 12; and James D. Boulger, *C as Religious Thinker* (New Haven, Conn.: Yale University Press, 1961), chs II, III, V. See also Laurence S. Lockridge, *Coleridge the Moralist* (Ithaca, NY: Cornell University Press, 1977).

3 'Your know that every intellectual act, however you may distinguish it by name, in respect to the originating faculties, is truly the act of the entire man' (*TT*, 29 July 1830).

4 On the psychological Trinity of reason, will and faith, see *LS*, 62; *AR*, 243 n. On the relation between faith and reason, see *AR*, 72–4, 301–3; *LS*, 47–8, 175–6. On reason and will (sometimes called speculative reason and practical reason), see *AR*, 181, 234; *LS*, 60, n. 2.

5 On C and the history of doctrines of faith, see: Barth, *C and Christian Doctrine*, pp. 31–3; Boulger, *C as Religious Thinker*, pp. 37–42.

6 C's idea of self is related in complex ways to his theory of the Trinity, on which his major statement is the yet-unpublished *Opus Maximum*. Barth discusses this material in detail (*C and Christian Doctrine*, ch. IV; cf. *AR*, 183, n. 2 ff.). See also McFarland, *C and*

the Pantheist Tradition, ch. 4, esp. pp. 235–44. On personality and reason, see *F*, I, 97–8. On personality and will, see *AR*, 108.

7 On conscience, see *LS*, 66–7; *F*, I, 150–1, 159; *AR*, 145–6. On sin, see *AR*, 248–50, 259–62, 273–4.

8 The distinction between reason and understanding takes two forms, explained at length in the *Statesman's Manual* (pp. 59–60 and nn) and the *Aids to Reflection* (pp. 211–25, and 'Appendix', pp. 353–4). Regarded *theoretically*, '. . . the Understanding . . . concerns itself exclusively with the quantities, qualities, and relations of *particulars* in time and space. The UNDERSTANDING, therefore, is the science of phaenomena, and their subsumption under distinct kinds and sorts, (*genus* and *species*). Its functions supply the rules and constitute the possibility of EXPERIENCE; but remain mere logical *forms*, except as far as *materials* are given by the senses or sensations. The REASON, on the other hand, is the science of the *universal*[.] . . . The Reason first manifests itself in man by the *tendency* to the comprehension of all as one. We can neither rest in an infinite that is not at the same time a whole, nor in a whole that is not infinite' (*LS*, 59–60). In its theoretical function, Reason discovers or invents theories, explanations in which all particulars are treated as a unified whole, as *one* not a conglomerate: 'from individual (or particular) and contingent facts and forms [Reason] concludes universal, necessary, and permanent Truth' (*LS*, 19, n. 1). The *practical* version of the distinction centers on morals, not inquiry. The practical reason is 'the power of determining the Will by Ideas, as *Ultimate* ends'; it is often equated with will or with conscience (*LS*, 61 n). This power distinguishes man as a moral being from the animals. The practical Understanding is 'the faculty of selecting and adapting means to *proximate* ends'; it is a more highly developed form of instinct (*LS*, 61 n). The two sets of distinctions are so closely related that C often discusses theoretical and practical aspects simultaneously. He calls the distinction between Reason and Understanding the '*Gradus ad Philosophiam*' (*TT*, 14 May 1830); it is the first point that a student of his prose must master – although the distinction is an ancient one. C himself directs beginners first to *F*, I 154–61, and then to *LS*, 59–93 (*CL*, IV, 851). One should also consult *AR*, 221–5, which richly illustrates the distinction, and relates it to the nature of language.

9 On self-knowledge and the knowledge of God, see *AR*, 79, n 2; *LS*, 68, n. 3. On the Incarnation, see above, n. 6. The passage in quotation marks is from the Nicene Creed.

10 For a statement of the progression from self-knowledge to knowledge of God, freedom and immortality, see *CCS*, 47 n; *F*, I, 112.

11 Another, more common way of describing this is to say that imagination mediates between reason and understanding and again between understanding and sensation. Commentary on this issue has usually centered on a marginal note in Tenneman's *Geschichte der Philosophie*, printed for the first time in *C on the Seventeenth Century*, ed. Roberta Brinkley (Durham, NC: Duke University Press, 1955), pp. 693–4. J. A. Appleyard, SJ, writes that before *Biographia Literaria* there is no discussion of imagination that gives the faculty a general epistemological function (*C's Philosophy of Literature*, p. 207). See below, Ch. 5, n. 27.

12 This philosophic consciousness (secondary imagination) is not to be confused with Schelling's *intellektuelle Anschauung*, which is a rare faculty whereby the mind catches itself in the act of creating the external world (see Shaffer, 'C's aesthetics', pp. 32–40; and Gian Orsini, *C and German Idealism* (Carbondale: Southern Illinois University Press, 1969), p. 202). There are two principal differences. First, for C the external world is independently real and existent, not a creation of consciousness. Secondly, for C philosophic consciousness is not the knowledge of anything fundamentally unconscious but rather an awareness of one's activity as a thinker, an awareness of one's *activity* in sorting, judging, attending or ignoring, believing, concluding. It is the ability to watch oneself think, and to reflect upon such observations.

13 For relevant discussions of symbol, see *LS*, 28–30, 69–70.

14 As McFarland points out, the relations among imagination, understanding and reason are not entirely clear even in Kant's own works; further complexities derive from the

fact that both Kant and C derive theories of imagination from Tetens ('The origin and significance of C's theory of secondary imagination', in *New Perspectives on C and Wordsworth*, ed. Geoffrey Hartman (New York: Columbia University Press, 1972), pp. 195–246). George Whalley sorts through the technical philosophic issues underlying the relation between C and Kant on imagination in *Poetic Process* (London: Routledge & Kegan Paul, 1953), pp. 46–63. See also A. O. Lovejoy, 'C and Kant's two worlds', *ELH*, vol. 7 (1940), pp. 341–62.

15 Among the exceptions is Michael G. Cooke, *The Romantic Will* (New Haven, Conn., and London: Yale University Press, 1976): 'In this story of an individual which modulated into a story of being . . . the presence of the will, though it has gone largely unnoticed, is radical and pervasive' (p. 28). And Geoffrey Yarlott is no doubt correct when he describes C's life as dominated by his quest to unite thought and feeling or power and strength, and when he notes that C 'tended to identify this want of strength with some atrophy or deficiency of the *Will*' (*C and the Abyssinian Maid*, p. 15). Yarlott's analysis of C's psychological difficulties suggests that the centrality of will in *BL* must have had a personal significance that might have given the work a tighter unity for C than it ordinarily possesses for us.

16 Mackintosh replies to C's charge of historical errors in a note to his *Dissertation on the Progress of Ethical Philosophy* (Edinburgh: A. & C. Black, 1836), note T-U. Mackintosh's commentary on Hobbes and Hartley in this work suggests that he would not have praised them so richly as C here claims. C's notes on the first five lectures of the second (1800) series attribute to Mackintosh certain materialist suppositions refuted in chs V–VIII: e.g. 'Makes Idea (of course) mean Image' (see *CN*, I, 634 and n). The story of Hartley's influence has often been told. Richard Haven argues persuasively that Hartley's linking associationist psychology to Christianity explains C's early interest in him. See 'C, Hartley, and the mystics', *Journal of the History of Ideas*, vol. 20 (1959), pp. 477–94; for a further development of the same general perspective on C's career, see also his *Patterns of Consciousness*. For a full and detailed history of C's associationism, see James V. Baker, *The Sacred River: C's Theory of the Imagination* (Baton Rouge: Louisiana State University Press, 1957), esp. ch. 2.

17 In commenting on the story of the serving girl, a review signed 'Oriel College, Oxford', complains that 'on such a vague and indefinite statement, no true philosopher could, we think, venture to found any serious speculation' ('David Hume charged by Mr. Coleridge with plagiarism from St. Thomas Aquinas', *Blackwood's Edinburgh Magazine*, vol. 3 (Sept 1818), pp. 653–7). Yet prior claims about will show that the story is merely to illustrate or at most confirm something already known. The facts about will that it illuminates are among those that experience confirms but cannot teach. This short, interesting review stands apart from its fellows in praising C's 'singularly acute metaphysics', especially in chs V–VIII. The review is not listed or reprinted in William S. Ward (ed.), *Literary Reviews in British Periodicals, 1798–1820: A Bibliography*, 2 vols (New York: Garland, 1972), or Donald Reiman (ed.), *The Romantics Reviewed: Contemporary Reviews of British Romantic Writers*, 3 vols in 9 pts (New York: Garland, 1973).

18 See *Enneads*, I, 6 [4], [9], trans. Stephen Mackenna, 4th edn, rev. B. S. Page (New York: Pantheon Books of Random House, 1969), pp. 59, 63–4; and see also trans. Thomas Taylor, in *Thomas Taylor the Platonist*, ed. with intro. Kathleen Raine and George Mills Harper, Bollingen Series LXXXVIII (Princeton, NJ: Princeton University Press, 1969), pp. 150, 158. C cites sun imagery form the *Enneads* again in ch. XII (I, 167).

19 For C on an author's obligation to remember his audience as part of his obligation to communicate truth, see *F*, I, 34–69. On this reference to mysteries as part of a pattern in *BL*, see Hunt, 'C and the endeavor of philosophy.

20 For an explanation of the consequences of object-oriented philosophies such as Locke's or Spinoza's, see McFarland, *C and Pantheist Tradition*, pp. 53–4, 69–70.

21 On the relation between fancy and imagination, see also Ch. 8, below, esp. pp. 133–40.

158 *The Design of* Biographia Literaria

22 For an explanation of the necessary systematic or logical openness of C's philosophy, see McFarland, *C and the Pantheist Tradition*, pp. 191–4, 53–7.

23 *LS*, 38; on popular philosophy, see also *LS*, 35–8 and nn; *F*, I, 34–67; *CN*, III, 3281. On the quality of popular writing, see *BL*, I, 25–7, 26 n.

24 See in particular the 'letter' in ch. XIII, discussed above, Ch. 2, and below, Ch. 5.

25 Haven, *Patterns of Consciousness*, pp. 36–7.

26 J. A. Appleyard, SJ, argues that C's theory of imagination did evolve from associationism. See 'C and criticism: I. critical theory', in *Writers and Their Background: STC*, ed. R. L. Brett (Athens, Ohio: Ohio University Press, 1972), p. 128. See also Baker, *The Sacred River*.

27 On Hobbes's originality, see Shedd III, 209 n; Shawcross, I, 229; Mackintosh, *Dissertation on the Progress of Ethical Philosophy*, p. 197. Shawcross's reference to Mackintosh's note 'S' is mistaken. The key to C's use of Hobbes may lie in Hobbes's commentary on wit, judgment and fancy, rather than in Mackintosh or mechanisms for association. C's use of both Hobbes and Descartes deserves further investigation.

28 'Schemes of conduct, grounded on calculations of self-interest, or on the average consequences of actions, supposed to be general, form a branch of political economy, to which let all due honor be given. Their utility is not here questioned. But however estimable within their own sphere such schemes, or any one of them in particular, may be, they do not belong to moral science, to which, both in kind and purpose, they are in all cases foreign, and, when substituted for it, hostile' (*AR*, 268). See also John Stuart Mill's famous distinction of the thinkers of his day into Coleridgeans and Benthamites ('Coleridge', in *Autobiography and Other Writings*, ed. Jack Stillinger (Boston, Mass.: Houghton-Mifflin, 1969), pp. 259–309, see esp. pp. 259–69).

29 The 'Essays on Method' in *The Friend* define the proper relation between methods of inquiry in the physical sciences and in the humanities (*F*, I, 448–524). On C's resolution of the competing ontologies of science and religion, see *AR*, 277, and C. Miles Wallace, 'C's *Biographia Literaria* and the evidence for Christianity', in *Interspace and the Inward Sphere*, ed. Norman A. Anderson and Margene E. Weiss (Macomb, Ill.: *Essays in Literature* Books, 1978), pp. 19–32.

30 John Arthur Passmore, *Ralph Cudworth* (London: Cambridge University Press, 1951), pp. 5–6. The reference may be submerged because C in *BL* defends Spinoza's philosophy as not necessarily incompatible with religion. In this regard, note the link between Spinoza and Leibnitz in ch. VIII's headnote. Cudworth's *The True Intellectual System of the Universe* may have been one of C's resources in writing *BL*. According to Passmore, Cudworth's book offers a 'sustained polemic' against Hobbes, and against 'aetheistic materialism' (pp. 3, 9). Cudworth, like Coleridge, insists on the continuity of tradition in philosophy, and protests the modern emphasis on originality and innovation (pp. 13–14). Cudworth also insists that Cartesian 'clear and distinct' ideas need no evidence (p. 9), an argument C adapts in ch. X. C's emphasis on the errors of Cartesian dualism, rather than the errors of dualism *per se*, may partly reflect Cudworth's admiration for the doctrine (Passmore, p. 8). Elsewhere, C describes Descartes' 'Mechanic or Corpuscular scheme' as leading to the philosophies of Berkeley and Spinoza – opposite forms of the same error (*AR*, 344 and n). Writing in the *Encyclopedia of Philosophy* (New York: Macmillan, 1967), Passmore also notes that opposition to fanaticism was a principal concern of Benjamin Whichcote, influential teacher of Cudworth and the other Cambridge Platonists (Vol. II, p. 9). See also W. Schrickx, 'C and the Cambridge Platonists', *Review of English Literature*, vol. 7 (1966), pp. 71–89.

Chapter 4

1 Walter Jackson Bate explains that C 'wanted to cut off the word "imagination" from any associations it still had with a mere "image-making" faculty which produces, separates, or joins together images derived from sensation' (*Coleridge* (New York: Collier Books, 1973), p. 162). He does so not by wrenching 'imagination' into an entirely new meaning,

but by more closely examining the relation of mind to world underlying the old definition. See also Thomas McFarland, 'The origin and significance of C's theory of secondary imagination', in *New Perspectives on C and Wordsworth*, ed. Geoffrey Hartman (New York and London: Columbia University Press, 1972), pp. 195–246; George Watson, '"Imagination" and "Fancy,"' *Essays in Criticism*, vol. 3 (1953), pp. 201–14; W. J. Bate and J. Bullitt, 'Distinctions between fancy and imagination in eighteenth century criticism', *MLN*, vol. 60 (1945), pp. 8–15; E. R. Wasserman, 'Another eighteenth-century distinction between fancy and imagination', *MLN*, vol. 64 (1949), pp. 23–5; Wilma L. Kennedy, *The English Heritage of C of Bristol, 1798: The Basis in Eighteenth Century English Thought for His Distinction between Imagination and Fancy* (New Haven, Conn.: Yale University Press, 1947).

2 For more on C's interest in principles, see Jackson, *Method and Imagination*, pp. 21–47.

3 See Shaffer, 'The "Postulates in Philosophy" in the *Biographia Literaria*', *Comparative Literature Studies*, vol. 7 (1970), pp. 297–313.

4 On faith and human intelligence, see *AR*, 61–2. On the grounds of our knowledge of will, see *AR*, 122. On the union of religion and morals re logic and language, see *AR*, 106–8, cf. *AR*, 129 n). On proofs of God, see *TT*, 22 Feb 1834; *AR*, 187–8.

5 'Nether Stowey' and 'a cottage in Somersetshire' refer to the same place.

6 Compare self-descriptions at I, 14, 62–5, 115, 137, 145–51.

Chapter 5

1 Shaffer, 'C's aesthetics'. Shaffer translates the relevant sections from Schelling's *System of Transcendental Idealism* in an appendix. The principal arguments of the dissertation reappear in three journal articles, but the discussion of Schelling and the *Biographia* is so severely condensed that the thesis remains preferable. See also 'The "Postulates in Philosophy" in the *Biographia Literaria*'; 'C's theory of aesthetic interest', *Journal of Aesthetics and Art Criticism*, vol. 27 (1969), pp. 399–408; 'C's revolution in the standard of taste', ibid., vol. 28 (1969), pp. 213–21.

2 *CN*, III, 4265 n. McFarland both analyzes and extends the work that has already been done in *C and the Pantheist Tradition*, ch. 1. The most detailed and reliable analysis that judges C derivative is Orsini, *C and German Idealism*. According to Orsini, C's 'rightful place in the history of philosophical ideas' is as a translator of Schelling (p. 221). One should also consult René Wellek's discussions of Coleridge in *The Romantic Age*, in *A History of Modern Criticism*, Vol. II (New Haven, Conn.: Yale University Press, 1955), pp. 151–87; and in *The English Romantic Poets: A Review of Research and Criticism*, ed. Frank Jordan, Jr, 3rd edn (New York: MLA, 1972), pp. 209–58. One interested in C's comments on the matter might begin with *CN*, II, 2375 and 2546; *CN*, I, 1695.

3 For instance, *CCS*, 44–5 echoes the Cis- and Trans-Alpine passage (I, 164–7); *LS*, 137, repeats the first half of the scholium to Thesis II (I, 174); *AR*, 108 n, repeats the definitions of nature, subject and object (I, 174); *AR*, 122 and 224 n, clarifies the comparison between the transcendental philosopher and the geometer (I, 171–3). Given C's habitual incorporating and rewriting of others' texts, his rewriting of his own work cannot by itself constitute evidence of dissatisfaction with the original. But one does find direct evidence of such dissatisfaction. As early as July 1817, C refers to 'a few opinions which better information and more reflection would now annul. But even these will, I trust, be found only in the lesser branches, as knotts [sic] & scars that may exist without implying either canker at the root, or malignant quality in the general sap of the tree' (*CL*, IV, 758). And in September of 1818 he criticizes Schelling's 'making all knowledge bi-polar, Transcendental Idealism as one Pole and Nature as the other', and laments his use of the idea in *BL* (*CL*, IV, 874). As I describe below, C's sharp division between transcendental idealism and the total philosophy does not successfully distinguish ch. XII's philosophy from pantheism (below, pp. 81–4).

4 On C's views of the relation between art and religion, see *LS*, 62; *COS*, 88–9.

5 See McFarland, *C and the Pantheist Tradition*, pp. 116–23.

6 See Kathleen Coburn, 'The interpenetration of Man and Nature', *Proceedings of the*

160   *The Design of* Biographia Literaria

British Academy, vol. 49 (1963), pp. 95–113, for an explanation of this theme in C's thought.

7   This belief about common consciousness probably underlies C's early interest in Hartley and associationism. See above, Ch. 3, n. 16.

8   Roman numerals following a page number indicate line numbers, which I will provide whenever such exact reference may be helpful.

9   See Shaffer, 'C's aesthetics', pp. 1–30, for an explanation of the technical issue with which Schelling wrestles. C translates his specialized references to geometry into an explanatory analogy.

10   J. B. Beer, *C the Visionary* (London: Chatto & Windus, 1959), pp. 70–1.

11   See above, Ch. 3, pp. 30–42, and Ch. 4, pp 61–3.

12   This traditional reference is a favorite of C's. See *LPR*, 94, n. 3, for a listing of other instances, and of his sources. For discussion, see C. Miles Wallace, 'C's theory of language', *Philological Quarterly*, vol. 59 (1980), pp. 338–52.

13   See McFarland, *C and the Pantheist Tradition*, pp. 53–8, 107–12. C's 'original realism' is not, as Appleyard claims, a naïve position to which he falls back because he lacks a theory (*C's Philosophy of Literature*, p. 196).

14   For thesis I, see I, 94, 174; for thesis II, see I, 168; for thesis III, see I, 168, 172–4, 178; for thesis V, see I, 66, 175–8; for thesis VI, see I, 94–5.

15   'Organic' is a more complicated and specialized term in C's thought than it later became in critical theory generally. See, e.g., *TT*, 18 Dec 1831, where he proposes 'a sheaf of corn' as an example of the 'inorganic'. The issue is explicated at length in the *Theory of Life*. On organicism generally, see, e.g., Barfield, *What C Thought*, pp. 41–62 and 210 n. 3; R. H. Fogle, *The Idea of C's Criticism*, pp. 18–68; M. H. Abrams, *The Mirror and the Lamp* (London: Oxford University Press, 1953), esp. pp. 167–77, 218–55; and James Benziger, 'Organic unity: Leibnitz to Coleridge', *PMLA*, vol. 46, no. 2 (1951), pp. 24–48.

16   Not all agree that these are equivalent terms, but the alternative is to conclude that there must be as many kinds of imagination as there are kinds of human endeavor. S. V. Pradhan analyzes the patterns of C's usage, and concludes this is the case ('C's "Philocrisy" and his theory of fancy and secondary imagination', *Studies in Romanticism*, vol. 13 (1974), pp. 235–54). Parsimony is better served by agreeing with Barfield that C shifts vocabulary to suit his context (*What C Thought*, p. 76). As an example, compare I, 167, xvii–xxvii, and I, 173, x–xxxi. I take it that in the second passage C refers to the effective development of the faculty, and in the first to its 'genotypic' presence.

17   In the *Philosophical Lectures*, C traces how philosophers and scientists, working from 'opposite' ends, discover the need to postulate a single force, which Christ reveals as the personal triune God.

18   My position depends in large measure on taking seriously C's division of all inquiry into three domains. Grosvenor Powell reads this thesis (in effect) as part of the total philosophy, and argues well that C does establish an infinite regress that badly confuses the distinction between God and man. See 'C's "imagination" and the infinite regress of consciousness', *ELH*, vol. 39 (1972), pp. 266–78. On the validity of this division as a bulwark against pantheism, see below, pp. 81–4.

19   For C's response to the 1815 preface as part of the genesis of *BL*, see above, Ch. 1, n. 4.

20   Arthur Lovejoy, *The Great Chain of Being* (Cambridge, Mass.: Harvard University Press, 1936, 1964), esp. ch. III.

21   Cited in translation supplied by Watson in the Everyman's Library edition (1965), p. 161, n. 2.

22   Cited in translation supplied by Watson, ibid., p. 162, n. 1. Compare a different translation of the same lines in a notebook entry, *CN*, III, 4189 n. The *dance* metaphor is present in the Greek.

23   This idea is explored at length in the *Theory of Life*. See also above, Ch. 5, nn. 6 and 15.

24   See *CL*, IV, 728.

25 McFarland, *C and the Pantheist Tradition*, p. 156.

26 See above, Ch. 3, n. 17.

27 These definitions are the *locus classicus* for arguments about C's theory of imagination. These arguments can be very roughly divided into two sorts: those principally concerned with the theory as part of C's philosophy, and those predominantly concerned with its role in his criticism. On the second of these groups, see below, Ch. 6, nn. 4, 5, 7. Arguments about the philosophical significance of imagination have more or less centered on the problematic relation between reason and imagination. To what extent do the qualities C attributes to imagination and all its works essentially derive from reason itself? What are the proper qualities of imagination, as distinguishable from the powers and elements it synthesizes? The questions are complicated enormously by C's intricate relations to Kant, to Schelling, to Tetens, and to others (see above, Ch. 3, n. 14). Principal studies include: Barfield, *What C Thought*; James D . Boulger, 'C on imagination revisited', *The Wordsworth Circle*, vol. 4 (1973), pp. 13–24; Jackson, *Method and Imagination*; Roy Park, 'C and Kant: poetic imagination and practical reason', *British Journal of Aesthetics*, vol. 8 (1968), pp. 335–46, 'Coleridge's two voices as a critic of Wordsworth', *ELH*, vol. 36 (1969), pp. 361–81, and 'Coleridge: philosopher and theologian as literary critic', *University of Toronto Quarterly*, vol. 38 (1969), pp. 17–33; Pradhan, 'C's "Philocrisy" and his theory of fancy and secondary imagination'. The questions remain vexing and, in the last analysis, probably without adequate answers. The powers of the mind are not independent programs which can each run the same computer. When one studies the mind in strict abstraction, it is easy enough to define reason, to define imagination, and to distinguish the definitions. In a parallel way, anatomy is distinct from physiology, from biochemistry, from pathology, and from genetics. But when one studies the mind not as an abstraction but as an act, then the tidy distinctions begin to blur. As C insists, when the mind acts, the whole mind acts; and poetry requires the richest, fullest mental activity. When a gleeful child runs pell-mell down the street, who can say what is due to anatomy, to physiology, to genetics? The more closely one studies the interactivity of reason and imagination, the farther one moves from abstraction to life.

28 Sara Coleridge observes that her father later lined out this clause in a copy of the book (Shedd III, p. 363 n). Shawcross's repetition of her note refers somewhat ambiguously to the 'sentence', leading some readers to believe that C had deleted *all* reference to primary imagination. *BL* provides C's only statements concerning primary imagination.

Chapter 6

1 My views on C's idea of language appeared first as 'C's theory of language'.

2 R. H. Fogle, *The Idea of C's Criticism*, p. 8.

3 Compare Wordsworth: 'If words be not . . . an incarnation of the thought but only a clothing for it, then surely will they prove an ill gift' ('Essays upon Epitaphs, III', *The Prose Works of William Wordsworth*, ed. W. J. B. Owen and Jane Worthington Smyser (Oxford: Clarendon Press, 1974), Vol. II, pp. 84–5; cited afterwards as *Pr. Wk W.*). On Wordsworth's idea of language in relation to his idea of poetry, see M. H. Abrams, 'Wordsworth and C on diction and figures', *English Institute Essays, 1952*, ed. Alan S. Downer (New York: Columbia University Press, 1954) pp. 171–201; Frances Ferguson, *Wordsworth: Language as Counter-Spirit* (New Haven, Conn.: Yale University Press, 1977); and W. J. B. Owen, *Wordsworth as Critic* (Toronto: University of Toronto Press, 1969). See also below, Ch. 7, nn. 5, 12.

4 R. H. Fogle, for instance, in his introduction to Baker's *The Sacred River*, describes C as offering 'a rallying-cry' and a 'trumpet call' to 'our famous New Critics' (p. xii). But C has a wonderfully complex relation to these critics, who agreed with many of his statements about the character of an artwork, but who understood the mode of relation between art and values in different terms. One alternative, then, is to argue that C's

criticism and his philosophy are incompatible (and, often, that his philosophy is a shabby, incoherent, inconsequent quilt of plagiarisms). The strongest of such arguments are by René Wellek (see above, Ch. 5, n. 2); for specific application to *BL*, see Appleyard, *C's Philosophy of Literature*, esp. p. 252. New Critics and Neo-Humanists alike none the less criticized C's work. Clarence D. Thorpe summarizes such criticism, and defends C in 'C as aesthetician and critic', *Journal of the History of Ideas*, vol. 5 (1944), pp. 387–414. For a lengthy and quite polemical account of C's relation to New Criticism, see Manfred Wojcik, 'The mimetic orientation of C's aesthetic thought', *Zeitschrift für Anglistik und Amerikanistic*, vol. 17 (1969), pp. 344–91. Wojcik develops his point in three subsequent numbers of the same journal, writing what ought to have been a book on the topic. See also 'C and the problem of transcendentalism', ibid., vol. 18 (1970), pp. 30–58; 'C: symbol, organic unity, and modern aesthetic subjectivism', ibid., vol. 18 (1970), pp. 355–90; and 'C: symbolization, expression, and artistic creativity', ibid., vol. 19 (1971), pp. 117–54. On the difference between C's concept of organic form and the New Critical account, see R. S. Crane, 'The critical monism of Cleanth Brooks', *Critics and Criticism*, ed. R. S. Crane (Chicago, Ill.: University of Chicago Press, 1952), pp. 82–107.

5   See, for instance, Walter Jackson Bate, 'C on the function of art', *Perspectives of Criticism*, ed. Harry Levin (Cambridge, Mass.: Harvard University Press, 1950), pp. 129–59, and his *Coleridge*, pp. 146–57; R. H. Fogle, *The Idea of C's Criticism*. M. H. Abrams deftly summarizes this approach in *The Mirror and the Lamp*, pp. 118–19.

6   See above, Ch. 6, n. 4. The error here, I suspect, is excessively assimilating C's view of art to that of the German transcendental idealists, esp. Schelling. Roy Park sharply and properly distinguishes C from his German forebears and contemporaries, and concludes that the secondary imagination is not free but subordinated to the moral vision of reason. See above, Ch. 5, n. 27. See also below, pp. 100–102, on C's distinction between the immediate and the ultimate purposes of art.

7   There is a considerable body of critical commentary attempting to reconcile C's philosophy with his criticism, much of it focused on the relation between imagination's role in cognition and its role in art. One error is particularly common: some claim that primary imagination provides access not to the day-to-day world but, rather, to a reality already translucent with value. Those who define primary imagination in this way then define secondary imagination as the specifically artistic power of making poems from the materials thus supplied, through a sort of transcendentalized mimeticism. This is the wrong route to a crucial distinction between imaginative vision and artistic production. C locates the distinction not between primary and secondary imagination, but between imaginative power and linguistic control over ideas and poetic forms. The best studies include Abrams, *The Mirror and the Lamp*; Baker, *The Sacred River*; J. Robert Barth, SJ, *The Symbolic Imagination: C and the Romantic Tradition* (Princeton, NJ: Princeton University Press, 1977); Stephen Prickett, *Coleridge and Wordsworth: The Poetry of Growth* (London: Cambridge University Press, 1970); Whalley, *Poetic Process*, pp. 46–63; and see also Ch. 5, n. 27. For an overview of the questions from the perspective of English literary theory, see R. L. Brett, 'Coleridge's theory of imagination', *Essays and Studies*, n.s., vol. 2 (1949), pp. 75–90. For the same overview from the Continental perspective, see Herbert Read, 'C as critic', *Sewanee Review*, vol. 56 (1948), pp. 597–624; and of course McFarland, *C and the Pantheist Tradition*.

8   The volume division was the printer's choice, not C's. See below, Chapter 8, n. 11. In this approach I am of course preceded by I. A. Richards. There needs to be much further study of these issues by one well versed in present-day philosophies of language.

9   On the Lockean tradition in linguistics, see Hans Aarsleff, *The Study of Language in England, 1780–1860* (Princeton, NJ: Princeton University Press, 1967), pp. 13–33; and Stephen K. Land, *From Signs to Propositions: The Concept of Form in Eighteenth Century Semantic Theory*, Longman Linguistics Library no. 16 (London: Longman, 1974), pp. 1–20. On the contrast represented between Locke and Wilkins, see Murray Cohen, *Sensible Words: Linguistic Practice in England, 1640–1785* (Baltimore, Md.: The

Johns Hopkins University Press, 1977), pp. 1–42. On the tradition in which C participates, see Ernst Cassirer, *The Philosophy of Symbolic Forms*, trans. Ralph Mannheim (New Haven, Conn.: Yale University Press, 1953), Vol. I, *Language*, pp. 117–76, esp. re Heraclitus (pp. 119–22), Plato (pp. 124–6), Berkeley (pp. 138–9), Herder (pp. 151–3) and von Humboldt (pp. 155–63). For Cassirer's delineation of the position underlying this history, see pp. 85–93. Cassirer would call C's work an attempt to define a 'metaphysical–speculative solution' that seeks 'to understand how the concrete totality of particular forms develops from a single original principle' (p. 95). C would respond that a 'critical solution' like Cassirer's is 'a cycle of equal truths without a common and central principle, which prescribes to each its proper sphere' (I, 181). It is no more likely, he would say, than the string of blind men walking a straight line without a sighted leader.

10 *Hermes; or a Philosophical Inquiry concerning Universal Grammar* (1751; rev. ed. London: W. Simprin & R. Marshall, 1816), pp. 113, 119–21; see also pp. 123–31.

11 Cited by Alice D. Snyder, *C on Logic and Learning* (New Haven, Conn.: Yale University Press, 1929), p. 79, 86.

12 ibid., p. 128.

13 See above, Ch. 1, pp. 9–11.

14 See above, Ch. 3, pp. 63–74.

15 See also the 'Essays on Method' in *The Friend*. Method and language are both essentially relational; method itself is concerned both with inquiry and with discourse. See also above, Ch. 6, n. 1.

16 The relation between language and mathematics had been variously explored both by philosophers and by those eager to make language a more precise tool. See, for instance, David Hartley, *Observations on Man: His Frame, His Duty and His Expectations* (1749; facsimile reprint in 1 vol., Gainesville, Fla: Scholar's Facsimiles and Reprints, 1966), I, 280–1. See also Land, *From Signs to Propositions*, pp. 128–54.

17 On C's etymologies and his relation to scientific linguistics, see James Holly Hanford, 'C as a philologian', *Modern Philology*, vol. 16 (1918–19), pp. 615–36; Joshua H. Neumann, 'C on the English language', *PMLA*, vol. 63 (1948), pp. 642–61; L. A. Willoughby, 'C as a philologist', *Modern Language Review*, vol. 31 (1936), pp. 176–201.

18 On C's blending of moral and literary concerns, see Peter Hoheisel, 'C on Shakespeare: method amid the rhetoric', *Studies in Romanticism*, vol. 13 (1974), pp. 15–23.

19 On C's account of their aims, see Mark L. Reed, 'Wordsworth, C, and the 'plan' of the *Lyrical Ballads*', *University of Toronto Quarterly* vol. 34 (1965), pp. 238–53.

20 On light as a central symbol of imagination for both poets, see Stephen Prickett, *Coleridge and Wordsworth: The Poetry of Growth*.

21 On how C's idea of this reflexivity differs from more recent versions, see R. S. Crane, 'The critical monism of Cleanth Brooks', in *Critics and Criticism*, ed. R. S. Crane, pp. 82–107. See also James Benziger, 'Organic unity: Leibnitz to C', *PMLA*, vol. 46, no. 2 (1951), pp. 24–48.

22 See also his study of *Romeo and Juliet*, COS, 75–97.

23 For defenses of Wordsworth, see below, Ch. 7, nn. 5, 12, 13, 20; Ch. 8, nn. 7, 8.

24 Cited in translation supplied by Watson in the Everyman's Library edition, pp. 182–3, nn. 1–3.

Chapter 7

1 Abrams, 'Wordsworth and C on diction and figures', pp. 171–201. See also above, Ch. 6, n. 3.

2 On C's role in the Preface, see *CL*, II, 811–12, 829–30, and Max F. Schulz, 'C, Wordsworth, and the 1800 "Preface" to *Lyrical Ballads*', *Studies in English Literature 1500–1900*, vol. 5 (1965), pp. 619–39. On the relation between Wordsworth and C generally, see Earl Leslie Griggs, 'Wordsworth through C's eyes', in *Wordsworth:*

Centenary Studies Presented at Cornell and Princeton Universities, ed. Gilbert T. Dunklin (Princeton, NJ: Princeton University Press, 1951), pp. 45–90; Thomas McFarland, 'The symbiosis of C and Wordsworth', *Studies in Romanticism* vol. 11 (1972), pp. 263–303; Prickett, *Coleridge and Wordsworth: The Poetry of Growth.* On the relation between C's criticism of the Preface and that in the magazines, see John O. Hayden, 'C, the reviewers, and Wordsworth', *Studies in Philology,* vol. 68 (1971), pp. 105–19. Those who defend Wordsworth from C's criticism are cited in notes below (5, 12, 13, 20); for a defense of C's position, see T. M. Raysor, 'C's criticism of Wordsworth, *PMLA,* vol. 54 (1939), pp. 496–510.

3 W. K. Wimsatt and Cleanth Brooks, *Literary Criticism: A Short History* (New York: Alfred A. Knopf, 1966), pp. 339–43.

4 *Pr. Wk W.,* I, 160–1.

5 Don H. Bialostosky, 'C's interpretation of Wordsworth's Preface to *Lyrical Ballads*', *PMLA,* vol. 93 (1978), pp. 912–24. As Wellek observes, Wordsworth's later qualifications of the intent to imitate the real language of men 'surely leaves all the leeway anybody could demand' (*A History of Modern Criticism,* Vol. II, p. 134).

6 *Pr. Wk W.,* I, 134. The italicized statement in the *Biographia* is a compound of two of Wordsworth's sentences.

7 ibid., I, 164.

8 ibid., I, 137–43, esp. I, 138.

9 Wimsatt and Brooks, *Literary Criticism,* p. 343.

10 See Nathaniel Teich, 'C's *Biographia* and the contemporary controversy about style', *The Wordsworth Circle,* vol. 3 (1972), pp. 61–70.

11 On grammar and logic, see my Ch. 6, n. 1.

12 For a defense of Wordsworth's objectivity, see Gene W. Ruoff, 'Wordsworth on language: toward a radical poetics for English Romanticism', *The Wordsworth Circle,* vol. 3 (1972), pp. 204–11; for a defense of Wordsworth's essential subjectivity, see Frederick A. Pottle, 'The eye and the object in the poetry of Wordsworth', in Dunklin (ed.), *Wordsworth: Centenary Studies,* pp. 23–43; for an argument that the real issue is the propriety of dramatic monologues, see Stephen Maxfield Parrish, 'The Wordsworth–C controversy', *PMLA,* vol. 73 (1958), pp. 367–74.

13 For a defense of 'The Thorn', see ibid.

14 *Pr. WK W.,* I, 124. See also Ch. 7, n. 5, and Ch. 6, pp. 95–6.

15 I have argued elsewhere that poems most fully meet the criteria for methodical discourse. See Ch. 6, n. 1.

16 Richards, *C on Imagination,* ch. 4. On the poetic function of fancy, see Baker, *The Sacred River.*

17 This passage echoes the opening paragraphs of the 'Essays on Method' (*F,* I, 448–9). The 'Essays on Method' argue even more clearly than the opening chapters of *BL* that genuine education does and ought to foster the development of imagination. On method, see Paul Alkon, 'Critical and logical concepts of method from Addison to C', *Eighteenth Century Studies,* vol. 5 (1971), pp. 97–121.

18 See Abrams, *The Mirror and the Lamp,* pp. 100–24; and above, Ch. 6, n. 3.

19 *Pr. Wk W.,* I, 144–8. For discussion of this same disagreement from Wordsworth's perspective, see Stephen Maxfield Parrish, 'Wordsworth and C on metre', *Journal of English and Germanic Philology,* vol. 59 (1960), pp. 41–9.

20 John Crowe Ransom, 'William Wordsworth: notes toward an understanding of his poetry', in Dunklin (ed.), *Wordsworth: Centenary Studies,* pp. 91–113.

21 Wordsworth, of course, did not contend that they were twins. See *Pr. Wk W.,* I, 134.

Chapter 8

1 John Livingston Lowes, *The Road to Xanadu: A Study in the Ways of the Imagination* (Boston, Mass.: Houghton-Mifflin, 1927), p. 49. See also above, Ch. 7, n. 16.

2 For an account of this urging, see David Erdman and Paul Zall, 'C and Jeffrey in controversy', *Studies in Romanticism*, vol. 14 (1975), pp. 75–83.

3 *CL*, V, 95. See also Park, 'C's two voices as a critic of Wordsworth', *ELH*, vol. 36 (1969), pp. 361–81.

4 See I, 87: by concentering the attention, will can render any objects 'associable'. Because this function is not bound by the literal contemporaneity of the original impressions, the genius's immediate impressions *and his memories* can be accommodated to imagination's ends. See also above, Ch. 3, pp. 46–9.

5 II, 106–7; see also II, 33–4 and n; II, 101–2; and George Whalley, 'The Aristotle–C axis', *University of Toronto Quarterly*, vol. 42 (1973), pp. 93–109.

6 On dramatic monologues and dialogues, see Parrish, 'The Wordsworth–C controversy.

7 Among the most astute defenses of the 'Intimations' ode are those by Richards and Ransom. See *C on Imagination*, pp. 130–7; and above, Ch. 7, n. 20.

8 At least parts of this treatise are present in *Aids to Reflection* (see Ch. 6, n. 1). I suspect that C's interests in language substantially merged with his interests in Biblical hermaneutics and the Higher Criticism. See below, ch. 9, n. 2.

9 Cited in translation supplied by Watson in the Everyman's Library edition, p. 268 n.

10 For an account of C's problems with the printer, see Grigg's introduction, *CL*, III, xlvii–lii, and his notes to some of the relevant letters, *CL*, IV, 657–660 nn.

11 See above, Ch. 3, and *LS*, 137; *AR*, 246 and n.

Chapter 9

1 McFarland, *C and the Pantheist Tradition*, p. xxvi.

2 For an account of C's place in Biblical hermaneutics and the Higher Criticism, see Elinor S. Shaffer, *'Kubla Khan' and the Fall of Jerusalem: The Mythological School in Biblical Criticism and Secular Literature, 1770–1880* (London: Cambridge University Press, 1975).

3 Boulger, *C as Religious Thinker*, pp. 5–8.

4 Note that arguments to and about political leaders are barely evident in the principal summary of his argument (*LS*, 43–9).

5 Peter Hoheisel, 'C on Shakespeare: method amid the rhetoric'.

Index